The Beauty Of Broken
By Angela Trainer

For Lily Douglas and Chloe Homewood.. see you in the morning.
All profits from this book will go to their charities - Lily's Legacy and The Everyone Project.

To find out more about Lily's Legacy (they plan to build a holiday respite home for children with cancer) - Scottish Charitable Incorporated Organisation # SCO52112 - go to lilyslegacy.co.uk

For Chloe's charity go to **www.everyoneproject.org**, providing mindfulness training for free to diverse communities in the UK

On The Beauty Of Broken...

"After Lily, my daughter, died of cancer aged 14, I could not face talking, reading or watching anything on TV about cancer. This book was the first time I did it.

Angela's story about her journey with breast cancer and navigating her way through her treatment is witty, honest and very uplifting. The way she coped and the tips she gives for others to cope really inspired me.

Now that I've read this book, I feel like I am not alone in the world after all.

Thank you Angela for living life, and for your love."

Jane Douglas

Mum of Lily Douglas the champion dancer, Teenager of Courage - Pride of Scotland 2021 winner and inspiration to all who met her

"Angela has a joyful knack for storytelling that draws the reader in. Raw, honest, insightful and funny, this book will no doubt inspire courage and bring comfort to so many."

Donna Ashworth

Author of To The Women and I Wish I Knew

"Looking and learning through the eyes of real honesty, Angela expresses her journey with such clarity.
The rollercoaster of emotions she describes is at times heart-wrenching as well as hilarious.
A super book for anyone navigating through the difficult times of life; laughing, loving and weeping. Nuggets of wisdom weave throughout each chapter.
A must-read."
Anne Rowan
C. E. O / Founder of Chris's House Suicide Intervention Charity

"Crisis catalyses change. Let this big-hearted, brutally honest account of a crisis traversed inspire your own change. It teems with life as real as a slap in the face - then fills you with love and laugh-out-loud humour mixed with wisdom, compassion and practical ideas (imagine Billy Connolly melded with the Dalai Lama).

It meets head-on the shock, deep stress, shadows, fears and deconstruction of the self that follow a major life-shift or severe diagnosis... then navigates 'the adventure' through the jungle of discoveries.

Then on to dealing with the floods of advice and treatments harsh and mild, sound and unsound, charting the stages of recovery and flourishing of a healing and spiritual journey.

This book can change the way you see your breakdown, your breakthrough, yourself and your life."

Dr David Reilly FRCP MRCGP HonDSc
Director of TheWEL Partnership of TheWEL Charity and TheWEL World
Former NHS Lead Consultant Physician, The NHS Centre for Integrative Care
www.thewelworld.org

On Angela's first book,
Love Never Dies

"Angela's experience of loss is not the same as mine and mine will not be the same as yours but   by putting her feelings into words she makes a key connection with every one of us who has had to let go of someone they did love and will always love dearly. The upside, if there is one, is that Angela is absolutely right…. Love Never Dies. My parents might not be 'here' but they are always with me."

Kaye Adams, Broadcaster

"Love Never Dies describes beautifully what we all feel before, during and after the loss of a loved one. It puts into words what we feel and validates our feelings making us feel less alone and more connected to others. It takes the fear from the dying process and makes it more normal, which it is, as part of the circle of life. I LOVED it!"

Dr Mary Frame,

Retired GP and retired Specialty Doctor at Marie Curie Hospice.

"Love Never Dies speaks to everyone who has experienced the loss of a loved one – and that is just about everyone. Angela brings the message of the power of love in a comforting and healing voice. Truly, a lovely book."

Caroline Myss, Author of Anatomy of the Spirit and Defy Gravity

CONTENTS

A Word From Angela
A Prayer
The Power Of Words

On Twists And Turns

THE JOURNEY
April 2019
May 2019
June 2019
July 2019
August 2019
September 2019
October 2019
November 2019
December 2019
January 2020
February 2020
March 2020
April 2020
May 2020
June 2020
July 2020
August 2020
September/October 2020
November 2020
December 2020
January 2021
February 2021

March/April 2021
May/June 2021
July 2021
August 2021
September/October 2021
November 2021
December 2021
January 2022
February 2022

COMFORT

The Last Word: A Prayer

Sir Ian

THE RETREAT

My Team
Thank You
Photographs

A WORD FROM ANGELA

I had never intended writing a second book.

Love Never Dies was a tribute to my father and my story of trying to cope when he was diagnosed with Pancreatic Cancer and died six months later – and help other people do the same, and realise their loved ones are always with them.

As a psychotherapist I knew the therapeutic value of journaling and processing deep and painful feelings. I blogged my way through and beyond and this became the first book.

Then came my own diagnosis and the journey through surgery, treatment, recovery and acceptance – a journey which is of course ongoing.

I was persuaded the social media posts I was sharing could again be helpful to others – but not just in dealing with cancer, in dealing with life and living in general.

And indeed it was the loss of several people very close to me which made me agree.

So my story may be about my own Breast Cancer journey but the lessons, the feelings, the advice and the guidance from those wiser than I can all be applied to ANY trauma. To life.

Loss of a relationship, a loved one, a job, a home, or just how low we can feel at times – I hope there will be something in the book to help you through any tough time.

The cover of this book is very significant to me. And it should be to anyone dealing with ANY kind of trauma.

I was looking in the mirror one morning at the scars where my right breast used to be.

My reaction was historically mostly distress, horror, deletion, ignoring, fast cover-up. As I am sure is the case for most women in my situation.

But not this day.

This day was different.

I saw beauty in the scars.

I saw the golden repair of Kintsugi – the Japanese art of putting back together and finding strength in the joins, which is the inspiration for the cover of this book. The repaired vessel is more valuable, MORE uniquely beautiful than the unflawed original.

Kintsugi means golden joinery. My scars were my badge of honour. I lived through it and I learned the deepest of life lessons - I survived and I soared.

I could see clearer than ever The Beauty Of Broken.

One must have chaos

if one is to give birth

to a dancing star.

By Nietzsche

THE POWER
OF WORDS

As a psychotherapist in the consulting room, I have always known the value of the positive reframe therapeutically.

Certain words and concepts have such negative attachments to them that we are beaten before we start by the power of association with defeatist emotions.

These words act like leeches of our power, as energy vampires on our system. They take us straight into the dark places.

I knew right from the get-go that I would need to break the chains of some of the language and concepts I was gonna come up against on this journey into the world of Cancer.

And there was the first!

Cancer.

I have Cancer.

I need Chemotherapy and Radiotherapy at the hospital.

All of these words have such negative connections and associations which triggered fear-filled and automatic reactions within and throughout my nervous system.

I knew I'd be damned before I even started if I didn't challenge the direction my body mind soul were heading in.

So I rewrote some of these words with a positive connection; I kept it light.

I had The Chancer - another chance.

I visited the Healthspital - a place of health-giving treatments.

I would have Ki-More Therapy – energy-giving therapy and Ray-Joy Therapy – happy energy.

I would see the Best Care Nurse - the breast cancer nurse.

Some other examples you could relate to your life:
Prognosis - Pro-Know-it
Divorce - Diversion
Affair - A-fall
Relapse - Relearning
Problem - Challenge
Redundant - Redirect-ment
Breakdown - Breakthrough
Retirement - Re-fire-ment
Menopause - Me-Now-Pause
Failure – Feedback
See what I mean?
By dissolving and dismantling these powerfully terrifying and intimidating concepts, I had a little bit of control over what I was feeding my mind and therefore my body.
We will ALL go through so much trial by fire, we would do well to guard the tongue and mind our language. The body is always listening and acting based on what it hears.

Challenge and change.
Reframe in a positive way what you are going through.
We all go through these life lessons.
Find a way to recognise the gold in the cracks, the value, the learnings in whatever we are living through.
This applies to ANYTHING in your life. Try it. You will be surprised at what may happen.

ON TWISTS AND TURNS.

9th April 2019

After a tricky couple of years, my dad's death, my business mentor of 30 years Michael dying from lung cancer, a changing of the guard in the clinic, a sexual predator with subsequent court case and a regular whack of life nonsense (and that was all before breakfast) I think my immune system waved a flag of surrender. There IS a limit to how much we can take. So it's time for surrender, humility, ask for help and gratitude. That spells S.H.A.G. to help you remember.

I've been tired for a while and I now have Breast Chancer. I have a four-six cm mass on my right breast and need a mastectomy on May 8. Ki-More-Therapy or radio to be decided at the

Healthspital.

I am ready. I think.

I'd find the irony of having just finished the editing of my book about my journey with my father's death from Chancer mind-boggling if it wasn't so real.

I'm positive, I'm open and I'm scared all at once but at least I won't ever feel a right tit again. But there may be tom-toms drumming.

I am not the pilot but I do co-navigate. If the pilot decides a different route, I will advise.

I will take all the Reiki, prayers, love, and positive thoughts going.

Don't DARE say "let me know if there is anything I can do" unless you MEAN it, because I will hunt you down and I will FIND YOU, and I will CALL YOU OUT!

I'm keeping a list of offending offerers.

Asking for help is tough but receiving it and digesting it is harder still – it's high time I upped my game.

Oh and I'm on the next book: you gotta find the silver lining after all. Love Never Dies -The Sequel.

ANGELA TRAINER

THE JOURNEY

APRIL 2019

GREET·PRAY·LOVE 1

What an interesting and fascinating white-knuckle, roller-coaster journey. Although much of the time I'm floating on marshmallow clouds of all shall be well, wrapped in the invisible soft fluffy comfort blanket of the love of many people.

Each day is like a lifetime, with sensory acuity increased to double the max volume. I feel as if I'm walking at times with one foot over the Veil and looking at life through a soft-focus lens.

If you are playing catch up, I was diagnosed with Breast Chancer at the Healthspital and have Purgery booked for May 8 with my beautiful counsel-aunt and Best Care Nurse.

Ray-joy-action and Ki-My-Therapy may be discussed later.

Not a spelling mistake in sight, negativity and its resultant fear clings to words and can change your vibe in a heartbeat.

I was aimlessly scrolling through a discussion post of

comments on the after-effects of Ki-more-Therapy yesterday when Sir Ian (cat) and I were jolted violently into the here and now by a thud on the bedroom window.

The offending pigeon flew off nonchalantly and seemingly unharmed but its almost kamikaze flight detour via our window rattled me out of my stupor and I changed channels on my newsfeed quickly.

The MESSAGE was timely and clear.

"Stay up here, don't descend into other people's stories and histories of their treatment disasters. You are not them."

The totem meaning of when the pigeon shows up significantly in our life is interesting. I checked it out:

"It could be letting you know that you need to stop and take a few deep breaths. Therefore you must let go of the turmoil that is currently surrounding you and take the time to find peace within you." Bingo.

"It can also be a message that you need to purify your thoughts. You are attracting what you don't want in your life by focusing on it." Bongo!

Now I know this. When you are drowning you need strong lifeguards and lifeguardesses around you, people anchored in strength and robust health.

When you are "severely off balance" it's sometimes not so good to surround yourself with others who are also drowning.

You can help sink each other with the fear and anxiety or put on a mask of positivity for each other's benefit - both draining your energy.

I've always told my sexual abuse clients to avoid "survivor groups" for the same reason.

You need to be able to surrender and let it all hang oot with folks who have strong shoulders to carry you and backs that have YOUR back.

NOT reading horror stories on your Social Meeja.

The circle of Healthspital Attunements has begun. I met Nurse Stephanie who does believe in angels and named her son Gabriel after her own Thyroid Chancer scare 10 years ago. SHE left our attunement (appointment) with a reading list and a good probiotic supplier contact I left having passed my pre-op so far.

Then I met my Best Care Nurse who will be my Anam Cara (soul friend) for the whole journey. My go-to mentor of the physical. She is spending her free time this weekend studying for a Health Psychology Masters Degree Module: her money, her time.

How hard are we gonna fight for this NHS?

Yesterday I had a check on my allergies, intolerances with Irene Maxwell McCabe at The Harvest Clinic. I need to up the iodine and I was right - I'm allergic to Penicillin.

And made sure I've got a plan for coated anti-inflammatory tabs, know to ask for anti-nausea tabs in advance of morphine, the value of charcoal tabs post-surgery to soak up and

carry away toxic chemicals, medicines, or for any eventual Ki-More-Therapy and the continued importance of multi strain probiotics.

We sourced totally natural organic chemical-free toothpaste, face wipes, rose water freshener, organic linseed oil, good green teas, natural crystal deodorant from Guava on Great Western Road, Glasgow. A fabulous place of all things healthy and got a lesson in a few Ayurvedic tricks and products to calm and soothe the soul while there from the shop owner.

Saint Caroline Miller (Homoeopath) has sent all my

Homoeopathic pearls for improved sleep, arnica for bruising, swelling etc.

But there are many - too many to mention - it's like the healthcare Oscars. Thank you.

I am blessed to have you in my life.

There are some benefits to having the Chancer. You wouldn't think so but there are some, I promise.

GREET·PRAY·LOVE 2

Another thing that they don't give you a prescription for as soon as you are diagnosed with anything but they SHOULD - especially for the Chancer - is Ultra-Sound Therapy.

It should be provided by the National HEALTH Service via vouchers for Speakers, dummy microphones, earphones, iTunes, CDs, downloads.

Ultrasound Therapy in the form of MUSIC, Sweet Music.

Musical vibrations penetrate the cells and fibres of our bodies and awaken the fire inside of us and we need that fire for the fight.

Dance and movement of any type is a sign of life in the body; an expansion and expression of the soul.

So I've been discovering karaoke backing tracks to all my favourite musicals on iTunes Store from Defying Gravity of Wicked, to The Lion King and through the years from Kiki Dee to Bonnie Raitt.

Kitchen roll tubes or HP sauce bottles make for fabulous fake microphones and snooty cats make for disdainful audition judges.

Husbands alternate from pure joy and a desire to cuddle and

participate to a slightly perplexed and anxious expression when you are still belting them oot an hour later.

This catharsis produces the endorphin effect which is mildly addictive - but in a very good way. These feel-good chemicals – Dopamine, Serotonin, Oxytocin, Acetylcholine (inner liquid Valium) are all mixed into a cocktail infusion and flushed through the body and mind on every level.

This is very good for everything but especially when you are dealing with The Chancer. We need to mobilise the Peace Corps in the immune system to flood and overwhelm, then see off the Chancer Cells.

I am making a Defying Gravity playlist or three:

1 Empowering Feck off Tunes:

"Bohemian Like You" by The Dandy Warhols - Try it, I defy you to sit still.

"Defying Gravity" from Wicked.

2 Greet and Release Tension Tunes:

"I'm Kissing You" Des'ree

"This Woman's Work" Kate Bush

3 Self Soothe and Relax Tunes:

Hans Zimmer "Elysium"

Local Hero soundtrack

The Beatles "Blackbird"

Music as Soul Medicine at the vibrational level where self-healing begins.

GREET·PRAY·LOVE 3

I'm currently working from a tick list with 13 days until lift-off and counting.

Tick lists are great for giving you a sense of control over the completely uncontrollable.

So today was "shorter hair day". Hair Dryers may be tricky for a while and my Medusa impersonation is not my best look for Healthspital visitors.

Plus, I think I needed a change. There needs to be CHANGE when you are dealing with Breast Chancer. I trained with Dr. Bernie Siegel over 20 years ago at Birmingham University and have handed out his book Love Medicine and Miracles to every person I knew who had Chancer. I had dozens of copies at home and in the Clinic which is probably why I couldn't find ONE when I was looking last week.

Until the clear out day-yesterday. One was found hiding in the bedside drawer among pristine unused journals.

Recently while up in Blairgowrie I was talking about buying a few copies of it from Amazon while in an olde worlde charity bookshop. How amazing if they had a copy.

Well, they didn't. Nope, they had one better - only a book by one of Bernie Siegel's mentors Larry Le Shan' "Cancer as a Turning Point" - a 30-year-old copy.

You need a good supporting cast - real and virtual - for this journey through the forest, and Bernie and Larry are in my crew for the duration. The pair of them are adamant about the need for change, for realising inner dreams and for creative expression in the medicine cabinet.

Today was also "New Bras Day". The wee catalogue they give you at the Healthspital is fine but some are SO expensive. Always someone looking to make a buck from misfortune. Prosthetic boobs you can swim with at £150? Are they mini-propellers, shark-repellent or what?

I could make my own out of Play-Doh with a raisin in it for £2. And I might.

Cue St. Michael. Ye dear olde Mark and his brother Spencer who live in a fort just off the M8 have been making Post-Surgery Brassieres for some time now – VAT-free, a fraction of the catalogue prices. You need a wee pocket inside to hold your prosthetit in situ - deliberate spelling. I can only imagine the hours of fun one could have without that wee pocket- landing in the soup, on the dance floor, caught up in somebody's hair extensions after a violent hug.

But needs must now if I don't wanna look like a burst balloon.

There are some really beautiful ones the boys have designed, with matching kegs.

Lord G enjoyed the impromptu Brafest fashion show yesterday, however modesty, FB rules and the presence of pervs online prevents me from sharing my delightful new wardrobe with you, dear reader

Nighties and jammies were on the ticklist too - easy to open, front-fastening, all the wee things you'd never think of but the Best (Breast) Care Nurse does.

And big shout out to Claire and Michelle who both sent me fabulous heart-shaped Mastectomy pillows for after and lovely L who has pointed me towards the soft and fluffy knitted prosthetit for my bra filler after.

All reactions are different and mostly fit the 80/20 rule that some people plan their diet around. You fill your plate with mostly good stuff and are allowed 20% not so hot foods.

80% of people are astounding, fabulous, incredible. The other 20%? Well, they are astounding too, just for different reasons.

That may reflect our OWN individual shadow side statistically.

Mostly we are all beautiful, loving, kind, wonderful human beings but we all have that Darth Vader aspect tucked away and hidden, ready to pounce. Sometimes the shadow side is more apparent when the sun shines, it's more exposed in the light. So at tricky times things can become very, very clear. What's light and feels good, what's not so hot.

My Darth Vader has been entering stage left. There has been more anger, frustration, self-pity around than normal. Okay make that RAGE, FECKED OFFNESS and DESPAIR.

That feels better! It's time to call in the big-shoulder persons with the wide-open hearts, huge ears and sealed lips. The people of THIS tribe are essential companions on a journey such as this and I have a few of them around me hovering on the periphery, waiting for my cue to enter stage left.

I suspect that already there may be some tutting and tsk-ing going on in the background about my posting on such a private, delicate and personal matter.

If so, I have two questions, why on Earth are you even ON my page? And why are you still reading such a long post? Do yourself a favour-feel free to exit stage right with my love.

Book two in progress.

GREET·PRAY·LOVE 4

Quartz makes up 12% of the Earth's crust and is used in almost every kind of technology, including time keeping (yer watch) electronics (yer radio), information storage and more. If it's possible for crystals to communicate through computer chips, then isn't it possible that this vibrational energy could be transformed in other ways? And with its connection to the Earth and its life-giving elements, it makes sense that crystals are universally healing, especially since they've made their mark in almost every civilisation before us.

I'm using them as part of my medicine cabinet of all that modern Healthspital medicine has to offer, using the teachings of the Spiritual traditions on healing - no matter the source and what the ancient healing systems have to offer too.

I'm having HOLY-ISTIC THERAPY as my approach.

I have them by my bed, in rooms I spend time in, in my water jug - but rinsed and cleansed daily and charged up under the sun, moon regularly. I can feel the energy they radiate.

If it's just my imagination. What does that mean? It's MY experience.

I can experience it. Doesn't matter if someone else doesn't or can't.

Anything that triggers self-healing in the bodymindsoul is really helpful in healing the Chancer away. Anything that stimulates the love-'em-phocytes (Lymphocytes)to flood the Chancer Cell Network with love to dissolve and dissipate over time. Love will always conquer the dark stuff - all the great spiritual teachers have said so from the start.

And allow the loving Auntie-Buddies (Antibodies) to flood the whole area with love and light energy clearing away any old unnecessary stuff and debris. Aunties are usually great cleaners.

I also use my rose quartz crystals to visually help me imagine my Chancer shrinking from all the love.

The first is where it started (four-six cm it's thought) and then I imagine it getting smaller and smaller down to a marble, then a pea then it's gone.

So inspirational reading is on my prescription medicine and ingesting positive affirmations. How perfect that Hay House are releasing a free online summit before and after surgery for the Mystery-Ectomy, daily videos of talks by their most inspirational writers on healing and spirituality.

The free gift sent was Louise Hay's film "You Can Heal Your Life."

Now I'm no daft, I know that spiritual healing doesn't always mean cure - but I'm giving this everything I've got down here in the engine room and surrendering the final decisions of navigation to The Pilot. Ably assisted I'm sure by my heavenly captain...dad.

GREET·PRAY·LOVE 5

The importance of accepting offers of help and assistance cannot be overstated in the process of releasing the Chancer Cells from the body. Some metaphysical experts see Breast Chancer as a "lack or loss of love", over-giving and/or imbalance in the emotional bank account. However, it is folly to think we KNOW completely what, why anyone develops Chancer - though there is now evidence-based science which describes the Chancer personality profile (See Dr Gabor Mate).

Sometimes it can be your Donaldo Ducko, part of your soul's journey and development, and, or the toxicity of the world we live in (anywhere from one in three to one in two of us may have an experience with Chancer in our lifetime - now DELETE THAT PROGRAMME).

Me, I think a combo of all of the above helped facilitate a hole in the castle walls of my compromised immune system after the last two-plus years of a few significant losses, a traumatic situation, prolonged stress and carrying too much for too long. My wee immune system was too tired and let down its defences for a moment or two and the Chancer Cell Movement moved in.

However the process of healing, love and joy can produce all sorts of magnificent improvements and alterations in the human condition and yesterday was one of those days for me. Allowing people to help, asking for and receiving help is on the prescription list.

I've got better at it over the years but this one requires total surrender of ego.

So when Frances offered to give up her Friday to help set up for Reiki one this weekend, I breathed deeply and said thank you.

Setting up, shopping, carrying, accompanying, listening. What a trooper.

When she offered after 6pm to give me a Reiki before she left, I breathed again and said thank you.

The love and support of others just seeps straight into the bone marrow.

GREET·PRAY·LOVE 6

Laughter therapy is essential in the Medicine Chest (which is really the heart, centre of the CHEST) to engage in true healing of any sort but especially so The Chancer of the Breast, which is right next to said heart.

The heart receives a wonderful massage when we laugh out loud and the vibrations carry like waves. We even use the words belly laugh: the big deep laughs that resound. It's just another form of Ultra-Sound Therapy.

Unfortunately, at this stage in my life, sometimes my bladder receives a slightly over rigorous massage when I'm laughing too hard. But perhaps that's too much information.

I awoke very early today: the Reiki one Tribe will arrive in a few hours.

So I made a big hot lemon water. This is great for alkalising a body which may be over-acidic and superb for awakening the liver, gall bladder and blessed kidneys which all have a big job to do in the weeks to come.

Laughter releases so many feel good hormones and chemicals in the system and is such a great medicine of the bodymindsoul.

So, I found a few photos and enjoyed making a daftie memory collage, for cheering me up after my Hope-eration. Photos that make me laugh and smile.

Everything does need to be in balance and there is a place for awareness and acceptance, tears and snotters, fears and what-ifs. Denial and repression of feelings overload a system already under strain and are not the way to go, but the secure baseline and our emotional scaffolding will be all the stronger for a healthy dose of the ridiculous, a holding of it all with a lighter grip.

They do say angels can only fly because they take themselves lightly.

MAY 2019

GREET·PRAY·LOVE 7

A Chancer diagnosis creates initial shock and awe. The shock wears off and after a while reality dawns but the AWE continues.

Life itself becomes precious beyond belief in all its forms. Everything seems more full of is-ness. I thought I was fairly mindful and alert B. C. (before the Chancer). But by comparison, I was playing at it.

I feel as if Gaia has outlined everything I look at with a fine black felt pen. There is a definition and clarity, I have only ever seen before temporarily but now see most of the time.

This clear vision extends to all of my senses. I feel more, hear more, taste and smell is attuned, thinking is sharper and more focussed.

Sometimes I even TALK more, can you believe that?

And I cry more deeply when I'm sad at belly level. It's not so often, but I am aware it's deep.

I really haven't got a lot to cry about. I've got the best Chancer to have in terms of successful treatment percentages. I've had a fantastic experience of NHS, McMillan Care and DWP, been carried on a tidal wave of love, prayer and Reiki, had a beautiful sacrament of healing this week and had our magnificent long-time-lawyer Mike navigate us through power of attorneys (which we really should all have at least after 50). I have a strong team of folks who have my back and part of this week has been spending time with them while I'm still fit and free of discomfort. We should avoid the word "pain" at all costs, too much memory luggage with it.

It's been a time of sorting and prepping. I'll be off for some time - we don't know how long - so there was a lot to organise. But tomorrow is my last day in Clinic for the foreseeable. Graham and the girls are steering the ship now.

And that feels right. I need to focus everything I've got on ME.

I took possession of my gorgeous crystal decanter and water bottle, my gift to ME from ME for the journey. Water and I are becoming even closer pals. Water in, water out is a good thing to do for Chancer healing, whether as tears of joy or sadness or as a powerflush.

WE are mostly water and we need lots to hydrate and to heal. But when we add the healing power of energetic crystals to our water, prepare to be amazed.

Let the magic begin.

GREET·PRAY·LOVE 8

There is a bittersweetness around these huge turning points in our lives and for me, since the Chancer life-agnoses, the sweetness is so far winning out. The outpourings of love, the offers of help and support, the beautiful cards, flowers, books, the sharing of hearts and the offers of soup, baking and much more. In fact, any painters, decorators, gardeners or ironing fans out there? I jest, of course.

Quiet you smart arses! I know Freud said there is no such thing as a joke. . it was ME who told YOU that.

So it's T minus three and counting until lift off.

I had a beautiful time yesterday which started with Michelle coming Thursday night with the gift of a gorgeous Mystery-ecromy pillow. Heart shaped to fit under the arm with a beautiful pink ribbon to tie on the shoulder, to relieve arm weight on the skin-art (skar for short) deftly mastered by the s-urge-you-on during the hope-eration.

And then a two-hour FaceTime with my long-time pal Kim in Sydney over the Rainbow in Oz. She is a high calibre top psychotherapist and boy did she put me through my mindset paces.

Lunch was with my dear friend Cherie, another master psychotherapist and doctor who finished off the job beautifully over her wonder-soup and crusty heavenliness. While reminding me that while good diet is important, in the Chancer healing, ENJOYING and taking PLEASURE in what we eat are crucial too, in targeted immune boosting therapy of the soul body mind. So I had another slice of that delicious crusty healthful rye bread but passed on the custard tarts.

My G has been a mahoosive walking hug. He is scared too - that's normal. Too much positivity can be equally toxic to the system, it becomes like emotional and spiritual Aspartame in the soul body mind. There are dangers in denial too.

He got me a beautiful painting called "Safe Harbour" the Christmas after dad died, it brings me great comfort now and reminds me of dad's song "When you walk through a storm.." and the equal importance of hope.

But laughter is a great refresher and my car registration plate game is in full flight with the Divine Intelligence playing along big time, I spluttered when I saw the number plate "..TYT".

It's always nice to have a place or space for your soul to express herself or himself creatively, a wee sanctuary spot.

I've got mine in my bedroom now and canny wait to see the NHS responses when it is transported to Wishaw General University Healthspital.

May God have mercy on their souls. They have absolutely NO IDEA what is about to land on the ward come Wednesday.

"What time are the drumming group visiting again?".

GREET·PRAY·LOVE 9

I like the word "GREET", it can be interpreted as "to have a greet", Glaswegian for weep or It can mean to welcome, to express a greeting of welcome.

I am learning to do both since I was diagnosed with Breast Chancer. To welcome in and to express and release emotions out.

Having never, ever claimed benefits for anything my entire life, I was resistant to the suggestion from my nurse that McMillan Care would send someone out to go through options, as we do not know the outcome or period of time off work and best be prepared ahead of time for all possibilities. It could cause delays later if things are required and I haven't signed in while I'm fit and able, apparently.

I knew I would not be eligible for much, having savings and rainy day money set aside for just such an emergency stop at work and being self-employed.

But I was still bemused by the hoops I had to jump through and the attitude of the DWP "form-filler", who it seems had quickly assessed that I looked alright, had no paperwork to prove I was ill and didn't look as if I needed anything much, so she would leave it and I could go to the job centre when I had made a phone call, that would let me download a form and when I had a "fit note" (sounds like a bloody wristwatch-step-counter-thing).

None of this was explained BEFORE her visit despite seven texts, calls (twice a day) to remind me she was coming and I'd better be in or a death squad would be round to exterminate me. The perils of them coming to you.

We got off to a bad start, she arrived 10 minutes before the end of the allocated time slot, she got lost. I had allowed two hours for our meet, it took up nearly three and a half hours of MY limited time, in the end.

I had been given poor info and had been honest that I was still working and intended to until a few days before surgery. This was a big mistake.

However, eventually it appeared she DID in fact have the form with her that I "should have downloaded once I had actually stopped work" (which was 4:30 pm that SAME day).

I listened to my pal Gabor Mate today. He was speaking about the roots of healing, about the health effect of repressed anger and our need to deal with anger constructively and healthfully.

But more than that, he was speaking about connection.

Connection with myself.

The fearful little child inside who is scared of all this change, of not being in control, of being at the mercy of the big people, of pain and suffering and what-ifs.

My scooping her up, that wee inner child in a loving embrace and soothing her with the assurance that I WILL be there for her and I will completely surround her with people who will love and support her.

Richard Rohr writes about how when we judge or criticise "the poor" and particularly people on benefits, we should remember that "we are ALL on benefits". We all live on the mercy of the Divine, the Universe, God, Gaia, whatever term floats yer boat.

We would do well to remember that. I'm living on handouts and sometimes emergency relief from the Great Mystery of Love every day.

When I stay connected, to and from a loving place, to all that is broken and hurting "out there", I am also staying connected to what is to be healed "in here" and vice-versa.

GREET·PRAY·LOVE 10

I met Kate, my pal of 45 years, and we had lunch at the top of the Campsie Hills in Katy Rogers Courtyard Cafe, one of my favourite oasis-places.

Kate has a home in Spain but is teaching here term-time, so we had a great catch up after the Easter break. The penny was dropping for us both of the enormity of the possibilities ahead.

I mentioned the Aspartame positivity knee-jerk "you'll be fine" responses given at times by totally well-meaning but misguided folks (by the way, I've done my fair share of it over the years). Versus an empathetic and compassionate reality check, with a secure baseline of positive focus but an honest appraisal of the gravity of the situation.

Sometimes in these situations with Chancer, we throw around soundbites to get us out of an uncomfortable hole.

"17 of my pals have had Breast Chancer and they are all still alive."

"You can always have a reconstruction and the wigs are grrrrreat these days."

"But you look so fantastic?!"

"It's the best one to get."

Mind you, that's all better than the stories of folk who are deid from it, the horrific complications and the war stories. You do need your wits around you in this earth school class 101 and a great radar with discernment scanner fitted, for who you should sing along to silently inside, while they wax lyrical about what a great thing to happen to one. Just as long as it's no them.

Still, that's better than the morbid curiosity of the car-crash watchers, who have a long list of questions to ask, and all BUT ask if they can see the Chancer, or even have a feel. The questions are endless.

So it was blessed relief to talk turkey (though they only have hens on the farm) with Kate. This is no cakewalk being embarked upon, though the pancakes were delicious and I took your advice Cherie, I enjoyed every mouthful.

And though focus, determination, resilience and lightness of touch, with laughter in spades is required, so too are vulnerability, expression of truth, surrender and total trust.

Next book (must be gonna write till I'm 100) is called "FEEL THE FEAR AND FEEL THE FEAR ANYWAY".

This is no time for dissociation. It is however time for connection - inner and outer, though they are the same thing.

So we visited Schoenstadht Shrine at the foot of the Campsies, where the Sacrament of Exposition of the Host was going on inside the tiny Tyrolean Chapel, and we lit a candle each. The solemnity of the ritual was time-bending and heart-opening. We were there minutes, hours or days.

I stayed on after Kate and the others who had been praying inside had departed, just me and Big J. Lo-ve. We had a good chat.

"All shall be well. . . and all manner of things shall be well" was how it began.

GREET·PRAY·LOVE 11

A loving friend panicked yesterday when I mentioned I had eaten a pancake at Katy Rogers' Farm, and put in an enormous amount of time and effort explaining the importance of evidence-based dietary changes that facilitate healing from the Chancer.

I was truly grateful. But I'm very blessed to have an on-site naturopathic nutritionist at The Harvest Clinic (Irene) who has pulled me through with a Christmas tree in time for the hoperation and healing and I'm prone to a bit of exaggeration on FB for effect. In reality I had a "bit" of my pal's pancake!

So, to put the record straight, since diagnosis I have been dairy-free and sugar-free (both of which "feed" Chancer) caffeine-free, alcohol nearly-free but for an occasional glass of organic red, red meat virtually-free, keto with a small k, and I rattle like a jar of vitamins and minerals because I have turned into one.

I end my day with alkaline base powder from the Mayr clinic and start by gagging down Dr Graham's Kermit-in a-blender juice. There are many combos of this enigmatic glass of snottery slime juice, broccoli and spinach, kale and broccoli, celery and kale or on feast days, all four.

This after my quark and linseed oil (shout out to Jack MindStore who reminded me) courtesy of the 3E cancer centre in Stuttgart, pioneered by Dr Joanna Budwig.

So mornings are busy in our house!

Diet is important for sure but I truly believe on its own it is not enough. It needs an holistic approach, holistic strategy.

We need the bodymindsoul engaged and recalibrated or we are rolling along with two wheels on our wagon.

Yesterday began with stunningly beautiful and restorative Reiki with Theresa and segued into a defrosting freezer day and some kitchen cupboard clearing. Boy, that was therapeutic, hacking the ice and thawing out.

It was a purging all of its own.

Then we went to buy some new life in the form of gorgeous tall houseplants for the bedroom, more lavender plants in pots for the garden and another tall Japanese Maple tree (acer) to mark the start of the journey. We will sink strong roots and stretch out our branches together.

G, however, was mildly concerned about the journey home in the mobile Beechgrove Garden.

On the subject of horticulture, Ashley, my niece gave me roses on 22 April - that's 16 days ago. I took a photo this morning, STILL going strong. They are however right next to my wee sanctuary space, crystal garden in my bedroom.

Making the bedroom a beautiful healing botanical crystal space is, I feel, really important. I will be spending a little more time there for a wee while. So we cleared all unnecessary stuff and filled with photos of loved ones, Himalayan salt lamps, cleansed crystals, sacred mementos, healing books, my new gorgeous plants and a comfy chair to sit on.

I may be so comfy, that I never leave this room - except I'd need to survive on Kermit juice.

I've never fancied nipple piercing myself, so today will be fun - I'm having radioactive isotopes injected into mine this afternoon.

Song for today is "I've got you under my skin" as I light up the sky and "Shine like a diamond".

GREET·PRAY·LOVE 12

Had my breast removed now. I awoke an hour or so ago to a room with a view that I was SO GRATEFUL and delighted to see!

And they provide wee cardboard pork pie hats to celebrate your awakening to Amazonian Warrioress status. The Amazons were an ANCIENT tribe of female warrioresses who, legend has it, cut off one of their own breasts so they could aim their archery bow more accurately. It was easier to get a clear shot at wherever they set the sights of their arrows.

Now apparently it's based on myth and legend but I still choose to believe in Santa so I'm happy to go along with this one too.

My G was soon smiling by my side.

During the whole process there was for sure a Heavenly Host of Angels around that operating theatre set - straight out of ER (but no sign of George C).

And with no pre-med in sight, my gran (Peggie), dad and my darling Liz were quite clearly outlined in the "trick of the light" at the foot of the bed. I felt them there as surely as when they were this side of the Veil.

God bless this place of Nurturing Healing Saints or the NHS as it is otherwise known. I have never seen so much care and compassion (except in the Harvest Clinic Glasgow) LOVE-IN-ACTION and consummate professionalism with a good

dose of self-sacrifice and courage mixed into the healing care cocktail.

Talking of cocktails: where's my Morphine? Self-hypnosis? I'll try the morphine please. Lucy in the Sky with Rose Quartz

Crystals.

GREET·PRAY·LOVE 13

(Lucky for me)

So I'm home, but not without a dash back in last night to Healthspital, my side drain was blocked and a little dodgy-looking - in that it was not draining. All sorted and full service with a smile on arrival at the Ward. Honestly WHAT a country we live in. So lucky, that's what we are.

I've started to share a few tips for those who are on the healing journey from the Chancer or who know, will know someone who IS.

Essential to the healing process is the healing of the bodymindsoul.

Too much emphasis is placed solely on the physical body. You are NOT your body, that's why you leave your overcoat behind you when you cross the Veil.

But the body is very important for manoeuvring around this Earth School and world of matter that we currently reside in. So it does need attention and needs to be able to work.

But to fully heal, we need to take an holistic approach, treating the bodymindsoul separately and together. We need to become whole and even Holy. Yes, I really did say that.

There are lots of ways to heal engaging in creativity, communing with nature, aromatherapy healing essences, use of affirmations, visualisation, mind guiding, laughter therapy, crying therapy, pet therapy, pal therapy, cuddle therapy crystal hydration therapy.

Watching the sunrise therapy.

All of these initiate unblocking of tension and dissolution of the pain body, and stimulate the production of Oxytocin, Serotonin, Dopamine and Acetylcholine (that lovely internal liquid Valium). These will create phenomenal results in your healing response and immune system boosting, in addition to any prescription from the Chi-mist.

Yesterday, I had a visit from two of my oldest pals. . . yes, they are both nearly 60, WAY AHEAD of me. Our first of our Women's ceremony and ritual-type thangs was established on this, my Healing journey…

The Robe Initiation - photographing everyone who visited me in my crazy Afghan purple psychedelic hippy dressing gown.

From now on, we have decided, all who visit shall be thus enrobed, captured on film and catalogued for my "Calendar Girls and Boys" which will be on sale in time for Christmas (for charity of course).

A heart massage through laughter is vital in dealing with Chancer. It acts as healing ultrasound waves in the tissues, vibrating away any little psychic dust mites of Chancer, or sub-atomic psychic-dandruff protons and croutons at a quantum level, after the Purgery.

So books, videos, cards that make for a jelly-belly laughter experience are to be highly recommended on the "lol" diet.

Eveleen Greer makes the most delightful little heart-shaped Karma Cakes for the beloved visitors who come to bring us good cheer.

Often they also bring homemade soup.

If they offer to bring anything, always ask them to bring good healthy soup, not chocolate. Unless they are very wealthy then just ask them for a load of money instead and make yer own soup.

Said heartful chocolate Karma Cake lovelies should NOT be ingested by the Chanceree though. No.

And the visitors will get fat, while you look great. Result.

However high cocoa content, good grade dark chocolate (85% plus) is full of amino-acids and antioxidants, delicious when melted and mixed into truffle balls or tiny cookies with nuts, seeds, organic peanut butter, coconut, organic cacao powder, chilli, Himalayan salt, grated ginger, grated carrot, coconut oil. . . you get the picture?

Nobody needs to feel deprived.

They tell me red wine is full of anti-oxys and aminos too. But stick to organic (Waitrose, Tesco, Aldi, Lidl) and remember it's just a wee treat now and again.

YouTube is full of fantastic mind medicine talks and workshops and at 5am this morning I started my day with Dr Wayne Dyer, who I interviewed and trained with over 20 years ago in Manchester. Where did the time go?

So this morning for 90 minutes, Wayne and I re-examined my mental toolbox and sharpened some saws.

Dehydration and the after-effects of drugs, surgery can be alleviated by water but crystallising your water makes it taste like a mountain stream and feel like the elixir of life. Invest in some crystals or a fancy pants wand or flask and a teaspoon of coconut oil in hot tea tastes fab but also greases the sluggish wheels of the waste disposal system.

Vitamin E oil is superb for rehydrating the skin and much more effective than those pricey jars of chemically toxic nonsense creams.

Thank you again Irene Maxwell McCabe for all your expert advice. Yer a marvel.

Just a few wee tips and updates, I'm sure there will be more.

TREAT·PLAY·LAUGH 14

It was time for a wee change of title (from GREET PRAY LOVE) although there are still intermittent tears of tiredness, mainly. Sleep isn't always easy with a mile of garden hose penetrating your rib cage and a plastic bottle of Buckfast strapped on to it, so I feel a bit like Sigourney Weaver in the film Alien "The Old Generation".

There are also sometimes scary monster tears. These are the most healthy of all of the tears. It's better out than in, and oftentimes reality really IS your best friend. My dear pal Moyra is a retired breast care nurse, who intuitively knew that today, NOW, would possibly be a tricky time. Thank you darling Moyra. It's not so bad, a wee abseil down and off the cliffs of morphine and adrenaline.

The biggest danger of the New Age, Woo Woo Movement, of which I am a fully paid-up member, and proud to be so, is that we ageing hippies often have great difficulty facing our SHADOW, the DARK stuff, DEATH.

The complementary health crew sometimes think they have the answer for everything and we don't. We just DON'T.

I am totally in awe of the people I have trusted with my healthcare plan, experts in complementary and traditional medicine.

I will not hear a harsh word said about pharmaceutical companies ever again. They have saved my life (although I know Big Pharma Business has its failings). Ach, I'll probably be banging on again about them and their policies within the month - who am I kidding? - but today, I'm sooo grateful.

I have a bag of white support stockings to stop a blood clot DVT, drainage equipment, even a wee cloth bag to carry it in, amazing pain relief pills, copious dressings, bandages.

And I've never been asked for a brass farthing. NHS - The National Healing Sensation!

For healing to occur "It takes two baby" in my humble opinion - conventional and complementary. I start reflexology treatment with Marion who is trained in ART (advanced reflexology for Chancer patients) and heavenly Reiki with Theresa, which I've had weekly since the kick-off. Irene and Caroline have been on my Naturopathy Team - Nutrition, Supplements and Homeopathy respectively. I'm very lucky, I knew all these guys already professionally and I teach Hypnotherapy and Reiki so I know how to apply liberally.

But many of these treatments are available through Maggie's centres, The Haven (Wishaw), Beatson Centres, Hospices - it's important to ask what's on in your area and it's free - for patients AND their carers and family.

And here's a nice wee story to end the day.

My mum and dad sang together semi-professionally and at every party and get-together all of their lives. Dad was always on guitar or piano and both sang in harmony. They were awfy guid! They sang many songs but my favourite and one of theirs too was "Feelings", originally by Andy Williams. Mum told me during her visit, that on the morning of my Master-ectomy, she opened her Inspirational daily reading book and the title of the piece for that date was... FEELINGS.

She received the gift deeply in her heart - thanks Dad.

Before my op they gave me no pre-med - but they DID wheel me right into the op theatre.

I was then advised that I had to roll over like a feckin' elephant seal, on to the operating table.

Oh bless the Lord and praise be that my nursing assistant, chief dresser and back scrubber had offered a pair of rather fetching fishnet, put-Bridget-Jones-in-the-shade, XXXXXXXL pants (though I use that term loosely).

A slightly finer net comprised the none too glamorous Hilda Ogden Style hairnet which had been placed over my flaxen locks, atop my head.

All hope of dignity was lost before the first "Hhhhhhuuuuupppp" was groaned as I hoisted and hummmphed myself across onto the table from the trolley.

Now, those of you who know me well will know I'm rather prone to maintaining a pretence at a sense of control in my life so this petty little humiliation had dented my somewhat already bruised ego.

I had to regroup fast.. what to do?

The eight or so members of the surgical team were all pretending not to have noticed my rather ungainly arse-over-elbow entrance into their world and were busy polishing cutlery and adjusting spotlights.

I cleared my throat - not easy when lying flat out on a butcher's block and in doing so I nearly choked.

"Can I have your attention please everybody before we start? I have a last request. I'd like you all to sing a chorus of a song as I am being operated on…"

I could read thought bubbles above their heads with the word "Groan" inside each one. They were obviously expecting to be asked to hold hands and chant a chorus of 'Kumbaya My Lord, Kumbaya… "

But no. "You should all know this song, it's a famous Scottish ditty by The Bards of Caledonia.. The Bay Titty Rollers. And it's called 'Bye Bye Booby'."

They fell about! It broke the ice and we all relaxed.

I kissed my fingertips, placed them on and blessed my right breast, saying "thank you for everything" to her and let her go with love.

MEET·REPEAT·TREAT 15

Another day. Another milestone. Losing the Cyberwoman look - it's drain removal day.

"You can take away my drain but you will never take my FREEDOM!"

I must admit, I think I'm now gonna miss my little companion of the past six days, we've been through so much together.

However, I have had a few human pals visit in the last couple of days and the "Ab-Fab-Dressing-Gown-Ritual" is going down a treat, I must confess dear reader. I think we could do it with an Afro wig too.. ahm just dropping a wee hint yo!. It will be tough to select just 12 winners for the annual Christmas Calendar.

Caroline and Chloe are coming to sit in the sun and chat about our Woman's Day mid-June, a wee compass point on my healing chart and it hurts when I laugh, so I may need to tune some of their zany chat oot. We will get them in the goonie, fear not.

GREET·PLAY·LAUGH 16

Laughter is a huge medicinal component in healing The Chancer. I now understand where the term "I was in stitches laughing" comes from. I nearly burst mine this morning during my four times a day Laughter Immersion Therapy Experience: Or LITE Treatment for short.

GREET·PRAY·LOVE 17

Well, what a week this has been.

Tuesday was the Counsel-Aunt's Results at the Healthspital (Consultant, Hospital for the un-enlightened) after my Mystery-ectomy (Mastectomy).

It wasn't the best news and it wasn't the worst. I had a buy one, get one free tumour removed (two for the price of one, joined in the middle). I never do anything by halves and I had a nymph node with little sleeper cells of interest too.

I love my nymph nodes - so we need to protect the rest.

So we see the On-Cellogist on the 11th to plan our journey to have some Ki-More-therapy over the next few months or so before we start some Ray-Joy-Therapy.

Now before you ask - was I upset?

Absolutely not, as you'd expect.

Totally stoic, was I so utterly brave?

It seemed so - but that wasn't true either. While I was busy comforting and reassuring everybody else, I was in complete and total undiluted, unadulterated shock.

I was "FINE".

"FINE" is great.. for a while. It puts the shock of gross reality into a reservoir and holds back the flow, until the system is protected, the banks are sandbagged high enough, to begin to allow the force of the situation to be channelled through the system - bodymindsoul, without too much collateral damage.

Thankfully my Lord G recognises all of these classic signs - jokes, banter, a light touch, chatting and reassuring trainee nurses - for what they really are. He sits and waits for the inevitable release of pressure, which eventually always follows and flows.

It doesn't mean we shouldn't laugh and joke. In fact we must! We have to lubricate the humour engine regularly. It is essential. We need those bio-chemicals of dopamine, serotonin and oxytocin, so laughs, fun, connection with others are all crucial in healing of any type.

So I knew the value of laughing and joking with my new pals at the "Feeling Good, Looking Good" make-up class at the Maggie's Centre on Thursday.

What an excellent service. They gave us each a huge bag of designer make-up worth well over £100 each, Estee Lauder, Clinique, Dolce and Gabbana among others, plus of course Boots No. 17 - which is also, by "chance" the number of this post.

The cosmetic companies all donate these products free all year and these three make-up artists (among dozens of others) are all volunteers, giving freely a few days a month to teach we 'Warriors of The Chancer' how to still look well to keep our spirits up, when we are in the throws (deliberate mis-spell) of Ki-More-Therapy.

The Maggie's Centre at Monklands is a haven of zen peace and tranquillity. G and I stayed on for the relaxation class after. It was bliss. I will admit I suspended my critical factor on how our students are SOOO well trained and what the obvious howlers in delivering relaxation are. At the prescribed BEACH in the visualisation (tut tut) of course I met my father on a Portuguese beach, promptly morphing into the one on Iona we had visited, so a few tears rolled - and he advised "all shall be well". New readers, he passed over two years ago.

But once I surrendered to the vibe, it was a real letting-go.

So yesterday we tried a wee drive (G, not me: I'm out of commission for weeks yet to drive after the Master-ectomy) to Fintry, Katy Rogers' farm and Schoenstadht Convent to light a candle or three.

My friend's brother is very ill with throat and Lung Chancer, another dear friend has a brother she may need to section into care for dementia. We are never alone in walking through these forests in our lives. But it was a glorious forest to drive and walk through with my beloved G yesterday. We need to seize all of these beautiful moments, making memories and put them in the bank of emotional savings.

And the poignancy of The Bee photo I snapped can't "bee" expressed here. I started my first book with a chapter called "The Bee Story". We spent a good hour there and returned restored and refreshed for the next chapter of our journey.

Speaking of all things natural I will never EVER get used to these breakfast juice combinations of Kermit in a blender, which Lord G has created. They are feckin' vile.

Spinach, kale, wheatgrass, broccoli, sprouts, ground birdseed, arsenic.

I think Ki-More and radio will be a breeze after them!

My niece Ashley brought me some roses on April 22. They are five weeks old on Monday and still blooming., all the way through the waiting game. Phenomenal.

And my dear pal Laura has been delegated headwear stylist for the possible follicle challenges ahead - meanwhile G and I go wig hunting and shooting today.

I fancy a Cher, a pink and an afro dreadlocks. You need to take advantage of every opportunity life throws at you.

And tomorrow.. my first book is born.

BLEAT·PRAY·LOVE 18

There is an unspoken shame and judgement that sometimes goes with Chancer (having Chancer), especially in some areas of the love and light brigade. The shadow side of life is often shunned and neglected in some tribes.

There is also a phenomenon of "The Chancer Olympics" where winners and losers are assigned their medals and trophies dependant on the fastest, strongest, toughest.

And sometimes, who suffered the most, longest, hardest

versus who did it cold-turkey.

I found myself enjoying a secret smug smile as I recounted to others how little pain relief I needed and so had cut down (ye know me being a Clinical Hypnotherapist and all that) until I rebounded and it came back and bit me on the arse.

Some of the shame and judgements may originate from the rather twisted New Age Nonsensical theory that 'YOU gave yerself Chancer' somehow (and that today's toxic world plays no part in the one out of two, or three max, people affected), or that by eating more mung beans and dancing naked with a unicorn under the full moon, wearing a bag of Scots porridge oats around your neck, in an amulet you will "cure it" – 'cos somebody knows somebody that did that.

Chancer in our culture today is a multi-faceted, multi-layered, bodymindsoul state of inflammation and of information (if we will but allow it to be), that requires, at the very least an Holistic, "approach each layer from each angle, gently and slowly, without stressing the system even further" method with no violence, judgement, criticism or any more INFLAMMATION-creating behaviours.

And let's acknowledge that NONE OF US ARE IN CONTROL OF THE BIG PICTURE, NOT A ONE!

Did you make the earth spin on its axis at 1000mph overnight? Or the sun rise this morning? Nah, I thought not.

There's a lotta stuff goes on that is nothing to do with our will or its perceived power, though our egos would like to believe otherwise. And yes, we absolutely are responsible for a fair chunk of our lives and our healing journey. Just not ALL of it.

The 12-step traditions have a great line - "you didn't cause it, you can't control it and you can't cure it". However you sure as heck can play your part in adopting a stance in which healing is most likely to occur.

There is no one system, one approach, one "cure" for a person who needs to heal from the Chancer.

The Chancer may be a messenger to reroute a life, a guide to new territories for the soul to navigate, a necessary journey of discovery, or even a soul's chosen way of dying. (Well, ye've got to die of something).

And of course it may be traceable to a toxic overload, emotional overwhelm over a period of time, or emotional fault lines which have manifested physically. A kind of perfect health storm.

It is more than likely that it will be a combination of approaches which take us back to robust health.

So do diet, nutrition and supplements help? YES. They help. My Naturopath calls them The Building Blocks of Healing, like the foundation level of bricks in a building.

Do other substances help, either by restricting or introducing them, whether dietary, homoeopathic, herbal, legal or otherwise? YES, it would seem so.

Does conventional mainstream medicine help? YES. Survival rates are increasing across the board.

Do treatments like hypnotherapy, massage reflexology, reiki, acupuncture etc help? YES, but only when in the capable hands of a qualified and experienced practitioner who works with cancer patients.

Does self-exploration (listening, counselling, therapy) with another, whether trusted friend or professional, through discovery of potential trigger points of loss of power and energy from the system, help? YES. But at the right time.

It is not the right time at the very start, when you are trying to process that this is more than a flu you've contracted.

But having a listening ear as you manoeuvre can be really helpful from the beginning. Just don't try to unpack your life too soon, for God's sake.

Does healing from emotionally-charged issues from the past, childhood or otherwise which may still lie dormant and drain the system, help? YES.

Do crystals in your drinking water work?

Does yoga work?

Does regular exercise work?

Do holy pictures work?

Do affirmations work?

Does writing a journal work?

Does visiting sacred or special places work?

Does singing Kumbaya in a circle work?

Do aromatherapy oils work?

YES, YES, YES!

Anything that you believe is helping to support you, is working on your behalf like a sacrament. It is an outward sign of inner grace.

Just don't give the power of healing away to the object, the pebble, the place. You energise these externals with the great love that is in and all around you and infuses everything at all times.

It is the healing power of love in its energetic form and spirit which transforms the crystal or the oil from pretty rock or nice perfume to vessel for healing (I owe Caroline Myss for that line).

This is where "prayer" enters the equation. Prayer, or call it loving thoughts, invocations, intentions, blessings, stillness and silence, long hugs, beautiful words, meditation, contemplation, communion with nature and life and the big picture, pure love.

The ultimate layer of the holistic approach to healing. The glue that holds everything else together.

But remember healing and curing are not necessarily the same thing. No matter how many mung beans you eat, meditation beads you count or candles you light, you will pass over the Veil one day, dancing with your unicorn or not.

MEET·PLAY·LOVE 19

"What a difference a couple of days make, 48 little hours."

So, fairly giant steps forward on day 19 post Master-ectomy. I was able to make it in chauffeur-driven style by Lord G, down to Helensburgh to surprise mum for her 21st Birthday at Loch Lomond Golf club with some of the family. Thank God not a club or putter in sight.

T'was a good catch-up with the next generation and a marvelling at the energy, resilience and force of nature that is La Mamma. A fireball.

I'm making great use of my heart pillows (gifted by both Claire and Michelle, one for hoose, one for car). These are made by beautiful Yorkshire ladies and mailed out free (or by donation) to mystery-ectomy patients anywhere in the UK with a gorgeous hand-written greeting on the card. They are called Jen's Friends and they run as a charity, in memory of their friend Jen, who wanted a lightweight pillow that fitted comfortably under her arm and could double as protection from invasive seat belts. Get one for anyone you know is undertaking this journey. It's invaluable for propping up a book, phone, laptop while resting too.

Tuesday, before my pal Kate came over, was my first outdoor

walk of any distance (two thirds of a mile) with camera. It was so liberating to widen my boundaries if a little scary too, for no rational reason. But the heart knows more than the head. And oftentimes the gut knows more than the heart.

My gut was cautioning me to take it slowly and gently, to not accelerate back into the fast lane. So I meandered and pondered my way around our wee circuit, turning back before I "thought" I needed to.

I bought a slow cooker. I had one years ago - used once then charitied away, but REAL FOOD is a REAL priority - so my new model was christened last night.

What goes into my body is now of vital importance if I am to adopt a stance where full healing can occur.

But let me tell you it's a bloody minefield/mind-field out there! (and it would blow yer mind). Everyone has a herb, pill, wonder food, diet, potion and view. I think I have a PhD in Nutritional Science now from all the hours of videos and trawling of research papers I've been directed to and then there is the big CBD with TLC debate.

Thank God I have a Naturopathic Nutritionist on site to help me sift through the maze.

I am practising the art of discernment now. One size does NOT fit all and the evangelists can be violent in their delivery, where it rapidly becomes an assault on the senses of a fragile and weary system trying to find its path in the fog, through the haze of pain and medication.

Gently does it lads, precious cargo onboard. You way-showers need to slow your delivery down, decrease the volume and calibrate to the altitude that the Chancer-challenged souls are flying at. Otherwise, in a knee-jerk reaction, you get muted internally. Too stressful.

And stress is the Big One - the one that can be felt from a great distance by a sensitive system that is trying to heal. In my humble opinion it is the primary requirement of the healing process.

I say this because it feels so immediately noticeable now on a physical level, now that I have landed back in base camp, how deeply sensitised I have become to things, people and situations that stress, inflame exhaust, drain, antagonise, irritate, overwhelm, deplete my energy system.

Not just my body but my subtler energy fields.

So, should we all just move to a private island?

Nah!

I'd have to take ME away with me, my chief stressor and irritant.

No, I need to take on board that the stress management we teach is fabulous, fantastico, shamazing in its breadth of current research, knowledge and application.

But I'm somehow now propelled on a journey down the rabbit-hole into the realm of a different type of stress, a bio-stress, so to speak. A soul-stress discovery and adventure which will require a different and deeper form of recovery and mastery. More than the oft-prescribed deep breaths, lists and visualisations, which are marvellous for mainstream stress.

But marathon climbs and ascents require bigger oxygen tanks and highly experienced Sherpas to guide us. After all, we are quite literally putting our lives in their hands.

So, onwards deeper still. There's work to be done. This weekend it's off to Samye Ling Monastery with Lama G for some deep diving and to see if I can join the community after my baldie.

EAT·EAT·EAT PLAY·LOVE 20

(How did we get to number 20?)

So yesterday, my niece and partner in crime Ashley took me Wig-Shooting.

The world-famous Judy Plum wigs was our hunting ground, after Ashley wedged her car on to a precipice in the car park, before we prepared for our expedition with a feast at Wagamama. It was hot, hot, hot in there.

Being out in the city for the first time in nearly a month was a surreal experience. It was jaggy and jangly. It was also very wet.

I was surprised at the assault on my ears from the traffic and people. I really don't miss the city or the buzz, just the facilities.

But it surprised me how vulnerable I felt - out of step, out of tune with the pace. I wonder if this is how older people feel in our culture, that they can't quite keep up with the speed and noise? We will ALL be old one day if we are lucky.

We had a very uplifting hour in the wig factory although there were some schoolgirl sniggers too.

On trying on a much longer style in a fetching mousy brown we all agreed that I looked like a psychopathic serial child killer or a terrorist in disguise from a 70s TV movie.

That broon trial was just a size test, and sadly one thing became clear pretty quickly after all my years of jokey wee asides, it has now in fact finally been confirmed that I really DO have a big heid!

JUNE 2019

RETREAT·PRAY·LOVE 21

After a fully immersed 23 days of healing from an enormous bunker of a wound inside and out, from my Master-ectomy, my mindbodysoul was thirsting for a wee change of pace and scenery. It was STILL all too busy, Healthspital and GP appointments, physiotherapy techniques to practice, prescriptions to collect, visitors to host and feed, research on supplements and treatments to do, personal therapy to source and start. Then of course there are calls, e-mails, messages, gifts to respond to, a busy Clinic to organise and manage remotely, with a triple whammy computer failure followed promptly by a heating boiler breakdown now it's cold, a cat to be cuddled… and a Lord G to be loved.

How did I ever find time to do therapy, teach training courses, run retreats, write courses, write a book, supervise, manage a busy clinic of 20 plus therapists and spend a full day a week with mum?

I just DID.

We just DO.

Until we don't; until we can't.

I've transformed in three weeks from being a nib-nosed Concorde, down through being a Boeing 747 (still powerful and carrying a lotta passengers) to a Cessna single propeller aeroplane with limited number of seats available, and shorter range.

And I am currently progressing to glider status (the one that needs a bigger plane to take it up).

Samye Ling Monastery is an old friend tucked sassy in the middle of nowhere in the Borders and Lama G and I arrived yesterday to spend a few days immersed in the healing atmosphere, soaking up the peace and being melted by the music of the birdsong. The chants of the monks and brown-eyed Buddhists (James Taylor) seeped into the cells, deep into the marrow of my bones and soothed every fibre of my muscles. The energetic vibration of the temple singing bowl being struck lifted my spirits alongside the wispy threads of incense, like smoky prayers being offered up to Heaven.

We meditated forever in the main temple and I maxed out my credit card in the shop. "It's my soul medicine", I explained to Lama G.

I am in love: with life, with him, with everyone, with my Tara (Mother of Compassion) with God, love itself, and with YOU.

MEET·PRAY·SWIM 22

Meet Bella the bowl. My new brass hand-hammered (beaten, not steamin') singing bowl.

I intend to use her for some sound healing.

It's not as strange as it sounds, pardon the pun. Ultra-sound Therapy is based on the same principle.

Sacred sound healing is the use of various sound "tools" to re-balance our energies on a physical, mental, emotional and spiritual level to promote health and well-being.

A singing bowl has its own unique vibration (resonance) and will, with the use of sacred sound vibrations (that can now be measured and photographed using high RMF equipment) re-calibrate itself to clear and transform blocked energy.

Sound therapy has been known to help -

·Reduce stress and tension.

·Increase energy and vitality.

·Release pain, trauma and blockages.

·Aid in overcoming negative patterns and addictions.

·Increase concentration, creativity and productivity.

And is just pure dead brilliant for meditation practice, as well as ringing downstairs to let him know I'm ready for a cuppa.

EAT·PRAY·LAUGH 23

Heart therapy is hugely important in healing from the Chancer. Laughter therapy is an equal first.

The company of those who make us laugh and smile, who warm the cockles of our hearts, is a major prime mover in kick-starting the Vagus nerve, reducing stress and boosting that all-important immune system.

So it IS true – you gotta laugh.

EAT·PRO·LOVE 24

I said to someone yesterday that I am on an ADVENTURE since this Chancer diagnosis, and she looked sideways as if I'd lost my XBox!

But it's true.

Now let me reassure you I have my moments, plenty of them. I have my 4am tribunals. But I had these before The Chancer - surely we all do. When you awaken in the dark and face the darkness, the unknown, the restless silence, the emptiness, the abyss.

I could tell you about my scar, the excess fluid that still slightly concerns me, the frustration of a GP who phones when it suits him (and I'm not free) - but I canny call back and get to speak to him about future meds. Then there is the heart scan that needs to happen but has been lost in space while I need to try all over again to explain I canny start the Ki-More-Therapy without it.

I could tell you about my disappointment in the unmasking of human beings, some of whom can be pretty woeful at such a time. The let-downs, the lack of support, the head-in-the-sand syndrome.

And I guess I just have.

But the focus of healing relies on where our attention lies most of the time and that needs to be on an altitude of gratitude, a day at a time (sometimes a momentino at a time). And not in needing to be Judge Judy or captain of the Universe. Life is a great teacher and things have a knack of going around as they come anyway - it's no oor job. Human beings are a pretty strange breed and are all just like me. We feck-up with amazing regularity and predictability.

So compassion is a useful tool at a time like this. When crisis hits our lives in so many different ways there are often WEIRD reactions that may surprise us. Some of our circle will dive bomb into self-protection mode, run for cover and hide until the bombs stop falling.

Some of our tribe may go out looting and shooting it up, taking advantage of the opportunities while there is a perceived vulnerability. A power steal.

Others still may rant and indulge in a dirty protest in the street, angry, chanting anti-war anthems of hate and spitting feathers, trying to fight fire with fire

None of this is helpful to the person trying to gather their resources for the "Mountain Less Climbed" that lies ahead. It is a steal of vital energy supplies and oxygen required for the journey.

So we must surround and protect ourselves, our Sherpas and fellow climbers, and undertake vital preparation, packing in fuel and food for these long, tiring, arduous and challenging journeys.

But it IS an adventure too.

The breath-taking views when we stop en-route; the realisation how far we've come, the camaraderie of the team overcoming each challenge one step, one crampon and ice axe at a time and we need to have a place of compassion for the suffering and misguided reactions of the folks above. We are ALL damaged.

Strength and resilience are vital. And we need everything we can carry but NO MORE than that.

We have no room for tourists, passengers and day trippers. You must be clear about who is in your team and have a relief team to take over when they need to rest, a team down in base camp is essential too - ready to launch a rescue mission if required.

You do not need a supporting cast of hundreds for a climb, just a few hand-picked, trusted and experienced Sherpas will suffice.

And good strong ropes and a map.

And a compass. Actually, we need all of the above for daily life.

Probiotics and prebiotics are essential for a healthy gut microbiome. They must be packed into tummies and rucksacks for the climb ahead. They will provide strength and resilience and support the whole system - but especially the immune system.

Fermented foods like kombucha, kimchi, sauerkraut, fermented veggies, sourdough, fermented miso and so on are all excellent sources.

And I spent three hours yesterday learning how to make some of them for myself from a true master, Janice.

She runs workshops from her beautiful home just outside of Glasgow and is a food scientist to trade so you are in very safe hands!

Two weeks till D-Day when the bombs go off.

Ps she also seems to have stolen one of my dreams on my lucky list, a hippie camper van called Bruce.. but I'm working on it.

GREET·PRAY·LOVE NEVER DIES 25

Some things are worth the wait.

It took three years to the month, but my very own book is available now in paperback print, on Kindle or on Audible Books with yours truly narrating.

Four and a half hours of me talking, it took over eight hours to record. G says it was a breeze for me to talk that long.

It's a heart-warming and hopefully inspirational book on loving, losing and living again based on my personal experience of my father's journey across the Veil. It's a book about love. There are many eclectic references to writers and commentators on the spiritual nature of our lives and an exploration of synchronicity and expanding our senses to include the senses of the heart, the eyes of the heart.

I was overwhelmed to receive endorsement quotes from legendary broadcaster Kaye Adams, Caroline Myss Phd and Dr Mary Frame (Marie Curie Hospice). It still feels rather surreal.

I didn't plan it. I was harangued into it but I am so grateful to everyone who pushed and supported every part of it. The thank-yous are all in the book but Monica, it started with you; and Mickey and Mark, it continues with you. I love you.

Profit share goes to Pancreatic Cancer Research.

GREET·PRAY·GREET 26

WELL, I NEVER EVER EXPECTED THAT.

I am utterly overjoyed and overwhelmed by your beautiful

heartfelt response.

I hate the word "humbled" - it reminds me of Ebeneezer Scrooge - but I'm on my knees, grateful and humbled as I read your comments.

It wasn't an easy book to write - it was scary. I felt very vulnerable at times, putting myself out there, putting my heart on a platter.

The cutting-room floor had pools of blood and guts and there were some tears and snotters en-route to the finish line.

But pulling it all together was mostly a load of fun and real joy and satisfaction with "pure dead magic people" who kept it real, did what they said they would do and told me when they thought I was talking shite. Which I often do.

Thanks Monica Smith - (it's all your fault) Shirley Reynolds (for lending us Dave).

Judith, soul friend and wizard, Kaye Adams - how many years now? - Caroline Myss (above and beyond) Dr Mary Frame - humility personified, Mark McMurtrie (the calmest producer in the world), and finally to my editor extraordinaire Mickey who couldnae make mince out of his words if he tried. "Right tit" indeed.

I loved every second! Here's to a robust and well-oiled book launch somewhere, some time.

Bless you all; you are in my heart and held in my prayers tonight. Every last one of you

And PS Mickey says: If you can leave a wee review on Amazon it helps get the message in the book to spread like ripples in a pond.

#loveneverdies

LOVE·PRAY·LOVE 27

Synchronicity is a huge subject but one that I find fascinating.

In fact as I wrote "fascinating" it came up as a typo of "dad I taunting". Now isn't that interesting?

So today I see my On-call-ologist, my go-to "Wonky-ologist" person who will get me straightened out.

A positive approach to Ki-More-Therapy as a healing tool of purging is crucial. Lots of tribes have used similar rituals throughout time, of chemical compounds to purge the body with yucky stuff, this is just another. Seeing it as a way to release blockages of any sort, allowing KI-MORE-THERAPY to do its job with a loving embrace feels important to me. Seeing it as a healing elixir, delivered with love into the body to free it of tired and confused cells which need to be released and replaced now.

BUT listen to this.

My appointment is at 11am on the 11th. My pal Helen pointed out that I posted the ad for the Audible version of my book at 11.11am the other day; my pal Laura (who hates this weirdo nonsense) said last night "funny - I noticed that". And my dad's birthday is the 11th, he died in the 11th month and my G has his birthday in November too. Then Sue commented online: "the number of likes on yer Audible ad is sitting at 11 right now!".

This was all within half an hour.

I looked up the meaning from numerology of 11:11 and came across similar interpretations:

"Some believe that the actual meaning of 11:11 is a number sign that angelic beings are close by. They come with love and protection, and they want to bring you clarity and guidance. So when you see 11:11, trust that it's an angel message for you to decode."

HEID·PRAY·LOVE 28

So after much ado, I finally decided on a wig for if/when the time comes. In fact I did a buy-one-get-one-free, so I have a spare if anyone wants to join in. Probably that'll be Lord G, but it's handy for when the original is being washed and dried.

And you have to think about all these wee things.

Some seem pretty quick to tell you that you WILL lose all your hair but that's not the best suggestion to make to folks, given my understanding of the power of suggestion as a Clinical Hypnotherapist. Maybes aye, maybes naw, but giving a direct suggestion when we are vulnerable and open is sure to have an unconscious impact on the patient.

However I've been fascinated by Buddhist nuns for years - two of my heroes are Pema Chodron and Cherri Huber. They are pretty bald and utterly beautiful in my eyes. So I'm a bit of an oddball on the baldie front and I'm hedging my bets with scarves, turbans, wigs and Buddhist wrap-around sheets. I may even take the veil. Or maybe I will go commando some days, just for the Heaven of it. It's all an adventure.

Who am I really? My looks, my hair, my boobs?

It's all a letting-go process so far, letting go of control, plans and body image.

But also a real "LETTING IN" process in abundance, letting in love, support, kindness and professional expertise above and beyond the call.

Today ended with a visit to the Cumbernauld FM studio to chat to Diane Goldberg for an hour or so live about my book Love Never Dies (she also lost her father recently, It was a lively wee blether and I was really chuffed to get to speak about it publicly for the first time on my home turf).

T'was a day with a difference but if you want to get ahead, get a wig.

HAIR·SPRAY·LOVE 29

So today I collected two new hairdos and a boob, in that order. My angel wig consultant Karen Patterson fitted me in at her home, as she lives near WISHY Healthspital.

She also has an extremely well-stocked gantry in her dining room. Shame I had the car, and my first Ki-More-Therapy tomorrow at 9am. Coulda been a swell party! She is truly amazing. Anyone looking at wigs for any reason should NOT go past her. She travels all over and does home visits for no extra charge. They are for fun too ye know.

We were lucky to get a wee tour of the day care intravenous unit when at WISHY yesterday, it really helps to acclimatise yourself to the places you'll be going and it helps me to work with these locations in my self-hypnosis as I prepare for procedures.

I'm working on a Virtual Cold Cap as well as Glove Anaesthesia for canula fitting and injections, control room of the mind for rebalancing tummy and gastric responses as my body prepares to detox any unwelcome rogue sleeper cells which have taken advantage (The Chancer) of the recent lack of auto-immune vigilance.

I suspect there was a gap in my defences to the traumas I've mentioned before, not least my father's passing, in the two years leading up to the onset of symptoms.

I think I literally "let my guard down" and the Chancer saw an opportunity to move in.

However in our dear green place - the Shire of Glasgow, with its rather limited sunlight and subsequent hellishly low levels of Vitamin D3 in its villagers - we now have Chancer rates of one in every two people being affected by one form or another. So my particular reflection above may be a little romantic in storyline. But I do think the emotional and psychological factors are ignored at our peril.

The whole is greater than the sum of its parts: we are bodymindsoul and need the three interacting to thrive.

Therefore THRIVING is my new compass point; less striving, someone else doing the driving, occasional jiving and a bit of ducking and diving!

I'll apologise NOW, that I won't be responding to messages individually when I'm in recovery. So please don't be offended. There are just too many people and although I appreciate every single message, I need to listen to tiredness as a messenger now and it can become a full-time job. I will do my bloggy thing of course. I'm absolutely delighted to get messages as long as there's no tears before bed that I didn't respond.

This is now time to purge, to release, to shake the tree, to heal and recalibrate on every level. To shed a skin like the snake.

It may not be pretty but it is a sacred ritual in many cultures, Western and indigenous, to use herbs and compounds to purge, detox and cleanse the body before purifying and healing can really begin.

I'm now discovering every tree in the Amazonian backdrop of the forest where they regularly film Outlander, near our house.

It is a sky canopy of green, it lives and breathes you.

I feel it will be an important part of my healing. Shinrin Roku means Forest Therapy and I've been exploring it this past year in practice, in workshops and in my reading on the subjects.

Now I know why.

I've made many boobs in my day but the freebies on our wonderful Natural Healing Service are amazing - only problem is my new one from the orthotics dept today is pretty pert and perfect, pointing beautifully upwards to the moon.

So I need some sort of scaffolded-type bra for the other one which is heading due South these days

JUST·EAT·PRAY·LOVE 30

And so it begins, deeper still.

And I don't mean on the rugby pitch. The fetching headwear is a cold cap worn before, during and after treatment if you choose.

I chose. It's a bit of a tiger for the first 10 minutes then eases off. It's straight out of the freezer every time.

But it seems to reduce hair loss or delay it at least.

I'm having a go at everything in the name of consumer research.

Sad to say, some of you will go through this one day and I am here to suffer for my art and do the Which Magazine review of Breast Chancer treatments.

Level one completed of the Master-Ectomy, the day finally dawned (7am departure) for stage two, Ki-More Therapy.

A beautiful five-day bed unit of peace and calm with a window view of a sunny garden, sandwiches (declined) hot cuppa and later homemade soup (accepted) and a complimentary foot reflexology from lovely Elaine who wants to train in Clinical Hypnosis and Mindfulness, during intravenous injections, due to a cancellation. We had a great chat. Perfect timing and heaven-sent.

Both G and I have now been referred to The Land O' The Monks Healthspital in two weeks for six one-hour sessions of any holistic treatment in the coming months. WHAT A NATURAL HEALING SERVICE IT IS BECOMING.

I've had a worse time at an expensive spa.

The nurses were compassionate, empathetic, gentle, patient and beyond giving.

Everything was explained, every drug triple-checked. The horse tranquilliser-size syringes were run through an intravenous line slowly, so nurse practitioner Lorna sat throughout the whole procedure with me, checking I was OK with every squeeze of each syringe.. all six. Oh and the Tizer ones make you pee red - glad she warned me!

The Chancer needs to be uprooted at its earliest physical incarnation by the most appropriate means known today but the toxic energetic baseline that assisted the germination in the first place is MY job. I'm on it.

I'm reframing that I've swallowed lots of tiny microbial/metallic search and rescue submarines on a temporary mission - it's only a week or two for each mission.

And they are off through the tunnels of my veins into my blood supply and organs to seek and find any sleeper cells who need rescued and delivered to the angels to be carried off for heavenly energetic recycling and rehabilitation. Just like composted old food or plants.

They just got lost, tired, hungry and confused.

We need more resources and input up here in Scotland, Vit D3 (and K to facilitate) on tap - the research is all out there.

Early and real nutritional education and training in schools, less exposure to toxic chemicals and pollutants, more Government-level control of the food and drink industry and more sunlight, please.

I took my husband for lunch afterwards. We passed some very synchronistic shop signs on the 100 yards walk to the Aroma Cafe.

What blew me away was halfway through my lunch I realised I was sitting next to a huge golden Buddha and a gorgeous mosaic painting with the letters AHMHTHP.

The woman holds a wheatsheaf, a harvest symbol, and stands under another favourite, a tree of life.

The symbology wasn't lost on me: I researched later.

AHMHTHP stands for The Greek Goddess Ceres or Mother Earth.

Point taken lads.

So I have a five-month contemplative angelic-induced Ki-More and Ray-Joy retreat to really explore what FULL DETOX and RECOVERY really means. And I am gonna use it well: my life depends on it.

My focus on pre and probiotic foods and fermentation will help thanks to a great teacher Janice Clyne daily walking will too.

I'm planning a moonlight bra walk for after, and G and I are going to do St Cuthbert's way (Melrose - Lindisfarne), 65 miles over a week or so, when it's over.

These plans are keeping me from thinking about chucking up.

I'm pulling back at work for the foreseeable to permit healing, redesigning my work/life balance, engaging in more creative projects, collaborating and creating outside of the box, more giving back and paying it forward. This feels like an inner stirring.

Today I am somewhat nauseous and trying to rest with a few mouth ulcers promising, a little tinnitus kicking in (side-effects). I'm on steroids and anti-sickness tabs for gastric games and have a slight metallic taste incubating (but hey we call that weight control aversion techniques in Hypnotherapy) and a wee bit of neuropathy - tingly, numb hands and feet

GREET·GREET·LOVE 31

I fell asleep sitting up in bed watching a Carly Simon interview about her book "Girls Like Us" on my phone tonight.

Don't believe all the hype, there actually ARE occasional times the shitty stuff is the only thing that helps you get to sleep, when you have pins and needles in your feet and hands, and itchy coos in your eyelashes though you should not rub them lest they fall oot. I needed distraction - nothing else would hack the Ki-More-Therapy side-show.

It's called whatever gets you through the night medicine.

It worked! Follow yer gut and stare at the screen until you drop.

However, someone else had other plans and I was gently tapped awake by an outstretched hand holding half a headphone set plugged into a laptop, and found myself looking into a pair of soulful brown-eyed-Buddhist-type eyes; no words and listening to a song.

Carly Simon wrote the lyrics "There's more room in a broken heart" decades ago. She's right by the way.

But Pink, who was here in Glasgow the other night, called me right out with this piece of genius on vulnerability and the messiness of the broken places - as someone obviously spotted and fed it right back up the line.

Truly blessed and duly grateful. Nite G, nite all x

JULY 2019

SMILE·PEE·LAUGH 32

These days I find, I've literally "gotta larf" EVERY DAY, whether I feel like it or not. It's like teeth brushing or peeing, it's a daily essential. My body tells me so.

I can FEEL the difference in my cells, in my marrow.

Doesn't mean I don't feel low, have a moan, a greet, misery moments (or hours, even days) during this Ki-More-Therapy and Chancer Treatment.

The last two weeks have been fascinating as I was pulled down into the undertow of a severe toxic reaction to the process of Ki-More-Therapy. It nearly killed me, never mind the Chancer cells.

I always said I was too pure for this world. We are currently re-evaluating the way forward with maths, bio-chemistry and common sense as our compass points.

These scary and shitty times need to be countered with

laughter infusions as if our life depends on it. Note – it does.

At the moment, there is plenty of material around: there's always Boris and Chunt on Blues at Ten and I'll bet you can use the antics of a few clowns closer to home to squeeze the juice too.

Larry David has been a nightly Laughter Therapist in the boxed sets of Curb Your Enthusiasm. I'm starting to talk like him and develop his mannerisms.

Billy Connolly always delivers. Peter Kay, I just need to look at that face.

Janey Godley's voiceover clips on Facebook, and on and on.

It's important for us all to know how to find our laughter muscles and work them but ESPECIALLY during Chancer treatment.

People can become awfy serious around you and drop into a deeper, slower, gravitas voice when they talk to you.

The ones who "know" us tune in and out, taking our emotional temperature and pacing our moods, leading when required into a lighter and higher vibration as necessary to avoid Gravititis, Humour Bypass or Smile Paralysis.

Now, let me clarify: force-fed phoney cheeriness, mistimed or inappropriate, aspartame, invasive or out of sync manipulations are irritating - exhausting even - when one is feeling like shit, in pain or in the grip of the fear. Do not do this, please!

But a bit of matching and pacing, gentle exploration of the territory with no sudden moves, testing the waters of humour, can lead to an opportunity that is not to be missed.

But the lasting and worthwhile healing benefits of a regular daily injection or three of our favourite comedy masters on our immune and nervous systems, and subsequent raising of spirits have now been studied and charted. See the evidence-based research, work going back to the early pioneers in Laughter Therapy: Norman Cousins; Dr Bernie Siegel (who I trained with in the 90s) and Dr Patch Adams among the thousands of clinical papers on the subject.

So remember, "When yer smilin'... the whole world smiles with you", including your inner world. Your white cells shine even brighter in the laughter and the light.

REMEMBER·PRAY·LOVE 33

Being in pretty much a state of isolation during Ki-More-Therapy (to avoid risk of Chemo Sepsis) has been two things, a very interesting inner journey hitherto never before experienced, and at times quite lonely too.

I've just had to cancel another three plans - a day of cooking fermented foods on Saturday with my inspiring friend Janice Clyne, and enjoying the graceful company of Kate Cowan. Then I had to pull out of my Beeswax Food wrap class on Monday, and I have Trevor Horn Concert tickets for the end of July. It's a no- brainer for risk assessment.

With the current Sepsis risks, antibiotic resistance and my lower than low immunity right now, it's a potential game of Russian Roulette.

I miss hugs and cuddles when family visit but it's no worth it. There are pretty potent viruses around the noo.

It's not forever.

Today my school pals Lorraine and Laura are visiting. Laura saved my life. She first spotted the indent on my boob while we were topless bathing on holiday in February. Her mum died with Chancer so she was well placed to comment. She eyeballed me and ordered me to get checked.

So I did. The rest as they say is history... but I may have been history had she not spoken up. Thank you Laura.

My partner in many a crime, Lorraine is 60 tomorrow. I wanted to mark it so I'm making my famous ginger and mandarin birthday cake in her honour. Sadly, I had to tell her I won't make her wedding next Saturday. It's three days after Ki-More-Therapy two and I could be on my knees if last time is any guideline.

She says she already thought so. There is always FaceTime.

For over 10 days after my first Ki-More-Therapy I couldn't have looked at anyone due to the extreme toxic reaction I experienced. It was beyond anything I SHOULD have gone through and it has now been confirmed I should have been hospitalised during that episode. It nearly finished me off. But it won't be happening again as we discuss modifications before we decide on the way forward.

Anyway, here I am with an eight-day window of feeling a bit better, though the bursts of energy are short so I am having the odd very limited visit, with nae hugs or kisses to prevent bugs and avoidance of weans or should I say 'germ factories They now give them live nasal vaccines which are dynamite for Ki-More-Therapy patients. So I missed wee Ella Bee's dance display. Papa explained to her it was because I can't go to busy places in case someone has a cold or flu and I could maybe catch germs.

She told everyone, "Gran couldn't come in case there were any Germans in the audience."

I'm so glad now I catalogued most of my visitors' beautiful faces in the Post-Mastectomy recovery phase.

I look through them and fill myself up with the beautiful and enriching memories of shared intimacy, unconditional love and connection; healing moments, reconnection and deep love.

This is Immuno-therapy: it boosts the white blood cells like nothing else. Pure love in a CELL-PHONE.

Revisiting THE MOMENTS in the memory bank account, the laughs, the kindness, is vital. It balances out and with enough immersion, obliterates the painful times, the scary episodes, the hurting places. Just in the same way, we are all working together to detoxify the Chancer Cells in Wishie General Healthspital and over at The Land o' The Monks Healthspitall. My team are neutralising the soil and digging up the weeds at the roots. Burning any rogue weeds that could otherwise destroy the garden over time.

Then we will remineralize the soil, mixing in lots of rich and fertile life, giving compost. Meanwhile, I am designing and preparing to plant out a new landscaped inner garden, wild in places, with an established inner temple and red tent. A new vista to be enjoyed, a new horizon from an elevated viewpoint. A clearer view of the horizons of this limited life.

We will bring some features from the previous landscape but a redesign is always going to be part of the soul prescription. It's what NEEDS to happen after a SHOUTOUT from the physical body.

It's exhilarating and exciting but for now it's a Vision Quest, mostly undertaken out in the desert, by myself.

But I'm never alone. I have love, God, La Mamma Terra, the Holy Spirit, Holy Nature for company always. We are never alone, not really.

And I have the beautiful photo-memories of the souls who walked me to the starting line and cheered me on my way.

MEET·NO WAY·LOVE 34
When it was suggested that I could be referred for six sessions of complementary therapy (massage, Indian head, reiki, holistic facial) during my Ki-More-Therapy treatment, I jumped at it. When it was suggested Lord Graham was also entitled to the same arrangement as my carer, he danced down

the corridor.

We were booked in for 9am Monday at Monklands Healthspital, Ward 16.

It rang a bell.

Yonks ago, I taught a nurse employed by NHS as a Complementary Therapist and funded by North Lanarkshire Health Board, on our Hypnotherapy Diploma. Ward 16 Monklands was where her clinic was, I remembered, as she was in our mailing list for years. Surely no way, after 16 years.

Yes way! It WAS Patricia McCabe we were booked in with and the Clinical Hypnotherapy Diploma I trained her for was still hanging proudly on her wall from back in 2002, alongside the Reiki training diplomas she completed with me at my home back in 2003 to Master/Teacher Level.

Tricia was later awarded an MBE for services to Chancer Patients.

She must've been seven years old at the time when she trained with me, cos she still only looks about 21. I feel very blessed to be in such safe and experienced hands.

The Circle of Life, eh?

Trainer's Teaching for Today

"Look out for the synchronicities in your life today. They are always around us if we slow down enough to notice. There is a constant stream of information and guidance available to us every day from the invisible realm - but we need to open our third eye, listen with our third ear, and see with the eyes of the heart.

It may be a random song on the radio that comes on with deeply meaningful words, a bird or butterfly that "speaks to you" in a comforting way a conversation with a stranger that has meaning for you, something a child says that resonates inside, the smile on a stranger's face, things from the past surfacing; bumping into someone. The permutations are endless.

Pay closer attention today and reflect on the meaning and patterns of the way things happen. I said, "Hey babe, take a walk on the wild side."

GREET·PRAY·LOVE 35

As I try to navigate the moving seas of Chancer Healing (12 weeks in,16+ to go), I find myself often in a parallel world of becalmed solitude, silence and utter mystery. Uncharted territory.

Some days I find I have been beached on to a dark and uninhabited island where there be dragons.

And there's nothing for it but to take a walk on the wild side. Emotionally it feels primal, at times I feel feral. My senses and nerve endings are on the outside of my skin. Survival instincts are locked on.

Ki-More-Therapy is a particularly vile treatment but injected with such love and compassion by Natural Health Service angels. So make no mistake, I am grateful to be able to access this treatment.

However, it is without doubt the ugliest detox procedure I have ever experienced and I've undertaken a few in the interests of research over the years.

I feel like a monster at times during the inner seek and destroy missions and I won't ever miss the darker than dark steroid-related moods, even though they are prescribed with love to keep my head above water. The world looks and feels completely different during the steroid withdrawal days for my previously "clean-as" nervous system.

When you have a life-threatening diagnosis, The Dark Night is a regular go-to destination and pit-stop. Fears, regrets and rumination become travelling companions when there is no escape or distraction from the shadowy recesses of the mind. There is a lot of enforced isolation during Chancer Treatment due to the risks of that dreaded Sepsis.

Shadow boxing is part of the territory.

"Hello darkness, my old friend, I've come to talk with you again."

My "Aunt" Irene (79) passed in her sleep last Thursday. She was a great support to me after my dad died - I've known her all my life and she adored him too.

I got the call an hour after I'd received a message saying my cousin Stephen (64) in South Africa had died the same day. I loved him like a big brother as a girl growing up. We shared a love of progressive rock.

It was a double whammy.

But then I had visits from two huge butterflies - one in the hall, one in my bedroom within 24 hours of the news - Macca (my Blackbird) following me around the garden the day after and the mysterious white rose which "appeared" in our hedge after 15 years which bloomed in November on my father's anniversary, choosing full bloom the same day soothed my soul somewhat. Synchronicity can be a healing balm at these crisis points.

Of course there has been a regular backdrop of guff and nonsense from the outside world playing in the background. You will have yer own cast of characters to deal with I'm sure, dear reader. So I won't share my endless line-up of "comedians" popping up day by day.

Poor me you may think. And you are absolutely right. Poor wee me.

So I am now responsible for consciously and deliberately wrapping my arms tightly around myself and discerning ways to hold me close, to self-soothe and comfort the vulnerable, terrified, groundless, shaven-headed baby whose life has been hijacked and blown apart by an April conversation.

During difficult and scary times I, WE, need to consciously breathe and welcome the life force into the body and mind by every means possible.

Some of my methods of choice are via the BREATH (just breathing better and deeper), Ultra-SOUND and music, vibration, tuning, healing touch - my own and others, active appreciation of beauty and NATURE, BIO-ENERGY FOODS and supplements, the presence of healing nature, healing spa waters, vigilant HYDRATION,

MEDITATION and PRAYER, HOMEOPATHIC remedies, culinary herbs and teas (Golden Turmeric lattes are so good for inflammation or Ki-More pain), Visualisation and Self-HYPNOSIS for release and relief, and setting of compass points, micro yoga and TAI CHI for big-babies (sometimes done in bed or seated in a chair), gentle movement to music, energetic field frequency HEALING via CRYSTALS, REIKI, trusted healers, consumption of good written and spoken WORDS from inspirational people across the centuries, REFLEXOLOGY, consumption of uplifting and inspiring images in film and TV, LAUGHTER therapy, HUGGING therapy, CRYING therapy, ART therapy, WRITING therapy, COOKING therapy, COLOUR therapy, music therapy.

It's ALL therapy when it helps you express or inflow more GRACE.

And by RELEASE through words, tears, skin, the breath, laughter, dance, physical release, detoxing, bathing, coffee enemas, intermittent fasting. Anything that helps us let go and stop holding on, in or down.

Shedding (like the snake with its old skin) the outgrown, outdated, outmoded cells and self before the preparation for the new ground which will need to be prepared, seeded and planted, after the clearing.

Who loves ya, baby?

WORK·PRAY·LOVE 36

There is an infused light around more often sometimes. I see a clearer light in the eyes of others. The birds seem to be singing louder. I FEEL the moonlight, my edges blur and soften in the raindrops when I venture out. I feel less contained in the boundary of my skin.

Am I finally becoming an enlightened master with the new Buddhist lack-of-hairdo?

Or is it toxic side effects from the Ki-More-Therapy pals?

When I'm resting, I drift in and out of deep states of Hypno-medi-sleep. I touch the edges of The Veil with amazing regularity and I contemplate the fragility of this short life.

Like me, you may have often gulped and raced headlong through your life at times, as if to escape the one sure thing, that this human life is impermanent.

But as my guy Paul Young sang in the 80s, "Everything must change."

I'm experiencing insights, feelings and memories not familiar in my "normal" range of awareness, nor within my previous reach. These usually occur during moments of surrender and extended stillness.

There is a deeper sense of big presence and my essence dancing together.

My connection with nature intensifies and so does my appreciation of the gift of the breath and how it breathes my bodymindsoul. I marvel at the gift and the fragility of life itself. It is all pure gift.

I sense my loved ones over the Veil around me so much - memories flow, my heart opens and widens as I touch their essences which live fully in my Heart. Love Never Dies. I think

I've said that before somewhere.

And I've dived deep again into the pool of grief, with the two recent family losses touching the hurting places.

We often think "I've dealt with that" but we don't DO grief, we just learn to carry it better.

Old wounds come up for air when we are immobilised.

I'm so grateful for all the self-imposed quiet times and retreats I've experienced. They prepared me partly at least for this split from my external identity, roles, career, persona, as I hurtled and tumbled headlong into this whole new life experience that began back in April and will continue for the foreseeable.

I've had time to think - too much time and I'm getting time to read.

Richard Rohr put something so simply:

"What mystics finally do, it seems to me, is heal within themselves the fragmentation that is evident in the world. "

He postulates that Instead of hating, excluding, or dismissing IT out there in other people or the world, they heal it in themselves.

When I see the good, bad, the ugly, the dark and the nasty in myself and also the soft, fragile, vulnerable and beautiful and delightful and I refuse to hate or ignore any part of it (the hard bit), I develop big deep sympathy, empathy, and compassion. I can really become a healer, in the service of love. It canny and disnae happen in reverse. Anything else is counterfeit, phoney baloney, fake, saccharin-coated pretence.

I can then, and only then, begin the skill transfer and upgrade to seeing and accepting the same in you, in others, and in the big wide world. The Shadow Self in all her glory (or his).

There are plenty of high-profile working examples at this point in our time of our collective shadow on the world stage for us to begin the work with.

It's MY and OUR hunger, thirst and greed for MORE in all its forms and disguises (EGO) that has driven us to this point on our tired and confused wee Planet.

Now what we gonna do?

How on Planet Earth can I develop the required ownership, collective responsibility, empathy and compassion needed to unpack this car crash scenario otherwise, but within myself? Without fanning any more flames of them and us.

It's not THEM. It's in ME. It's in YOU.

We need to grow up, to show up. And work with something far more powerful than our puny and brittle little egos. Some may say it's too late for US to solve it, here on Planet Earth - hope never dies.

Until I put the "H" letter first, and make it Planet Heart, on the inside and the outside, the miracles we need will elude us.

But love has boundaries too and sometimes love says "NO". Tough love. Love will always conquer fear and its derivative hate.

Despair, outrage, blame, indignation, scapegoating and drama are all FEAR-based.

Focus, reflection, contemplation, ownership, forgiveness, responsibility, pro-activity, firm boundaries, energy conservation, connection, compassion, empathy, Grace (not force) are all LOVE-based.

Miracles do happen and they grow best planted in the soil (and the soul) of Love. Expect a miracle today!

REST·READ·PRAY·LOVE 37

Maybe it was the hot weather, maybe I slightly over-extended myself, or maybe I just had a nice blank dance card today but I'm having a two-thirds of a day in bed today. Because I can.

I missed Kim's birthday afternoon tea on purpose - too many people, too restricted a space (Sepsis alert) but we did have a lovely meal at Wagamama early last night, just the five of us and including Dame Ella Rose. I wanted to treat ER to something as we have limited contact just now (Sepsis, Weans-germs alert) and she wanted a sparkly baseball cap. It fitted me, and you know what they say.

So we have in fact celebrated that you are 37 years old, Kimberly.

How did that happen? The age I was when I first met yer dad and you were a wee teenager.

That led to the stirring of lots of "heart photographic memories" as I sorted and sifted through some of the beautiful photos and memory videos stored away in my inner library.

I then felt moved to find some of the actual photos, the girlie get-togethers when they were all younger, just delightful wee ladies-in-waiting, budding and bubbly and bursting with blossomness.

My windows are wide open in the monsoon rain, four hours and not counting. The garden loves it and so do I. I love the cool just now as I rest in bed. I say "rest", but I'm practising lots of deep breathing, I'm meditating, praying, reading, drinking lots of crystal water.

I've had lots of nice message chats on here with Caroline, Ashley and Shonny. Shonny shared a wee video from "Aunt" Irene's cottage and some notes she had written in the day or two before she passed over. Her woodland burial is on Wednesday. I'm hoping I'll be able to make it for a while - it's outdoors.

I had a visitor just before her messages. Another stunning butterfly flew into my bedroom and stayed a while. I had just been talking to Ashley and I managed to capture on film.

Ash decided it was from grandad.

I think it was a sign from them ALL over the Veil. That "all is well, and all manner of things shall be well"- Dame Julian of Norwich.

I shared my current reading list on a group I'm involved with this morning and Dame Julian was one of them. I sent a photo of my live books.

I just realised it reflects my spiritual nomad soul. One is by a female Jewish psychotherapist Auschwitz survivor, one a Tibetan Buddhist meditation master, one a deceased priest and writer who lived with the L'Arche Community, and finally a female 14th Century English anchoress (enclosed hermit).

I think I've covered a few bases there. They all say the same thing mind you.

Be still and know that I AM.

Let it go.

Forgive everyone - especially yourself

Love the ones you're with.

Stop and smell the flowers, coffee, rain, chocolate cake.

Have a braw weekend lads.

REST·PLAY·LOVE 38

So, before the next cycle of Ki-More-Therapy rolls around again, and before I say goodbye to Aunt Irene on Wednesday at her woodland burial, we agreed that my first sleepover away should happen somewhere spectacular, and it did.

Last time we were there a few years ago, Dad had given us a Christmas voucher and Archerfield didn't disappoint this time either, their Fletchers spa has a bespoke "made for Life Treatment" especially for Chancer patients - totally pure and organic products designed for lymphatic issues and total comfort of the lack of a booby type.

It was divine. I will be back - when the Chancer treatment is done.

I am, on Thursday, attending for number three of Ki-more-Therapy, halfway through in a few weeks. Though I've still got Ray-Joy-Therapy to follow for four weeks after.

It has taken until just recently for the enormity of the situation to finally sink in. This is no cakewalk, no walk in the park. It is not a tick list of treatments, a chore to be gotten to the end of so life can return to "normal".

I appreciate now that I am not the same woman who started out on this trip back in March of this year and the events that have unfolded have both expanded my heart beyond its limits and left me breathless. They have also had me on my knees with my head in my hands in despair. I have been uplifted, overjoyed, astounded and delighted by the support and care of so many, and the other stuff folk were there too but thankfully not in equal measure. They are always there aren't they - the sour and the bitter - just to balance the sweet.

But yesterday and today were about butterflies and beaches, dressing gowns and going commando, resting and restoring, laughing and loving, history and misty vistas.

Injecting pure pleasure into my system in the window of time I have, before the next intravenous infusion occurs on Thursday.

Bring it on.

"Ain't nothing gonna break my stride."

AUGUST 2019

GAG·PRAY·LIVE 39

Halfway through the treatment sessions. Woo!

Rough day due to medication changes but will have less steroid rage and doom, gloom withdrawal hopefully in the days to come.

It was a four-hour Ki-More-Therapy intravenous session today as a result. We were both knackered after it.

Downside - more sickness and nausea and uber-detox symptoms. I feel really lousy since.

Upside - nae appetite - jeans that will fit.

Result!

BLEAT·SAY IT LIKE IT IS·LAUGH 40

I'm paraphrasing here but I love the writer Jeff Brown's musings. I've added some Glaswegian for effect.

We all know those airy-fairy, float a foot above the ground, dark cherry and chocolate voiced, angelic wannabe-goddesses in dresses with tiny mirrors sewn on, who always have a soundbite or four to provide straight outta either the Celestine Prophecy, Louise Hay's Dial Up Your Condition or even – woe is me - The Secret. Wish they'd kept it.

And YES, I recognise myself in here too before you start off with a feckin' defensive projection. I still have those frocks.

So when they remind you in the midst of a trauma, crisis or illness – YES, INCLUDING A LIFE- THREATENING ILLNESS - that "you choose every experience", punch them hard right in the face.

When they wake up, remind them to say thanks to you for "actualising their dream" and being part of their karma, remind them to forgive you before the bruises show, that the pain is an illusion and just to come back to "the noo" (by Scottish mystic Eck Fart Toley).

When they try to get up, you should push them back down saying, "Everything you see and experience is a reflection of you. You have issues around violence. I gave you a gift. Be grateful. Namaste. Om Shanti."

If they get angry, remind them that anger and judgments are low vibe emotions and there is never anyone to blame. Advise them "you are trapped in the matrix and seeing the world through that limited viewpoint."

Steal their wallet, demand their PIN number, then they can learn another valuable lesson about attachment and manifestation.

Then run like hell!

SMILE·PRAY·LAUGH 41

For a million reasons, these recent days I need to fill up on nonsense, daftness and laughter, which normally comes easily to me.

Life continues to surprise and amaze me - as do some of my fellow humans as outlined in Snooze at Ten or on the other channel The Ten o' Clock Blues.

But I'm sure dear reader, you - like me - have your own

personal Daily News Channel that never fails to deliver, on the happenings in your own tribe, and in your own community.

Humour and laughter can be as prone to constipation as any other part of our anatomy and my laughter channels don't flow so easily during the uphill climb and stumble on the cliff path of Ki -More-Therapy.

I need to work the laughter muscles hard - and often by day 14 in my three-week cycle they will kick in again by themselves. But I need to keep them "warm by force" during the dry season.

God bless the folks who have been born without the laughter and humour muscles or settings. I pray for you – really. But when I miss out on humour bubbles, I really miss them.

Never take your sense of humour (the seventh sense) for granted. Feed and water daily and place in direct sun.

EAT·PRAY·SAIL 42

It's easy to lose hope. It's easy to become overwhelmed. To rant and rail against our circumstances. I regularly and often feel a sense of despair overtake me, especially when I'm tired, when things go wrong, and on days where it seems like too high a climb with the Chancer.

On days like those, I find the words of Clarissa Pinkola Estes very comforting and empowering. She rattles my Chakras, straightens my spine and strengthens my core. I feel reminded of who I am and am reminded that I am part of a team. When I walk through the storm I never walk alone.

I paraphrased, shortened and edited a fair bit. She writes beautifully and poetically but it can be too flowery for some. Apologies to the purist fans. The cropping and alterations are all mine.

"We were made for these times.

We are in shock about the state of our world. We are bewildered and enraged over the degradation of people, especially the vulnerable and our planet, that's happening on a daily basis.

The hubris and arrogance some engage in while endorsing callous acts against those who are vulnerable, heinous acts against children, elders, the poor, the helpless, is breath-taking.

Please don't spend your spirit dry by bemoaning and bewailing these difficult times.

Especially do not lose hope.

WE WERE MADE FOR THESE TIMES."

LOVE·PRAY·EAT 43

I write from bed after Ki-More-Therapy number four on Thursday last (with two to go).

It had a bonus ball of Bisphosphonates as an infusion attached to strengthen bones and protect them from osteoporosis and Bone Chancer. Weight-bearing exercise, vitamin D and supplements may have done most of the work but exercise is not quite on my feeble radar at the mo, and I take no chances with the Chancer these days. I knew, like always, there would be potential "reactivity". There was.

Think getting a team of plasterers in to sand, fill, pebbledash and seal the exterior of yer hoose, a fair wee bit of disruption, ladders and paint pots everywhere and messy dust sheets lying about all over the joint for a while.

So I was delighted that I got a window of opportunity in amongst the "mess and dust sheets" stage to go over for an hour or two on Saturday night to my brother's house.

He had a new smoker to try out, he said. I thought he was pulling my chain when he asked if I'd like to come over for a "smoke-out."

It was good to spend time with some of the younger generation - they are all scattered now at different ends of the country, at unis and in new jobs and some sadly couldn't make it. You were missed Kells, Rachie and Squidge.

We are now the "auld adults" eating in the house to avoid the midgies, while the young ones are happily being eaten alive under the stars.

Social interaction versus isolation is highly correlated in the effectiveness of recovery and healing but it's tough to get the balance right. I chose to rest in bed until 5.30pm so I could be upright for a couple of hours - but it was worth it. The next day was a "gentle day" and early night. Today I'm buggert.

Getting the balance right in the energy stores while in recovery and healing from Chancer or any other health condition else is always gonna be an art form, not a science. Gently does it. I've had my fingers burned from doing more than I could in the past.

Getting rest hours in the bank, learning to say no, maybe, can I let you know at short notice or not?, reflecting afterwards on what helped or hindered, sometimes specifying an hour visit would be good and enough when you're tired, having a gate-keeper to evict persistent overtime-offenders, not pushing the conversation or feeling the need to entertain, letting others carry the visit, dropping the hostess role, kicking people oot , accepting offers of help - all of these strategies go towards making social interaction a part of healing and recovery in the long-term when we have been pole-axed by whatever means.

Learning to RECEIVE, to take in and take a back seat really - like the auld-yins.

PRAY·LOVE 44

Today was a not-as-good-as-it-could-have-been-day.

That's to be expected for this stage in the cycle of detox by Ki-More-Therapy.

So today I spent time sitting WITH the yucky feelings, and time absolutely not.

I've developed a new technique and it's called "MINDLESSNESS".

With this tremendous new and innovative approach, one consciously travels into the PAST and the FUTURE and spends only minimalist amounts of time in the present moment. Then when the bleugh symptoms have calmed and settled, before they roll around again. I won't bore you by listing, but this time they surprised even me in their variety and eclectic nature.

So I spent a fair part of today planning next week, next year, my upcoming and new year 60th birthday extravaganza, my festival of life year, next year. Camper van studying, project planning, The LUCKY-LIST making.. you get the picture.

Then I spent other times today also totally NOT in the present moment, squeezing the juice out of the last few weeks or so of fun and joyous times. Dunno about you but I think sometimes I don't fully appreciate events without a review and debrief, and enjoy them on a deeper level in the remembering.

So I flicked forwards and backwards as required and managed the distraction of the present with reasonable aplomb, and at other times just sat square in the middle of the fire.

Had some cool and fun times in the last wee while though. Here's a few memories I dined out on. Sound healing and reflexology with Caroline Arlene delivering the stunningly beautiful patchwork healing blanket she knitted me along with Suzy and the gorgeous candle, jams, bath bomb basket, all handmade by them, Nathan's 18th birthday dinner, Schoenstadht with C, Laura for lunch with her mahoosive pomegranate, L babysitting me overnight, oysters in Helensburgh with mum, Ash and Aiden by the canal, Dougie and Gordon reunion.

Thank you all for helping me make memories I could use therapeutically and medicinally.

SEPTEMBER 2019

BURN·ACHE·CURSE 45

I'm not gonna lie, this last week has been the worst. Crap. Awful. Hellish.

I won't do it in French and German but it'd probably sound more authentic.

I've tried to distract myself from the shapes of the light on the bedroom ceiling in a thousand different ways.

I've even become inexplicably and deeply interested in politics so I could have a safe and reasonable place to justify and target my ever-expanding sweary-word vocabulary.

There's no a bit of me that hasn't been affected this last load of

Ki-More-Therapy. Any more Ki and I will be airborne. This is an extremely thorough detox indeed.

But it was a combo cocktail of two drugs (including the one for bone density) that only has to happen as a double this way once, that did for me. Just as well - it wasn't happening again this way regardless.

But watching the sand artist on Britain's Got Talent doing her thing for Children with Chancer Week burst my heart wide open. I have a whole new viewpoint of THAT WALK for the kids, for the parents, the wider family and for the staff who do the work. This line of work is not for the faint hearted.

When you are in this Chancer treatment system, you are part of another Universe. You are surrounded by health professionals of differing titles and a variety of roles, radiographers, tea trolley ladies, complementary therapists, nurses of all varieties, doctors, consultants, auxiliaries, receptionists, helpline advisors, chaplains, porters.

These folks are Earth Angels and Ultra-Uber-Exceptional Human Beings of Light, strength and wisdom who have titanium backbones and hearts on fire. They are healing warriors and warrioresses - working on the very edges of life and death.

I've never known such fearless eye contact like it before. They look deep into your very soul as they impart info, listen to your laments sympathetically, deliver news firmly but kindly, both welcome and unwelcome. They must eat iron-girders for breakfast for their resilience and strength.

Dave has been sending me a sample of his vast and eclectic taste in music of all genres and centuries - one a day for months now, from Wagner to Coldplay, Abba to jazz, Nordic progressive to piano concertos. Shirley generously lent me her husband's incredible expertise here and not for the first time either - he did the final proof-reading and much more of my first book.

But today he sent me the marvellous words below. They sustained Nelson Mandela for 33 years of incarceration on Robben Island when he had no hope of release or escape. They strengthened my feeble heart and breathed life into my spirit.

"I am the master of my fate

I am the CAPTAIN of my soul."

We are never alone for long when we are in pain or difficulty, if we reach out and when we suffer, we are in connection with all those thousands of others out there ALSO suffering - maybe not in exactly the same way - but

"EVERYBODY HURTS SOMETIMES!"

We are not alone.

EAT·PLAY·LOVE 46

It had been a really rough ride, this cycle of Ki-More-Therapy - but for a variety of reasons. Stress doesn't help my immune system concentrate on the job at hand and this last few weeks there have been some stoaters on my path.

These included a well flooded clinic due to upstairs neighbours who didn't respond for 24 hours of pouring water gushing through their bathroom floor, gross professional incompetence and infantile behaviour of the BoJo/Trumpton crazy-making type (work-related), car audio system packing in just outside of warranty - £700 to replace - drama lamas seeking the spotlight; heating breakdown in the clinic this week and unfair and unwarranted £60 parking ticket to boot (G had entered the wrong car reg).

All fairly inconsequential and trivial on their own. Combined in the middle of a course of Ki-More-Therapy, not so much.

I have no words. Well I do but they are not very nice words so I'll stick to feckin' keech of a shift.

However, as I started to turn the corner for my few days of feeling normal-ish, things came into perspective and re-aligned.

No lasting damage to the ceiling in clinic, Gene Kelly school of tap-dancing footwork around Bo-Jo II and The Trumpettes, Arnold Clark picking up the £700 tab for a new audio system, drama llamas deftly dealt with by usual altitude adjustments, Vinnie the heating angel scrambles in at 5.30pm at night to sort out, Maureen hangs back late to let him do his magic and parking ticket taken on the chin and now paid for with joy and pleasure, much less painfully after the heavenly windfall courtesy of Monsieur Clark et Co and Marion is the glue that holds the roadshow together with St Graham steering the ship.

We were ready to split for a window of rest and recovery and a change of scene for the 48 hours of window I had. So we headed off to the Far East for a weekend of divine light, butterflies, angel feathers, Mr Blue Sky, Fife coast sunsets and foodie delights.

It was just what the doctor ordered and helped reset my immune thermostat before Tuesday's Consultant pow-wow and Thursday's Ki-More-Therapy, No. five.

Should we have warned the hotel of my sensitivities to certain subject matter perchance, ahead of our arrival? Too late, dear reader.

The reading material provided in the room for the discerning traveller had me in the first five minutes – it was suggestions of 1000 things to see before you die!

I was in fact delighted that I had seen most of the ones suggested in Scotland so I only have around 983 to fit in afore I shuffle off this mortal coil, which I have no intention of doing any time soon.

Was everything even MORE beautiful and breath-taking given the rigours of the last few weeks or so? It's hard to tell. But life is life innit and we learn to surf and wait for the waves if we want to enjoy the ride.

There were beautiful things to celebrate this cycle too, not least the mad fun on here with Jacob Cream Crackers posts, St. Angela, The Angel Graham and The Holy Harvest Church (my new online business and range of spiritual accessories for the discerning enlightened ones) and the surprise visit of my darling pal of three decades Senor James Flynn from Australia.

It was so lovely to hook up with Shona McDonald Neal and Phil today - who had literally arrived home an hour earlier from a month in Croatia and meet wee Medo the Persian Princess in person. Could've chatted on but some folks need to work tomorrow and it's not us.

We stopped en-route here for a cuppa at a place in Dalkeith called The Restoration Yard. That's how I feel, RESTORED. Bring it on.

Keep your altitude up when you are juiceless, any which way you can. Humour, laughter, fresh air, sky-watching and infusions of good people helps and remember to give equal airtime to the things that are going right - even if it's just access to clean drinking water, and moderate weather fronts.

WORK IT·PRAY·LOVE 46 (B)

Many recent Studies from UCLA, among other highly valued seats of learning, underline the importance of gratitude and openness to the blessings that ALWAYS surround us no matter WHAT is going down in our lives.

I tend to get stuck mostly when I engage in comparisons to my imaginary parallel life over there somewhere (which disnae exist by the way) and my current reality, my life situation today.

What is even more crazy-making is when I audit my life against YOURS and compete and compare all of the ways in which yours is better, happier, fuller, enviable.

Conclusions are often drawn that I must be deficient, am no trying hard enough, am being negatively Karma-ed, punished by the Big Man with the beard and pointy finger cos you are having much more in the joy, fun, happiness, fulfilment department than I am at any one point in time.

So tomorrow when I revisit Wishy Healthspital for my fifth Ki-More-Therapy and probably my 30th visit since kick-off in April.

I will work it! I will consciously experience gratitude for every service I am offered from the researchers who pore over the hot microscopes and petri-dishes, to the hard-earned taxpayers who pay for my treatment; to the nurses and doctors who studied so hard for so many years to learn their craft to the cleaners and tea-ladies who've been on their feet since sun-up to make me more comfortable during my visit; to the pharmacists who laboured over exam papers to dispense my healing medicines so I can alleviate my symptoms of the Big Detox, to the wonderful complementary foot massage I get from Elaine, to my pal Theresa, giving up her free time and sharing with me her wonderful Reiki when I get home to help the process along.

Then there's my handsome chauffeur and re-birthing partner Lord G who holds my hand and distracts me from my darts practice/canula fitting; and Sir Ian the cat who purrs healing vibes into my tummy when I nap or rest after; to my family, friends who gently support from a watchful distance afterwards sending tom-tom drum and smoke signals to each other to avoid overwhelm.

And yes, I always bless (and Reiki) my medicines. They are energy too.

And they will interact with MY energy to purge, to soothe, to boost, to relax, to restore, according to their role. So I use crystals to purify and charge my medicines before I start on them when I get home.

I quietly bless each nurse and doctor who helps me heal; I silently pray for the other patients; I bless the Day Unit as I come through its doors.

I bless that BELL which folks ring at the end of their therapy, as I pass it and every soul who has ever rung it. I enter that mindscape of GRATITUDE.

It helps. It heals. It stimulates oxytocin, serotonin and dopamine in my mindbodysoul.

They are all stress and pain relievers.

It only makes complete sense.

But it FEELS GOOD TOO!

I rise. I elevate my spirit. I raise my altitude. Just writing this I feel better than when I started it.

I activate my resourceful self, my resilient self. I am realigned.

Having an attitude of gratitude changes the molecular structure of the brain, keeps grey matter functioning, and makes us healthier and happier. When you feel happiness, the central nervous system is affected. You are more peaceful, less reactive and less resistant.

Now that's a state of being worth having when you are going through ANY challenge life has put in front of you on your journey.

What can you turn around in your life today and for the foreseeable? What will you handle better with the mindset of blessings and a grateful heart?

AWE·PRAY·BELOVED 47

Tonight, look up. The HARVEST moon will be beaming her love down on our beautiful planet and our divine selves.

It's a great time to leave your crystals, oils and sacred objects outside to be charged with that powerful energy that controls tides and oceans, and optimum planting and harvesting conditions.

Oh yes, and the fluid levels in our bodies - but more importantly our BRAINS and associated mood swings. Hence the word lunatic.

It's also the equinox and the official start of autumn, and an unusual one in that it's a Micromoon. Last year it was a Supermoon as it was really close to earth, this year it will be 14% smaller in size as it's 30,000 miles further away.

It will be at its peak at around 5.30 am. Will you set your alarm, get up with a duvet and a hot drink and sit outside in AWE, marvel at the magic of the Cosmos and the sheer mystical magnificence of it all? And why not recharge your own soul batteries. See you out there tonight.

Cue Linda Ronstadt "Somewhere out there, beneath the pale moonlight.."

PRAY·PRAY·LOVE 47 (B)

ON GOD.

How very dare I? Well, I dare.

I woke up this morning with random thought and recent readings mingling and felt moved to share.

Richard Rohr talks about God being a VERB, an experience, an interactive relationship, not a static notion or rational answer to a question. So, if asked what I'm doing today, my reply will be "I'm away oot to God the world, and I'm probably going to be God-ding most of the day. Well that's the plan anyway!"

What if there's a wee bit of God in us that wants to find herself? How awful if we ignored that longing inside and outside, though as quantum physics now tells us, that's really the same thing.

What if the longing, the constant craving for that sense of connection and security we all seek, IS the point?

What if the searching IS the meaning and it's not that we've failed because we don't know, can't be sure, are still seeking and exploring, looking for answers.

What if our EGO (though it does a marvellous job in so many areas, got us outta those swamps, and works on so many levels evolving us and getting things done) has no effective built-in braking system and can become a relentless and ruthless driver. It drives us towards "perfection" and other ridiculous ideas that don't exist.

Dr Wayne Dyer used to say, "If you knew who walked beside you, you would never know fear again." What if that's true? How would I do things differently without the fear?

What if I actively practised changing channels in my head and my heart, from the "lack channel" and the "self-pity and resentment channel" to the "gratitude" and "sense of awe" channels. They are ALL there on your inner remote control, where you put your focus, you will BE but this requires daily practice to establish a good quality signal and reception.

There are ways of the heart which function like keys unlocking the chains, padlocks and the prison cell we find ourselves in, so the breeze of eternity can breathe on us and in us.

Gratitude and appreciation breathe grace and blessings into our lives.

DON'T·EAT·PRAY·LOSE 48

A good friend and mentor gave me and Lord G some powerful advice during his last months before he passed. He was latterly a psychotherapist and a monk, formerly a Yorkshire roofer and builder in between a psychiatric nurse at Broadmoor Security Psychiatric Healthspital. He had eons of life experience and wisdom. He taught us both how to meditate many years ago.

He said if we are to develop spiritually at all, one of the things we need to learn in life is HOW TO BE A GOOD LOSER.

We can translate and find this same theme in the ideology of taming the tiger or ego (Buddhism) and in controlling the desires (Hinduism - Bhaghvad Gita) and watching the appetites - or primal drivers (St John of The Cross, Christianity).

Some folks think it was Dr. Gabor Mate who came up with the term Hungry Ghosts to describe addicts. He did add we are mostly ALL of us addicted to something or someone.

But no, the concept goes way back to Chinese Buddhism. The hungry ghosts were depicted in early Buddhist iconography with long thin scrawny necks and big malnourished hungry bellies because they could never receive sustenance, they roamed the earth enduring endless unsatisfied cravings as nothing could pass down their tiny thin throats into their huge empty bellies. Permanent hunger and drive, ravenous desire, constant craving.

Strike a chord? Hit the spot? Get the picture? Make sense?

When I'm ingesting Lord G's healthy raw juice breakfasts and supplements I can often resemble the Hungry Ghost.

I've been on a huge learning to lose journey this past six months or so. The good loser aspect, not so much. I obviously wasn't paying enough attention to Bro. Peter's guidance.

In April when I was diagnosed with Breast Chancer I had never felt better, just returned from the best ever holiday, had two very successful Hypnotherapy training courses about to launch, an innovative Empowered Women's Day Project at the Caledonian Uni selling out with future follow-on plans lined up.

Plus my book ready for publishing and launching, a charitable project simmering gently on the back burner, lovely retreats on Iona (facilitating and participating), Reiki training weekends booked way ahead and a spring and summer of fun and sunshine.

That was the plan.

You wanna make God laugh? Tell her your plans.

In a matter of weeks from diagnosis of a double tumour, I was learning to lose. Among other things:

I lost my dignity (the grace of humility) being bathed by nurses, baring my arse in those crazy Healthspital gowns, yon white bandage-impersonating stockings, involuntary post-surgery, Post-Ki-More farting and of course having my boobs - later boob - felt by most of North Lanarkshire's Medical personnel - and a spatchcock check or two down below for good measure.

I lost a perfectly good back tooth - "just in case it acted up" in the next three years while on bone strengthening chemicals which prohibit teeth-pulling. I haven't lost a tooth in 30 years, and probably didn't need done - but precautionary.

I lost my hair - all of it, within weeks.

I lost my right breast, only a wink remains.

I lost my sense of smell and taste.

I lost sensation in my fingers, toes, hands and feet (this should return).

I lost my ability to drive for six weeks then two weeks out of every three because of side-effects of Ki-More-Therapy.

I lost four people to the other side of the Veil and attended three funerals in three months: an aunt, a cousin, pal's brother and family friend.

I lost a third of staff members from the Harvest Clinic. By June, seven members of staff had handed in notice to quit - the biggest staff exodus we've seen in a matter of weeks, and nothing I could do about the dominoes falling from a sick -bed.

I lost the ability to sit in sunshine (I'm photo-sensitive, risk of skin cancer now). Sun irritates my skin now, even through clothes.

I lost people. Some vaporise off the face of the earth, others run for cover - canny handle it, don't want to be around it (we all know it's contagious), some put you on a tick-list and check in that you're no deid yet, some cross the street when they see you coming. I like to holler "COOOO-EEEEE! HULLOOOOOO!" with accompanying windmill arms as I cross too. See, I told you I was not yet a GUID LOSER - Scottish version.

I lost my identity as Dr Harvest-Wise-Wumman, dispenser of wisdom to Western Europe. I have been in the clinic once since May for an hour. All else dealt with by phone or Dr Graham Harvest.

I lost control of my legs (temporarily for short wobbly periods).

I lost control of my emotions - courtesy of senor steroid and accompanying roid rage.

I lost control of my other emotions courtesy of fear, terror, sadness, grief, anger, frustration, et al.

I lost IT! The clinic computer packed in (three callouts), Clinic flooded by upstairs' flat students and heating broke down. All within eight weeks.

I lost CONTROL. My life was pretty much in THEIR hands, part was in mine. But in truth it's always been in God the Mother's hands.

Poor me. Damn right.

What's the message from the Universe? Away 'n' raffle yer vision board.

It's called Life.

We're most likely gonna get ill one day.

And yes, one day we shall all pass over that same Veil, that is assured.

So the sooner we learn how to be a good loser of the little

things, the better prepared we are gonna be for the bigger things to tame that tiger, to learn how to control those desires, to manage the appetites and senses. Not a welcome approach in our ego- celebrated, have-it-all by yesterday, love and light, airbrushed, beautiful and abundant, prosperous, magical (bullshit) world these days.

Have you seen our world after 50 collective years of affirmations of "I can and I will!"?

We could but we didnae.

It's been a long rocky climb for me with still a way to go. It's a giant life-size board game of snakes and ladders Himalayan Mountain Style - with many soundless ravines to fall into and plenty of dark caves to get lost in. Often you are completely on your own – Sherpa-less and the silence is deafening and relentless.

Oftentimes the invisible quilt of love wraps around me; the presence of Big Deep Love that can hit me like a tsunami when I least expect it carrying me along, the intimacy of a personal relationship with the divine which nature provides as a portal, the voice of sacred love in the little synchronicities, the eyes of a beloved friend or family member.

The whisper of God sounds in a timely song title, a casual expression spoken, a standout line in a book, acapella birdsong, a curious and lingering butterfly - these all catch me when I fall. But not always on my timeline.

These act as a supportive harness and they anchor the way forward.

Everyone I know is climbing their own mountain. They are learning to lose too, to roll, to fall, to slide and to get back up.

Some have stopped to enjoy the view, are sharing a picnic and others have set up camp for an extended stay. But we are all travelling on the mountain - whether by the gentle gravel path for a time, or on a steep climb with crampons, pickaxe and ropes.

I have friends in severe pain right now - physical and emotional. Some watching adored parents and family members touch the edges of this side of the Veil, others are grieving those recently travelled to other side, fathers, wives, aunts, friends, husbands, brothers, sisters, sons, beloved pets, some are awaiting results, diagnoses, treatment plans, others still are battling depression and anxiety. There are relationship fissures for some in my circle, heart-bursting break-ups for others.

Maybe the traditions and my old teacher have it so right after all. Maybe we all need to learn how to become GOOD losers, to surrender this illusion of control and learn how to fall easier and softer. To practise our falls, loosen our grip and see where we roll, where we land. Who will come and help soften our fall?

It's all a big adventure, grim at times for sure but oh my - the view at others.

CHECK·PRAY·LOVE 49

I just got the okay from bloods check yesterday to go for my last Ki-More-Therapy tomorrow.

It was in jeopardy as I've had that lousy virus of coughing, sneezing and spluttering for over a week. I'm choosing, as reminded by Irene, to see it as a cleansing, a release, a flush-oot.

I must be shining on the inside now.

I'm still weak and hacking but apparently my blood is stronger than strong and I can take it tomorrow. A huge thanks to my Reiki-blaster group on Messenger who've had my back, especially in last few days of doubt.

So tomorrow, if no decline, I get to ring that bell even though the hard bit is to follow over the next few weeks with Ray-Joy therapy daily until mid-November.

My wee Chancer was well-hidden but with more diligent checking perhaps I would have noticed sooner. My pal Laura noticed that indent on my boob while topless bathing on our apartment terrace back in March. I thought it was a bra mark.

If I'd picked it up sooner, it would have been a different treatment plan altogether.

If it hadn't been picked up at all?

Don't be like Ange, check yer pumpkins regular and often.

Until you hear the magic words, "You have Breast Chancer", you have absolutely NO IDEA what you would do to spend more time on this beautiful planet with the people you love.

RING·PRAY·LOVE 50

So I finally got to ring the bell after all, despite concerns about the lurgy I had developed.

What a beautiful surprise when I came out of Ki-More-Therapy number six to find my brother Chris had brought mum up from Helensburgh (round trip of 120 miles for him). Lucie made it over too at such short notice.

Dougie was in collecting his mum Christine from a nearby ward by chance after over a week's stay and the happenings continued as he was just in time too.

The family managed a beautiful lunch at Crossbasket to celebrate the conclusion of this part of the journey. I still have "reaction/recovery" from the chemical detox to pay for over the next few weeks (a bit of a quicksand descent) then 15 sessions of daily Ray-Joy Therapy (you get a bell to ring after that trip too), followed by rebuilding the immune system, rehabilitation and reorganisation of life. It's not over when the doctors stop, that's when the deeper healing starts.

Wake up calls are turning points, and the bell can also be seen as a symbol of a call to AWAKEN.

This type of journey isn't just for those of us Dancing The Chancer, this is for all of us who know we have a wheel fallen off of our wagon, whether physical, emotional or spiritual.

What do you need to start, stop, detox, re-commit to, eliminate, continue, endure and how and when will you honour and celebrate? Ring YOUR bell.

GREET·LAUGH·LOVE 51

I worried a bit when people consistently commented on my positivity, my strength, my fight and my humour during my healing dance with The Chancer. Superwoman, eh? Er, naw thanks.

This would be a totally false impression of reality and I believe we should always make reality our best friend, even when it's not pretty.

This journey, which has a ways to go with treatment yet, has so far been a harrowing, magnificent, inspiring, devastating, horrific, beautiful, healing, destructive, hellish, magnificent, powerful, terrifying, desperately lonely, completely overcrowded, enlightening, joy-filled, becalmed, isolated, deeply healing, supportive, soul-stretching, mind-bending, visionary experience.

And I've no desire to relive it.

I'm crap the noo but I will rise again. I'm getting awfy good at this resurrection shuffle. The cocktail of Ki-More Detox is powerful and strong and it's on the seek and remove mission right now. Immunity is lowered as the purge of any remaining tired and confused damaged cells is undertaken yet again. And they are swept up and carried off for recycling outside of my energy body and energy field. Just like the falling leaves being swept up this Autumn.

It doesn't need to be A BATTLE!

It doesn't need to be A FIGHT!

You don't need to be A WARRIOR!

You don't need to KICK CHANCER'S ASS!

It's tough enough just to get through the appointments and the treatments without having to take a superhuman stance.

It's good to fall down, to wail, to release, to give in to the despair.

We are not machines. We are not computers. You are not being negative.

You will not die from having a good greet but you might from the effects of repressing emotions if you don't. Tears soften the heart. In fact, you will release toxins from your system in the process.

Letting go is part of the whole healing cycle.

Hauding it in is NOT the way, nor being a soldier.

These turning points in our lives, whether because of a Chancer diagnosis, a physical or emotional health breakdown or any major shift in our relationships, family situations, work life are not mistakes to be erased or disasters we must urgently despatch. They are the natural challenges and experiences that every soul who has walked the planet since the history of time has faced in some way, shape or form.

The Dark Night is an opportunity for a spiritual transformation.

When things fall apart, I must not add SHAME and BLAME to the challenge of negotiating my way through the landscape of life. It's ok to fall, it's important to fail, in fact it's crucial. It teaches me humility. It teaches me compassion for myself and others. Falling and failing are essential and elemental parts of my life skills.

It's essential as an awakening to all that matters. It's an opportunity to receive, to lean on, to learn new stuff about yourself, people, life. To deepen your relationship with yourself and others. With the bigger picture. With love.

And when it hurts, you should cry.

Big boys DO cry and so do big girls.

There were always gonna be twists and turns, dark woods and thick forests, wild animals, vultures and thieves. Along with the birdsong, angels, seascapes, starry skies, sunsets and the wise ones to guide and protect us on our way.

It's still a world of duality we live in here on Planet Earth last time I looked. The dark and the light.

DEATH·PRAY·LIFE 52
(Not for faint-hearted)
You are gonna die one day. Fact.
I am gonna die one day. Fact.
But only the really strong of gut are willing to go near the subject of death and dying with someone who has a diagnosis. Is it tempting fate to even sniff around the edges? Some in the health and positive thinking fascist society would run from the word DEATH. There, I said it.
I said it again. And look, I'm still here.

The truth is, I could get hit by a bus next week.

But I have found myself in recent months "clearing out", organising better, explaining things others don't know or need to know should I be unavailable in the future for any reason. Putting my house in order.

Negative thinking? I like to think not. More a WAKE-UP-CALL to that best friend, REALITY.

It's easy to think we will live forever. I happen to believe we do, just not in these clothes.

I listened when my teacher recommended that we keep death on one shoulder as a soulmate and a reminder to live fully on this Earth.

Chancer treatment is a destructive process. You die a little with each treatment. But in time you learn to trust the rebirth of your system as you gain strength again in time. It's serious big-time ebb and flow, dark moon - full moon, sunshine and storms. Just like life.

It helps to really tune into nature for supportive guidelines and metaphors.

Beautiful May reminded me the other day of a metaphor I used when teaching students Reiki, how children respond to the words "Will I kiss it better? There, is that better?"

I've been kissing my hands and transferring those kisses to hot spots since, with success.

Autumn reminds me that I need to let go so I have been clearing out over the past month or so. I sifted and sorted through lots of paperwork including some of dad's stuff the other day. It was tough seeing his signature on things, wee notes with smiley faces he had drawn for me, scribbled messages. But if the trees can let go of their leaves of fire, so too can I. I let go.

When we acknowledge/breathe fresh air, shine some light upon and let go physically of stuff and things; when we let go emotionally of "the holdings" the denied thoughts, the sat-upon feelings, the terrors, the ragings, the guilty secrets, our leaves golden and glow with fire.

Before the gentle release and fall into grace where they are transformed into new life energy.

When I look up from my life and check in with my spiritual sat nav, I may need a re-route. The soul will gently guide us, one way or another to where we need to be.

The process of transformation and letting more light in mostly ain't pretty and is rarely done sitting on the meditation cushion, tinkling your tingsha bells or lying prone on the yoga mat according to most of the magnificent teachers I've met or read. These do help root and prepare the ground, and shake the bough, however.

It's mostly a process of guts and glory, tears and snotters, dragons and dens. In 30 years of working with people as a psychotherapist, I never yet met one client who made a truly worthwhile connection, discovery or recovery by tap-dancing, or by waving their arms through some fun and giggle sessions, or without a handful of Mr. Kleenex's finest by their sides.

It's a peeling back and stripping away job. A shaking down. A complete rewiring and replumbing project. It's not easy - nothing worthwhile ever is. Despite what the wishful thinkers would want you to believe in their "wonderful" books, from Gremlin to Goddess workshops, Early Bird online courses £17.99 with and free bonus personal FaceTime live from my bath.

So if you are struggling today, regardless of whether it's a physical challenge, an emotional crisis or your spirit feels like a burst balloon - know that you are not alone. You are part of a huge community of people who are too and some very deep shifting will be happening if you allow it to teach you what it can about this short life. Maybe as you watch Autumn do her thing, she will whisper some guidance into your ear for the next step on your path.

EAT·THANK·LOVE 53

Regular inventories of things to be thankful for are part of the immune boosting medicine bag for all ails. The Chancer healing is no different.

Depression, sadness, lethargy, tearfulness are part and parcel of all chronic illness but the side effects of the chemical cocktails of Ki-More-Therapy are legend.

Gratitude practised religiously and diligently is a wonderful antidote.

The beautiful gift boxes free-from just about everything inflammatory, except healthy life-giving ingredients and love, with handmade macaroons and cookies from my pal Kate Cowan.

Family catch-up after their hols.

Dan celebrated his 15th birthday.

Molly donated some of her hair to the Little Princess Trust for children who have Chancer. They use it to produce wigs.

Meeting Dougie's mum at Wishy Healthspital after I'd rung that bell.

Aiden discovers the tooth fairy.

I discover the health benefits of fresh rosemary in a gin and tonic.

The offer of a personal Melatonin courier delivery from the

States by Clare.

Two mahoosive jars of homemade fermented sauerkraut from Caroline (Andrex chilling in the fridge).

Candles lit in various foreign churches by loving and kind peeps – Lorraine, Christine, Marion.

Beautiful movies of the sea filmed just for me by pals on their hols.

"These are a few of my favourite things" this past few weeks, while enduring the descent.

SHINE·PRAY·LOVE 54

This recent full moon is the Huntress Moon, the Blood Moon, or the Winter is Coming Moon, or the First Frost Moon. I love these names, given by the indigenous peoples who lived close to the land, to differentiate each Moon from the other. They ALL have their own name.

Most people at least know the Harvest Moon, which was in September (my favourite). Sitting under the full moons, exploring the night skies, tracking the patterns of the stars, helps me expand my senses and connect more fully with the heavens above.

St. Francis of Assisi called the Moon "Sister Moon" and referred to the sun as "Brother Sun". He saw the divine and the sacred in every living thing. He named everything in nature and had a personal relationship with all of life.

When I extend my awareness, expand my energy field and deepen my connection to Nature, I blur the edges of my boundaries and sense of separateness with a spiritual eraser. I have a deeper awareness of the divine energy animating all of life. I fall back into my true nature. My wildness. My untamedness.

St. Francis wrote the prayer/song The Canticles to inspire us become "more deeply aware that we live within one web of life: our common home".

"We praise you for Sister Moon and the stars in the heavens you have made them bright, precious and fair."

Amen

MEET·GAB·LOVE 55

I was so happy I surfaced in time (just) to meet up with Grace who had flown up from Landan Town specially to make me smile and she brought the sunshine with her.

She's more used to Marbella Marina but the Auchinstarry houseboats on the canal hold their own boho chic charm.

Michelle you played a blinder as the chauffeur, driving Miss Gracie halfway round West and Central Scotland to make it all possible.

Grace and I go back 50 years to primary and I shared her bed every few weeks while I trained in Clinical Hypnotherapy in London 35 years ago, over a two year period. That's a pal.

Life and distance got in the way for a chunk of time but here we are in our autumnal phase of life. Shared histories make for deep roots.

Michelle is a very recent friend - I've only known her almost 40 years so we are still getting to know each other.

Life is a quilt and the colours of the different threads, textures and patches create a heavenly "embroidered cloth, enwrought with golden and silver light" (Yeats, no me).

Good Deep Heart Medicine.

LAUGH·EAT·LOVE 56

Social isolation is highly correlated in recovery rates for women with Breast Chancer. Bet you didn't know that.

But it makes perfect sense.

We wummen are sometimes a bit neglectful at nurturing and taking care of ourselves, SELF-SOOTHING. We often run about after everybody else, neglect our own needs and lose touch with our own social networks and interests. This is pure folly when it comes to matters of health.

So I am taking NO chances on this front and am now eating my way around the West of Scotland with my pals and sinking deep taproots into my relationships while socially immersing myself in the company of my pals near and far.

Gotta up those percentage points.

40% higher recurrence rate of Chancer and 60% higher mortality rate if you are socially isolated.

Now I'm not, but I do live a wee bit out in the land time forgot and I had got a bit over committed work wise these last few years. That's been rectified from the get-go of this diagnosis.

Self-nurture is crucial to heal but receiving from our friends and family is imperative in the recovery stakes too. There is no place for stoicism here, don't be a hero. RECEIVE. C'mon girls get those connections going and maintain them as if your life depends on it. It does. Reach out, risk it for a biscuit, recontact, join up, join in, invite, call up, write, make the first move.

Laughter is vital and there was lots of that, retail therapy must be up there on the healing chart too. I'm sure it is. So Caroline's Nellie Elephant and my Buddy the Buddha plant pots are actually self-medicating tools.

The robin sang his greeting as we parked and saluted us again as we left from exactly the same branch and position. Funny that.

CHAT·PEE·LAUGH 57

So Caroline comes for a visit yesterday and I visit the loo for a tinkle before we head out for lunch. I'm searching for the telephone number of the lunch venue to check and book a table as I'm sitting on the loo.

I'm surprised when a screenshot comes on my phone saying The Three Witches.

Chloe Homewood is another member of this Witches' Coven and is visiting her mum in London this week. It looks as if Caroline is making a "group telephone chat" from the kitchen to Chloe and I'm included, so I accept. We have no secrets. We need to tie up dates for our visit to Holy Isle Retreat Centre next spring, that'll be why she's called her up, I muse.

We are all earthy women so I click accept as I sit there on the throne and join in.

"Hi Chloe" I declare as I see her face beaming at me from part of the screen, Caroline's questioning look, with hindsight, filling the other section.

"You've just caught me sitting on the loo having a pee," I laugh nonchalantly into the phone, while it slowly dawns that we are on video camera as I'm tinkling merrily in the background in confirmation.

Just at EXACTLY the same moment, Chloe scans her camera lens around her mother and three children directing them to "say hello to auntie Ange" who all look extremely startled, nay HORRIFIED, on my video screen at my raucous Glaswegian echoing announcement of my current preoccupation.

It couldn't get any worse.

You'd think.

But just before Chloe - who by the way had been the instigator of the call by - cut me off abruptly in my prime, she announced

"ANGELA, WE ARE ON THE TRAIN INTO LONDON."

This was accompanied by the sound of raucous laughter from the rest of the carriage patrons en-route to the City who've heard the whole feckin' thing in the quiet carriage.

Caroline heard and watched the whole disaster unfold on her phone screen helplessly, from the other room - literally a train crash.

Ye couldnae write it.

RISK·PRAY·LOVE 58

It was Dr Bernie Siegel who realised he was able to predict survival rates from Chancer back in the 80s and 90s (when I was lucky enough to train with him down in Birmingham University).

He identified what he called Exceptional Chancer Patients, despite their diagnoses. These people defied all predictions and odds and displayed robust recovery, leaving many doctors scratching their heads.

One of the many traits he identified in this group was their forward-thinking and planning, and commitment to post treatment goals.

So I've been invited to be a speaker at the upcoming Ted Talk Day, which is running in Cumbernauld. How could I refuse?

With such a fabulous line-up of 15 international and homegrown amazing speakers for women, great entertainment and the sharing of a huge variety of ideas and perspectives.

I'm speaking on This Woman's Worth in addition to 14 other contributors from a hugely diverse background of personal development, medical, scientific, therapeutic, writing, performance and entertainment backgrounds.

It will be a day to remember.

The talks are Ted Talk standard 18 minutes each, now that WILL be a challenge for me. I can talk for Scotland.

RETREAT·PRAY·LOVE 59

I'm just setting off on retreat, all by myself, until Friday over at the Carmelite Convent.

It will be a pretty much silent time.

I have my own wee tiny flat but will join in with the community for prayers.

I spent yesterday afternoon at the medical centre due to a pretty bad fungal infection on my foot, Ki-More-Therapy side effect. It split deeply and bled. Big sepsis risk of infection. So I was seen in minutes, anti-bio-ed and given more bloody steroids.

I was dressinged, bandaged, and blood tests done to check for infection. All over a wee cut on yer foot. But believe me, these Natural Health Saviours (NHS) come into their own when your life is at risk. They are outstanding.

The receptionist even came out to apologise that I needed to wait an hour to get my dressing done, having seen the doctor at 20 minutes' notice without an appointment.

I was offered a blinking house call to save me travel which I refused of course, being perfectly capable. No private health care system would operate with that level of efficiency.

We called from home at 1.30pm to ask for advice. By 5.30 pm, I was back home chewing on my meds, having been seen immediately by the doc, had bloods taken, the nurse had cleaned and dressed my foot, got prescription cashed and had driven home.

I am ready now for some soulful input, solitude and silence and Lord G will benefit too from some space from me, my health weather reports and being a chauffeur and carer.

We've been pretty much joined at the hip since my diagnosis of Chancer (the reindeer nobody wanted to know) in April.

It will be good for us both to have some private catch-up time "Let the winds of heaven dance between you."

I'm hitting a pause button between extreme gratitude for the Ki-More-Therapy I was given access to and the next stage of treatment starting Monday: Ray-Joy-Therapy.

I will have a laugh too at the convent - they are really switched on, bright women and I'm having some spiritual direction while I'm there, it's a kinda therapy for the soul. Pretty tough work, the ego hates it. Keep a daily journal for a month of the lies, the untruths, and the embellishments you've indulged in. That's one I've been given in the past. Go on, try it as a nightly review. Very, very sobering and insightful.

So, my darling pals, I won't be responding to the outside world until the weekend. I will probably post a couple of wee posts of insights or share a little of this mysterious journey but don't be offended if I don't respond.

I will be praying for y'all, and the beautiful souls who have supported me on my journey. I'll include all the gorgeous card-senders. I have every last one of them and read a few of them daily to bolster my spirits. Thank you for being part of my healing journey. Big hugs.

AWE·PRAY·LOVE 60

That's the word. AWE.

Yesterday, I left the Carmelite Convent where I'd been on retreat since Tuesday, in silence, by myself. The services and some daily spiritual direction being the only outer punctuation marks during the inner journey.

I liked what someone called the sisters: "The Karma-Lites."

It's been a deep and wordless experience, I couldn't even begin.

Being on antibiotics all week pulled me physically down and

I was already weary from six sessions of Ki-More-Therapy but I was advised by my Anam Cara (soul friend) who was my spiritual director to "SLEEP and WEEP". So I did. BOTH. A whole box full of man-size in five days.

My prayer time was just "to sit" to not even TRY to pray. To follow the edicts of St. Teresa of Avila (who set up her community in 1562) and St. Therese of Liseaux (The Little Flower) who both knew real health challenges in their lifetimes.

The experience of being prayed FOR by a community of Women of Prayer with an average of 50 years' experience of constant prayer in an enclosed community, was like being surrounded by the weaving of an invisible golden cloak of protection and light. I swear I could FEEL IT and I could TASTE IT, even during the night.

Not once was a big thing made of this unspoken process overtly, it was happening under the radar all the time I was there. I could experience being held like a child in a deep loving embrace and it was confirmed later when I asked that that's exactly what had been going on.

I read the suggested sections of the books offered with gentle suggestions of compass points, newly discovered beauty in Isaiah, reconnecting with John of the Cross in The Dark Night of The Soul and Therese's Little Way and her Story of a Soul.

I entered into St. Teresa's Interior Castle. I travelled into The Silent Land.

A place of constant prayer has its own healing energy and presence.

Love grows where contemplation and sacred practice is planted. Silence highlights the birdsong and sound of the bells calling us to prayer.

I had daily squirrel visits to my window. Deer grazed 30 feet away. And of course a photo-shy Robin led me on my walk, branch-hopping while he whistled.

I feel restored and renewed before my daily Ray-Joy Therapy begins today.

I feel unburdened, less fearful.

I feel the hearth of my inner living room has been rekindled with "a little straw" not a BONFIRE and FIREWORKS, just a gentle heart-warming glow.

The Little Way of the Little Flower.

I experienced gentleness.

Preciousness.

And restorative deep love in my heart and in my soul.

Some thoughts I explored that you may like to chew on, or leave on the side of yer plate if ye don't fancy them.

I'm like a sponge in the ocean - immersed in what flows through me. The more I remember this, the more connected I feel, the more I am fully ME, just as I AM.

Sometimes my damaged thinking has an arthritic grip. I need to loosen it and open my palm gently. Then I can sit soft in the silence and depth of the present, and the presence of love.

When I'm connected and transformed I breathe in the mystery of love and she breathes in me.

Silence cleanses my mind and my heart and blesses my tongue.

There is something in us deeper than any pain and fear. When the chaos of my mind is stilled, I touch this constant and loving presence.

Awaken my soul.

GREET WITH LAUGHTER & 'MEET-RAY-JOY' 61
Yesterday was my first of 15 daily Ray-Joy-Therapy sessions (Radiotherapy) at the Land 'o the Monks Healthspital.

It's a magnificent new facility and everyone, and I mean EVERYONE was tremendous.

But I did have a chuckle to myself at the wide and robust "privacy screen" provided for one to disrobe in discreet modesty. This is before being handed a piece of kitchen roll (okay, I exaggerate - bedroll) to cover yer wink.

All before trying to lie down spatchcock-style, on an extremely shiny (therefore slippery) black XXL kitchen chopping board and assume the position of a horizontal chubby and ageing ballerina on point. Promptly followed by having your boob stump drawn on with felt pens by two complete strangers colouring by numbers, with colder than cold hands as they ask "how ye doin'?".

They slide me around on the chopping board telling me to play statues and not help them (I've got my feckin' arms stapled into some S&M arm and wrist cuffs overhead - how am I gonna help anybody?).

After a few minutes of this folly they surrender, ever-so-slightly out of breath ("ok Angela, maybe give us just a teensy bit of help" in a voice an octave too high), having under-guesstimated my deceptive body weight. I give some much-appreciated assistance in order to get things suitably in alignment and positioned, with the spaceship enterprise hovering in anticipation above me and here's me with the Patrick Stewart lookalike hairdo too!

The actual Ray-Joy was over in a minute or three and utterly fine. There can be side-effects but one should delete that programme. Heat in the area treated, sunburn-style, broken skin, sepsis has to be watched due to lowered immunity, exhaustion over the piece and risk of lymphoedema. BUT with good skincare, Aloe Vera and Aveeno lotion, plenty of hydration, rest and gentle Tai Chi and yoga arm movement to keep lymph working and some magical homoeopathic remedies to aid and assist protection, I'm full of hope and intention for a great result.

I almost laughed out loud when after drawing on my ex-boob, heaving my stationary frame about, and having had their their faces at closer than close proximity (12") to my wink, the gorgeous Ray-Joy-Graphic-ers demurely placed another wee square of kitchen roll over me, to protect my dignity as I got up and walked over to the "privacy screen" to dress!

I used it to wipe the tears of laughter away.

So beautifully done - all of it.

My God, She loves music and this anthem came on the radio when we started up the car as we were leaving.

One down - 14 to go. "Keep on moving."

NOVEMBER 2019

SIT·PRAY·LOVE 62

INTERLUDE

25 sleep nights and counting

Caroline and Chloe.

This was a very, very good idea to retreat to Samye Ling again, girls. My Chancer journey started there back in April before surgery, and my treatment finishes on November 15, before we go.

My baldie hairdo is utterly perfect and of course I will be wearing red sheets to carry it off.

Thanks so much for suggesting and organising. Grateful.

Namaste!

READ·TALK·LOVE 63

I've been asked by Ali, Chaplain at University Healthspitall Wishaw (I call it Wishy Healthspital) to participate in their Absent Friends Festival with a book reading. They have copies of the book that I wrote and distribute to people who've experienced loss and are grieving. I'm very flattered and well chuffed. Who'd've thunk it?

November is the historically the month where we remember

those who have passed over the Veil and it also happens to be my dad's third anniversary this month, so I couldn't refuse.

I'm speaking a little about the book and reading some extracts from it, then Ali will facilitate a discussion around the subjects in the book.

Here's to all of our loved ones over the Veil.

Love Never Dies.

RANT·PRAY·LOVE 64

People post all sorts on here, and I usually manage to scroll on. But this week was an exception.

Sometimes I get triggered by the health fascists, you know them, they know it all. Their way is the right way, and the ONLY way.

They haven't a clue, nor a real interest in the facts of the reality faced by Chancer patients and their families.

They have no interest in complexities, exceptions to their self-proclaimed rule and they have usually feck all personal experience of what they are talking about. But THAT don't stop them.

Oh No.

So I'd had enough of the Chancer experts, the ones with a few part time training courses behind them, who dismiss those who have, have had, or will decide to have Ki-More-Therapy or radiotherapy or surgery for that matter, as "deluded dimwits". I usually cross the road to avoid them these days.

But when I saw a guy who is in the midst of Ki-More-Therapy treatment being rounded on, nay bullied, on FB by three or more of these chumps, who hadn't even read properly the research paper they were bandying about as evidence, that "Chemo makes all Cancers worse, kills you, and there's no point in it at all "or words to that effect, I pulled my knickers on over my tights, tucked the tea towel into the neck of my jumper and here was my reply.

"As someone going through treatment my views have dramatically changed with regards to these discussions.

Firstly, there is no such thing as "Chancer" in and of itself.

Chancer is a continent. There are thousands of different countries within that continent.

There are a myriad of different types of Breast Chancer, for example, and differing causes from hormonal changes to toxicity to immune dysfunction to combinations of all and others.

Eg : I am ER + Pr + . But I am not HER2+, which my next door neighbour was. Another friend was only ER + and neither of the others.

We all had different treatments and combinations of same. Some lumpectomy, some mastectomy, some radiotherapy, and a wide variety of different Ki-More-Therapy approaches. We humans come in all shapes, sizes and genetics.

Your one size fits all blanket judgement of Chancer and Ki-More-Therapy is waaaaay over-simplistic and extremely distressing for those going thru treatment. At best it's far from helpful. At worst, downright dangerous and destructive.

We are not idiots. We know there are risks and we are living with the consequences of the decisions we make every day.

These headline-grabbing press articles are generalised and globalised by people who don't read the detail, this article refers to one small study involving PRE-operative Ki-More for example.

But the snappy title doesn't specify that.

There is no such thing as "Chemo".

It is a continent too. The type, the combinations and dosage required are myriad and again numerous.

It's often people who have never been touched personally by cancer, or the decisions around treatment protocols, who have the loudest voices and the most dogmatic views.. Ahm jus sayin'."

And In response to flimsy protestations later that same day.

"I truly hope that neither you nor any member of your family ever finds themselves in a position where you have to test your belief system in reality.

I see many children with leukaemia and myeloma on my own personal travels with Chancer and I chat to their parents negotiating these percentages, which some cast aside in a rather smug and cavalier fashion.

I too have had to make decisions based on 2% increase in efficacy here, an extra 3% likelihood there. These are people's lives we are talking about.

Believe me these 3.5%s and 6%s all add up when you are faced with your child's mortality, or your own.

And most of us will take every chance we can get when we are.

The luxury of predicting what we would or wouldn't do IF we, or our loved one, had a diagnosis is lost when staring that diagnosis in the face. We start to take the maths very seriously indeed.

Blanket generalisations made from bits of research are unhelpful, and headline-grabbing PR pieces with misleading titles are dangerous and scaremongering. As therapists, we both know the power of words on vulnerable people's psyches and Chancer patients are extremely vulnerable people.

But they, and the nurses, doctors and consultants who treat them are also intelligent people who have weighed up the pros and cons of their own bespoke and specific treatment.

They courageously make tough and unthinkable decisions about how best to take their chances at life, at this current point in time given where they are at, with what treatments are currently available. Or give the same chances to their children."

And later still..

"PS: On the Toxic theme: having any form of surgery is toxic, the chemicals are potentially life-threatening, but also life-saving.

When you say you don't believe in healing anything by using toxins, would you refuse surgery, anaesthetics, pain relief?

Aromatherapy oils can be toxic.

Allergens in food and the environment are toxic.

Living in the city and breathing in these days is now toxic.

I often wonder where the line gets drawn on the toxicity argument."

The toxically baldy one walks away, shaking the dust from her sandals.

TED·TALK·LOVE 65

Around two years ago at this time, I and two friends delivered The Empowered Woman Day at Trades Hall in Glasgow, which was well received. In June this year, four of us presented Women 4 Women at The Glasgow Caledonian University.

I'm awfy excited that I've now been invited to be one of the speakers at TEDx Talks on Thursday Dec 5 at Cornerstone House, Cumbernauld.

My theme will be The Curse of Perfect - Are you ready for love?

*TEDx is a non-profit devoted to spreading ideas, in the form of short, powerful talks (18 minutes). TED Talks began in 1984 as a conference, and today TEDx events help share ideas in communities around the world.

EAT·PRAY·FLOW 66

I'm defying gravity the noo - MERCURY TURBOGRADE.

And I'm not complaining.

In spite of all the Mercury retrograde warnings, there's a fair wee bit of flow flowing right now.

So two more bookshops said yes to stocking my book Love Never Dies, just as I approach my dad's third anniversary this weekend: Hyndland Books and The Crystal Shop in St. Andrews.

I did my first book-reading gig on Thursday and I really loved it, felt really nice to share and though a small and intimate group there was a heartfelt response and the participants seemed genuinely moved by the experience. I certainly was.

At the weekend, we checked in to our favourite hotel in St Andrews but there was a dodgy smell in the room, and it wisnae me.

Was it a) Damp? b) Drains? or c) Graham? Ah wait, he wasn't even in the room yet.

Lord G expressed our concern to reception, especially with my suppressed immune system and associated health risks. We were offered another room. Oh yeah, ONLY the best room in the hotel. Le Suite: the room with les windows with le view!

On Sunday, as we kept a wee silent minute or two in remembrance of the souls who didn't make it home from the hell of battle, I turned around and looked out of that same window... just as two mahoosive deer sauntered past only 30 feet away.

And finally, as I checked in with my pal about meeting up for a pre-theatre on Monday before the show, which we both had tickets for. Dougie casually mentioned "eh it's not on Monday Ange it's on Sunday."

I had six tickets, £150 worth.

I'd booked and paid for a lodge for the family to celebrate G's birthday this weekend. We stay till Monday and would miss it.

However, D and I at the same time remembered that ATG tickets changed the time of the performance months ago from 1pm to 7pm. Could we pull it off?

We did! They happily refunded every penny due to their having changed the performance times, and it "not suiting" now.

Love it when the flow flows...

GREET·PRAY·LOVE 67

A short one. I'm almost, but not quite, without words. It's nearly 2am and I am sleepless in Condorrat.

Today, Friday, is the day of my last treatment for Chancer, at the same interesting time as all my other Ray-Joy-Therapy appointments, 12:12pm. I looked up the significance of the combination in Numerology.

"12:12, is a reminder to be aware of your thoughts and keep a positive state of mind. So seeing 12:12 is a message for you to be conscious of your thoughts and focus on positive thinking to attract the right things into your life for your highest good."

How the tectonic plates shifted on the fateful last day of March, with THAT letter. 33 weeks ago and different experiences and treatments during each one of them.

Manmograms, Diagnosis, the telling of, to family and friends, dealing with reactions -mine and theirs, Mastectomy, results, drains, infection control, decisions, Ki-More-Therapy, blood results, scans, fungal infections, antibiotics, low white cell count, radiotherapy, hormone blockers.

All infused with and surrounded by love.

It's not over. Consultants, prescriptions, nurses, needles, appointments and scans are gonna be my fellow travellers for a while yet, until I get my training wheels off. My diary has lots of wee stars for Wishy Healthspital in it yet.

But I lie here in the early hours of this momentous day I will never forget, on the brink of having my life back and that feels like another leap into the unknown.

Tomorrow is for thank yous, prayers of gratitude, hugs, releasing tears and another rite of passage bell-ringing ritual.

Lots of thank yous to give. G has endured all of this crazy-making detour and derailment with me and still does. We head from Wishy to North of the Wall to celebrate his birthday at weekend with the family. My thank you to him.

Thank YOU. For being here. For reading my ramblings or even tut-tutting your way through, for giggling, growling or groaning, for responding, supporting, indulging and for playing along with me.

I'm not finished. I still have things to share about the trip that may be of use to someone.

Returning home later I was treated to a golden sunburst of a sunset. A sense of closure of a cycle.

And to top it off, I returned to a special delivery of a small package. I was speechless. Chloe - the timing was everything. I shall wear my silver angel wing bracelet with pride tomorrow as I ring my bell and get my wings.

RING·PRAY·LOVE 68

Numb.

Why do I go numb?

Probably one of the biggest days of my life, and I go numb.

But Friday was the last day of eight months of Chancer Treatment Therapy and I got to ring the second bell.

David turned up as a surprise.

And G presented me with a ring I'd admired a while ago.

It's by a jeweller who makes casts in silver of sea shells. I loved the symbolism of the barnacle seashell. It's used as a simile in humans for being tenacious, I've since read.

For me it symbolised the Chancer and how something beautiful can be made out of anything even an unwanted attachment on the underside of a boat. They are usually scraped off and despatched.

But my Chancer, though unwanted and unwelcome, needing removal and despatch, was also a gift.

It brought many lessons and much deep healing on different levels.

I got another CHANCE and a chance to do things differently.

A heart attack or a stroke may not have given another chance.

Many people didn't wake up this morning - I did. I get another CHANCE at life every time I open my eyes, still breathing.

There are many people I know who have crossed over the Veil since I was diagnosed (Aunt Irene, David M, Noreen A) and some I didn't know so well, but I owe it to them (we all do) to remember - we have another CHANCE today.

I have some photo memories of Friday, one of the most important days of my life that I will be able to take in fully, when I thaw out enough to exhale fully.

WRITE·TALK·LOVE 69

I'd given myself one or two wee projects this side of the New Year, to exercise my brain muscles a little, which is crucial after eight months of relative vegetation, other than reading Healthspital appointment letters and side effect lists.

I'm pretty exhausted now which is par for the course it seems. Symptoms don't end with the last treatment date. Everyone is different, every Chancer is different, treatments are different, dosages are different, age and stage will impact too.

So what your Auntie Mary experienced and how fast my Uncle Willie recovered or declined have little meaning in the grand scheme of things.

Everyone's journey with the Chancer is pretty unique, a bit like life, I guess.

So it makes things a little tricky when trying to plan ahead or to risk committing to things. I find these days I need a 'get out clause' in everything I plan, a PLAN B and an evacuation procedure factored in.

My energy levels can drop like a stone in a heartbeat.

My symptoms still involve challenges with my eyes and reading, neuropathy, joint pains, radiation burning and rash, fatigue, internal inflammation and nerve pain. And the blessed exhaustion which hits me like the overriding, overruling, automatic-braking system, that it is.

But all of these are a joy and a pleasure after the rigours of Ki-More-Therapy. That was a swim the Channel six times effort.

Ray-Joy-Therapy was a pleasure by comparison.

Yes, I'm still cooking on the inside, I have a charming rash to remind me I'm not home free, am a little itchy and bitchy at times, and have tender, limited movement due to inflammation.

But the girls were all so lovely and gentle with their soft, cool hands - apologising for their temperature on my weary and nuked body. I'll know and remember those faces, seen daily in close-up for nearly four weeks, for the rest of my life.

And there was Yoko, the guide dog of Patrick, blind but there for prostate treatment with radio (yes, I said Patrick - just like my dad's name). Yoko was there to greet me before and after 10 of my treatments. A joy indeed.

And as for the banter in the waiting room from the Prostate Cancer Guys, waiting for their Radio-Ga-Ga, their dodgy bladder stories were priceless. A few close-run happenings myself after some of the laughs.

So I will miss some aspects of the last while, strange as that may seem. Mostly all the people.

However, the appointment letters still arrive on a regular basis. Uncle-ologist next week, Best Care Nurse check, bone density photoshoot, the blood appreciation society meet-ups, bone-strengthening Ki-More-Therapy, Her-Moan control tabs checks.

Lots still to do. Along with my Magic Medicine Practitioners in Homoeopathy, Nutrition and Vitamin Supplements, Reiki, Reflexology and Manual Lymphatic Reflexology.

These work in at least equal partnership, in my humble opinion, if not in fact preparing the ground and stabilising the whole process.

I'm seeing someone too.

Not a new love - a talk-to person.

There are things you can't always say to your loved ones, friends and colleagues - no matter how much you might want to. You can only burden so many folks for so long with your fears, worries, feelings and stuffed-up emotions.

There is always gonna be a backlash after a time like this, and I know the value of dealing with loss, and grief and stumbling into the future with an Anam Cara (soul friend) who's been around the block a few times.

Having a witness, who we don't need to protect to these deep times of soul growth can be invaluable and essential.

We all need a safe space from time to time a recycling point. I've lined up mine.

I'll share a wee piece I wrote a few years ago, which I will include in my TED talk. It may be familiar to some of you as I've used it before on women's retreats and days but I think it's worth the re-share. I'm STILL working and nudging towards it myself, it also applies to men, and everyone on the rainbow, gender, race and age spectrum too.

A "Bold and Brilliant Woman" shares from her heart and she does her share.

She is open to counsel from those she trusts - but SHE discerns what is right for her.

She displays humility: she feels equal to, not better than, others.

She doesn't carry her self-worth in the clothes she wears, her handbag or her hairstyle.

She carries herself with dignity and is in touch with her vulnerability, her soft place. She allows her tears to flow.

But she will rise as a she-wolf to protect herself or others. She is not static, she waxes and wanes like the Moon, she is in touch with her connection to Mother Nature.

She has no need for perfection, and little interest in competing or comparing.

She knows how to laugh, especially at herself.

WALK·EAT·TALK 70

A day of four halves today. I have a bone density scan coming up soon, it seems osteoporosis is a real risk factor after the treatment I've had, so they check.
What a country.

If I'm at risk, they will prescribe big time calcium but bone density is helped by other things too. So I'm playing MY part in helping my bones to strengthen and dense-up.

You could play along too if you like, especially the girls that are hitting menopause or afters, when the bones may begin to shapeshift a little.

I've been on Vitamin D3 and its wee pal K2 since this journey kicked off, as we Scots particularly are totally depleted in D due to our location on the planet in relation to the source of light. I am consulting Dr David Reilly FRCP (formerly Glasgow Homeopathic Healthspital and Integrative Care Centre) who suggested I ask for a blood test to check my levels. They were WAY too low at 50 something. He wanted me up at 120-140 or thereabouts for good immune function.

NHS doesn't consider you have a problem unless under 30/40.

Lack of Vit D is implicated big time now in Chancer, MS, and many auto-immune disorders. D3 needs a hand from K2 to do its job properly.

I also take a half-teaspoon of fermented cod liver oil (Oceans Alive Website). Cinnamon flavour as it's bleurgh on its own, as a good back-up food source of Vit A and D. Great for everything, but especially Sally Skeleton.

You can do a Vit D check with a kit bought online or ask your doctor. You are entitled to one check a year.

I won't let it drop down there again. I will be seeing David for several sessions throughout my treatment privately to experience his TheWEL (Wellness Enhancement Learning) programme, to bring about transformative change and to share in his ideas on the healing holism paridgm. We will be looking at every aspect of the compass of my life – physical, emotional and spiritual. He is the consultant physician who led the creation of the NHS Centre For Integrative Care in Glasgow.

WEIGHT-BEARING EXERCISE is good bone health medicine so I'm out now in the morning and chatting to the sheep and trees as I pound around the paths and fields. walking and putting my bones under pressure.

For good measure I use a couple of very light hand-held weights for a few minutes on my arms for upper body and lean on my wrists, hands and arms when on all fours a couple of times a day. Looks pretty nuts in the supermarket.

So after a good start in the mists of morning, Michelle and Laura arrived for a few hours of chatting and eating lunch while doing health check comparisons, mid-to-slightly-more-than -mid-life complaining about getting older, complaining about men as per usual, the weather, reviewing Netflix latests and the role of the Monarchy.

We do chat about other much more interesting stuff like sex - or the lack of it – drugs (medicinal and naturopathic) and rock n roll but that's not for this book.

Mich brought a really lovely surprise gift: a camper van money bank! And reminded me I have a dream to fulfil.

Laura brought her blessed homemade Biscotti biscuits for coffee dunking and tooth chipping if you forget.

While waiting on M, Laura and I were upstairs for all of 10 minutes and were greeted by a beautiful visit from a red admiral butterfly in my bedroom (window not been open for weeks) and seconds later a cheeky wee robin staring right in at us on the branch outside the window. We both knowingly smiled at the synchronicity, Love Never Dies, we have both got a few folks over the Veil.

I came home to work on my TEDx Talk for next Thursday. I had 35 minutes worth of Wisdom and culled it all back earlier this week. Too much Wisdom isnae good for you.

A Ted talk is routinely 18 minutes and not a minute more. I got it down to 20.

Then yesterday I added a couple of wee interesting bits and pieces, thinking I'll trim a little later.

When I timed it again it was back up to 35 minutes.

Who says I talk too much? Even in print. Where's the chainsaw?

MEET·PRAY·LOVE 71

A mahoosive honour on Thursday, and amazing divine timing. We three only got to meet individually with Lama Yeshe who is the head Monk or Abbot, here at Samye Ling Monastery in Eskdalemuir.

It was surreal because Chloe has tried to arrange this for me all year but it's been impossible. Lama Yeshe has been very ill himself and been in Healthspital - he is 76. We got a meeting on the last day before he begins a four-month silent retreat.

Howzat happen?

Chloe and persistence for one but the last day he was seeing anyone and he's hardly seen anyone this year?

He was a delight, a young boy in an older man's body, twinkling and shining.

We had a good chat. He shared wisdom.

We laughed heartily for very little reason.

I loved him.

I feel so privileged and really blessed and I know how really lucky we were.

By chance – ha - after finding a pic of him with the Dalai Lama, this post from the past I wrote some time ago appeared in my memory feed, so I guess I 'suppose I should share it.

"Suffering in this life is unavoidable" - all traditions and religions agree on this. Sometimes, we New-Agers like to pretend it's not and that we can "affirm" our way out of this fact.

I laughed out loud when a therapist friend (and husband) told me recently of a client who had declared "I've been looking into this affirmation thing you've been suggesting and I've come up with one that works for me: all men are Bastards."

I don't think she had quite grasped the concept.

So difficulties and suffering may be inevitable while we live and breathe but how we respond and react to that suffering is pure choice.

We are free to choose our response, if we work on our knee jerk reactions of old and justified reactivity.

When we hit the PAUSE button.

When we step back and surround difficult situations with a blanket of compassion for all involved (usually a lot of damaged, wounded souls), inject some humour into same, add a healthy dose of humility, drop our unreasonable expectations, a dash of generosity of spirit, a ladle full of forgiveness and downgrade the whole scenario from Red Alert - "It's' the end of the world" - to Amber - "This is pretty lousy, hellish, unpleasant... but in time with the right support, attitude and grace - I'll handle it."

The Dalai Lama and Desmond Tutu had a week together and discussed this suffering theme in relation to joy. Some of these factors were considered to be the pillars of joy.

I call it the scaffolding.

When I'm weary, feeling small, when tears are in my eyes, if I can go through the above checklist and apply it (and it will often require external support to do so) I am able to transform my response to the pain and difficulties in my life.

With generosity and humility I see my connection to all others. I recognise my place in the world and acknowledge that at another time I could be the one in difficulty.

With a sense of humour and ability to laugh at myself we do not take ourselves or others too seriously.

We can find the acceptance where we don't push the river, don't force life to be other than it us. There is a gratitude for all that we have been given.

And as the Dalai Lama put it, "Helping others is the way to

discover your own joy and to have a happy life."

Tutu gave this blessing: "You are loved with a love that nothing can shake, a Love that loved you long before you were created, a love that will be there long after everything has disappeared. You are precious."

And love says "Help me to spread love and laughter and joy and compassion, as you do this you will discover joy. It comes as the gift, the reward for this non-self-regarding caring for others."

DECEMBER 2019

MEET·GREET·LOVE 72
(Signed off yesterday by Oncologist!)

No need to see him again.

Breast Nurse will monitor, IV bone-strengthening treatments every six months, hormone blocks for 10 years, and yearly photos. I'm aw dun and was singing "When you're smiling" and "You never walk alone".

When we went to place our wee gratitude pebble in the Waterbowl at The Sanctuary in Wishy Healthspital, when we bumped into Tosh Lynch (Head Chaplain for Lanarkshire, our very good pal and originally student of Hypnotherapy with us over a decade ago). So we all had a cuppa, a catch-up and a sit down, stand-up comedy routine. He likes to copy my hairstyles and this time was no different.

Then at the exit doors we bumped into PATRICK and his guide dog YOKO. He got Radiotherapy at same time as me but over in Monklands Healthspital. So we met up every day. He had just got all clear too!

Went to Wagamama to celebrate and did some retail therapy in M&S.

As we left, I bumped into my neighbour Linda, who went through exactly the same treatment as me over 10 years ago.

She has been an inspiration when things got me down.

CO-incidences? I like to think not. It's Angelic happenings. All within 3 hours.

I think I've already had my Christmas gift... Life.

SLEEP·PRAY·LOVE 73

Who knew that delivering a Talk that was EXACTLY the prescribed 18 minutes long by TEDx Talks could be so tiring?

But it was...

It was a very exciting day and so rewarding and uplifting. I met some really incredible women backstage and then listened to their stories onstage. Honestly had no words. Some women are true Amazons.

And the thing is, you'd never know if you saw them walking around your local supermarket: whether here in Scotland, in London, Birmingham, South Africa, or Noo Yoick. Yet they all had a story and an idea worth sharing.

Many thanks to all involved, I'm truly blessed and duly grateful to have been a small part of the big wheel that was TEDx Woman Cumbernauld on Thursday, with its 200 beauties in the audience.

TED's Ex - I've no idea who you are (Ted is the loser, believe me!), but you're doing a sterling job, and thanks so much for having me.

WALK·PRAY·LOVE 74

Lindisfarne Island (or the Holy Isle) is a magical place. It was originally called, in Roman times, the Island of Healing and amazing herbs and tinctures were grown and dispensed here over the centuries.

I came for the soul-healing.

There is only the call of the seals and birds, the coal fire, the words in books, the call of the church bell and the whistle of the wind to distract you here.

But today we were busy!

We joined the Advent Adventure walk across the Causeway while the tide was out, before it crept back in and cut the island off completely again overnight from the mainland, an experience worth watching.

It took two hours to walk, or should I say squelch across. Some do it in their bare feet but wellies are needed, not walking boots, because the sinking sands do exactly that - and did to a couple of our hardy crew.

We stopped seven times to breathe and pray and sing.

It will live in my heart forever.

As we looked back across at the poles that marked the tricky and at times scary journey we had made across, the metaphor was not lost on my G and me. I leant on him at many points on the journey, mostly when I got stuck and he had to pull me out. We nearly went down at a couple of really slippery and slidy spots, fear overtook us once or twice, it seemed a long way ahead - would we make it across in time?

But we did. It was further (and deeper) than it had at first seemed, looking back.

But we made landfall and the road ahead looked easier. Love and comforts ahead drew us on homemade spicy pumpkin soup, beautiful music recently recorded by Anna our host, laughter and warm company, big congratulatory bear hugs from Andy who'd invited us along.

I will sleep tonight.

PRAY·PRAY·EAT 75

Just eaten the Hanoi Bike Shop and had a Hanoi Beer to celebrate!
I got my Christmas Gift tonight.

My husband casually asked me just over two weeks ago "what's that on your back?"

It sent an earthquake down my spine. I have always had a thingy, mole-type thang there the last year or two but now he was noticing a change in shape and colour.

It was much darker. And turns out now there were two.

We got straight onto the GP, got an appointment for a couple of days later, were immediately referred to Medical Illustrations for a photograph to be sent to Consultant Dermatology, but all of this took over a week. Superfast? Yes.

But a million years in time when you're where I am and have been. It may have been another four weeks or so before we got seen with Christmas etc in between.

So we paid.

We got the last available appointment this side of Christmas to see a consultant. Phew!

It was absolutely the best £150 I've ever spent to reduce the stress and anxiety factor on my newly acquired nervous system balance, which I had just begun to enjoy.

So Dr Herd - and yes, he was a good listener - took one look and reassured me, "it's a @&&?!@&£@&" and it's completely benign. But I will burn it off anyway with 'Hellish-Stingy-Burny-Feckin-Murder-Inward-Burning stuff'."

He didn't actually say that last bit - but it was and it does.

But "All I Want For Christmas" is what I got tonight... peace of mind.

So thank you to the Healing Island of Lindisfarne, St Aiden, St Cuthbert and St Mary for keeping us both relatively stable and sane; for filling me up with trust and love again to handle whatever may have come - but thankfully didn't; and for the Earth angels by my side.

You know who you are.

EAT·SING·LOVE 76

"Whatever lifts the corners of your mouth, trust that." - Rumi

"I have been a seeker and I still am, but I stopped asking the books and the stars. I started listening to the teaching of my soul." - Rumi

"Christmas - a time to make room for others in the stable of my heart." - Me

MEET·STAY·LOVE 77

Afore all the New Year goal setters and visioneers get intae ye, let me just say something.

You don't need to change, you simply need to embrace and connect with the bruised and weary wee child-soul that was chewed up and spat out, all of those years ago, firstly by them, then by you.

Don't beat her or him up any more than they already have been. Just sit there a while beside them. Be there.

Wrap them up in a cosy blanket of hugs, look deeply in their eyes and tell them you will be taking over now.

Say out loud in a soft Southern Californian accent: "You're just too tired now darling, you've done your best. And you tried your very hardest but I'm here now and I am finally up to speed and on the case. I make the decisions from here and some things are gonna change. The bullying stops today from them, but more importantly FROM ME."

Take them gently by the hand and lead the way, slowly, carefully and always checking that little frightened child is not being left behind again.

I like to share what I harvest myself, fresh from the fields.

By Angela Trainer, Dec 2019

JANUARY 2020

DRINK·BIN·LOVE 78

This is a tough time of year for most folks. It's dark, it's cold. The coffers are also empty for most. It's a time of low ebb and we are vulnerable. Anxiety and depression often peak around this time as our defences are squeezed on all fronts. Absent friends and family have often been keenly missed over the festive period and everything can feel out of kilter.

The turbo-charged hype of December often leaves an abyss in its wake. What goes up must come down. Our immune systems are under assault. We're tired.

Here are a few easy-peasy things you can start today that really WILL make a big difference within a very short time.

1) Hydrate properly. Go NOW and boil a kettle, drink a large mug of boiled water, cooled. Even better with a slice of lemon (or fresh ginger - good for digestion). Repeat regularly through the day. We simply DO NOT drink enough water in the winter months and it leads to all sorts of problems. We need to flush the bugs out of our gut.

Did you know that stress leads to dehydration, and guess what - dehydration leads to stress.

It is a vicious circle. We may think we are drinking lots of hot drinks but tea and coffee dehydrate us even more.

Commit to six or more BIG mugs of warm water with lemon, honey and lemon, ginger and give your inner engine and bowels the gift of a home spa break.

2) Go throw out/recycle some clutter, just one wee totie bag, a shopping bag size is fine, or a wee bin-liner size of auld make-up and train tickets. Now. It takes minutes but feels good.

Letting go is good for us, it creates inner and outer space. We hold on too much and we calcify.

Do this every day for the rest of January. Join the "bin a wee bag a day for 30 days" challenge.

3) Leave out some of the lovely bath/body stuff and a candle beside the shower/bath, have a spa break in candlelight today/ tonight. Music is good too. A wee 15 minutes of indulgence can be a huge act of self-soothing. Do the whole thing: the scrub, the face mask, the conditioner left on for more than a nano-second, the body lotion. A healing ritual of self-love.

4) Get out for a short oxygen and natural light bath. A 15-minute walk will do for starters. Make it pointless and aimless. Go and "waste some time" just breathing and being, feeling your body move and breathe. Your feet kissing the ground

with every step.

5) Sit and read one of those books you never get time to - you know the one. You've been meaning to get into it for ages but.. there's always a but. Just 15 minutes a day of reading is pure gift for your busy thinking mind, even if it's last thing in bed at night.

6) Perform an invisible act of kindness every day. Do something lovely for someone else without looking for gratitude or repayment. It may simply be to smile at a stranger, chat to someone in the supermarket queue, or let someone else have the parking space. Phone a lonely friend, family member, send a gratitude card acknowledge someone, invite someone for dinner, offer Reiki or massage to another - ideally someone you know!

Giving it away feeds the soul.

Happy January: raise your spirits! The other kind, that is.

RETREAT·PRAY·LOVE 79

I came on retreat to the Carmelite Convent in October to rest between Ki-More-Therapy ending and Ray-Joy Therapy starting. Quality recovery time and preparation at a soul level. Before I left, I intuitively knew to book in, after new year, for a few days. Naively, I thought it would be a retreat of gratitude, a time of celebration and a time of forward planning now the treatment was behind me. Hah!

Er, that'll be a naw.

A part of me knew I would need this time but I was oblivious as to the why.

I am knackered.

I moved from treatment ending to Christmas and celebrations in one fell swoop. And the tsunami of the exhaustion of the previous nine months of relentless hospital and doctor visits arrived as a tumultuous thundering wave or six over a series of days.

It was as if I had somehow managed to park most of my tiredness, doubts and fears, anxieties on ice. I had packed them up deep into the heart of an enormous iceberg in my very own inner Narnia.

But when this Arctic fridge store instantly thawed not long after the clock struck midnight on New Year's Day, it produced a flash flood, releasing anything and everything that couldn't be processed or dealt with at the time of crisis.

I was pole-axed, discombobulated and bewildered.

I shouldn't have been but I was. I thought I had handled everything so beautifully.

See what thought did?

Humility is usually learned from our arse hitting the deck.

So the wiser old soul inside likely knew what she was doing when she booked some silence, solitude and spiritual direction for January.

And so here I am.

And here is an explanation borrowed and abridged and re-jigged by me from Richard Rohr on why I'm here naturally indwelling for a few days.

"When I go to my own depths through the silence, solitude and contemplation of retreat, I uncover an indwelling Presence. It is a deep and loving 'yes' to the love and to the life force that is within all of us. Love is the very ground of my being."

Some mystics have described this Presence as "more me than I am myself." My true self. My connection to big love, higher power, Mother Earth, Maya, Gaia, God, Allah, all that is, The Mystery, The Mysterons.

The paradox is that this true self is immortal and indestructible and yet it must also be awakened and chosen, it must be consciously received.

It needs to be recognized, honoured and DRAWN UPON to become a living presence, like drawing from a wellspring. It needs worked. It needs feeding. It needs pruned. It needs direction.

We are all divine souls but we surrender and awaken in varying degrees and stages.

Grace is not created by our actions or behaviour. Sacred love is naturally in-dwelling.

When I live out of my ego, my reputation, image, role, possessions, etc, these things will fail me. They always do in the end.

But my true self will always guide me, if I create enough stillness and space to listen.

My true self is pure compassion. And from this much more spacious place, I find I naturally connect, empathise, forgive and love just about everything.

We are made in love, for love.

Do you recognise your need for some stillness, space, silence and contemplation? Winter is a great place and time to find it. Especially at the Lunar Eclipse of the Wolf Moon.

GRIEF·LOSS·LOVE 80

Stars reach our eyes long after they have "died" light years away. Our planet is struggling and parts of it are scorched. Magnificent animals are dying, some to extinction and our water supplies are polluted.

Endings and loss affect us all every step of our path through life.

Grief is not restricted to the loss of a parent or a pet. Our old dreams may die. Friendships are lost in the changing seasons of our lives. Relationships end. We retire and we move away from people, places, roles. Our children leave home. Things change and end. We have to deal with endings and loss on a regular basis.

Grief is neither a system failure, a control tower error, a slip and fall to be righted or a hurdle to be jumped over.

I've been studying the Mystics in recent times and am currently going for long walks and chats with St John of The Cross of The Dark Night of The Soul, a 16th century mystic and poet. It's much more uplifting than it sounds, and the wisdom is timeless.

The skill set of healing through grief and dealing with a broken heart is a necessary part of our soul's development. There is a divine intelligence embedded within us like an eternally sparking jewel which recognises the value of the punctured and sacred heart, broken open in vulnerability. Naked and open.

Working with loss and disappointment is not about fast-tracked recovery.

It does not require a Teflon coating of the heart, nor a life lived in protective isolation, and a striving to become invincible and unbreakable.

We are all broken open, punctured, wounded and left scarred in our lives, and usually way more than twice.

The heart is bottomless - vast and beyond wide and we can learn to dive deeper still in her endless oceans of love, learning from of the gifts of grief and loss.

As the ego dissolves in the depths of confusion and shock, the shoots and eventually the fruits of grief and endings becoming more tangible and visible.

In time, the boundaries and sharp edges of grief become blurred and she becomes soul friend, shining her torch on unwalked, virgin, fresh pathways. Her light also shines on the previously menacing, dark corners of our lives. They wilt and shrivel from the exposure. We however grow bolder and stronger with our emotional muscles strengthened.

There is a light in the darkness that only loss and the felt experience of the pain of grief can teach us to trust and know.

But we don't travel a straight trajectory on this path. It winds around, it spirals and circles, it twists and performs figures of eight in various combinations.

We can begin to learn to trust this mystical dance in the shallows and then in the depths of loss.

We can begin to discover how we navigate this gateway into this mystery of life and love; in trust and with deep reverence.

Difficulties, suffering and loss can become opportunities for us to receive the gifts of grace deep within us, the jewels in the treasure chest deep within our heart.

MEET·PLAY·LOVE 81

I was having a pensive, if a little emotional morning. "It's all too beautiful" as The Small Faces used to sing.

The sky is china blue, the sun squinty bright, the birds chasing the breeze and Sir Ian is supine sunbathing like a Sumatran tiger.

A brisk-ish walk for me on the flat of the road avoided a Dancing on Ice Spectacular.

I'm nearly 60. It's a matter of days now. G asked this morning how I felt. To be honest, I'm looking forward to the bus pass and doing a tour of the whole of my ain country with someone else doing the driving. I just pray they will ask for ID when I go for concessions.

But I still can't believe it, nor do I feel any sense of connection with the number.

Maybe the numbers don't matter because time doesn't really exist.

I've met 14-year-olds with the ancient wisdom of sages and 90-year-old teenagers with a twinkle that would dazzle you. I've also met a lot of midlife adults who really need to grow up.

Maybe I need to grow up.

They say if you spot it, you've got it.

So I was thinking of the lovely week G has planned: a family dinner tonight in town and overnight stay, a few days away next week at a heavenly spa and a meal with the Rowdies next Saturday. I was feeling very, very lucky and blessed beyond the boundaries of all of it.

I was also sad. Someone won't be here to share in it (and for a while there I thought that might have been ME). Had they not picked up the Chancer when they did, it could've been a whole different playing field

But of course I was thinking of my Dad. Although he passed over the Veil three years ago, I've bought myself a gift from him. There will be an empty chair at the table in my heart.

So I'm pensive and pondering while I put my things in an overnight bag, happy and excited with a bittersweet coulis on the side, when I hear a strange sound behind me...

Yep, bang on cue: a January butterfly on the inside of my bedroom window ledge.

And he let me hold him. Love NEVER Dies.

TALK·PRAY·LOVE 82

So back last summer I was asked if I'd speak at TEDx Talks Women in the first TEDx for women event ever outside of the Capital.

I was so afraid the Chemo and steroids would stop me from being able to show up. But it was a goal drawing me on and having some goals during this kind of treatment and any form of healing and recovery are important as long as they are FLEXIBLE goals.

Maureen Hascoet, in full command, was tremendously supportive and patient, reassuring that if I couldn't be there it would be okay.

Now, before you say anything, my talk and delivery was far from perfect but THAT is really the point I'm making. However, it was recorded, produced and packaged perfectly by the amazing team and I send a million thanks to all who helped a dream become reality, especially under the tricky circumstances. I send my love and gratitude to the production crew and volunteers - especially Godsend Frances (who gave us all restorative Reiki on the day).

Link available on home page of www.harvestclinic.co.uk.

GRATEFUL·PRAY·LOVE 83

Some days ye just breathe in and think, I can't believe all of this. I made it to here.

And after a wee rest and breather there, can I send out a mahoosive thank you to you? You know who you are.

Your birthday messages, blessings, cards, presents and

presence, gifts and hugs - real and virtual - were all received with wide open arms and placed deeply in my heart over the past week of celebrations. I felt like the bloody Queen (just hope I didnae look like her).

I can't find room for any more joy - I'm fit to bursting, but I'm working on it.

It's been a year or three of bittersweet contrasts, three terminal illnesses and anticipated deaths including my dad's, two sudden family deaths, dramas, deceptions, betrayals, crimes and court cases and to top it off my own Chancer journey. In other words, LIFE.

But my God, what an abundance of material to stretch and grow from.

My God has furnished me with phenomenal people and opportunities to turn each situation around (EVENTUALLY) and to crawl back when I couldn't bounce.

My eyes have been prised open to a wider, bigger life screen than ever before and my pain threshold, physical and emotional, has been burst through its former limits. My emotional capacity has extended its range and the depth of my capacity for and to love has grown exponentially with that expansion. I've been on the unconditional love express.

Suffering has such great value and meaning in this human life of ours although you would pass the chalice given the choice and the chance.

I have never known so much love and support in my life and often from the most unexpected places.

You have just helped us raise OVER £1600 for Chris's House suicide charity in Wishaw (my dear friend Anne Rowan founded in memory of her son Christopher whom she lost to suicide many years ago) and I'm planning to walk 5K in May on their Walk of Hope to raise more funds.

My book was published, Love Never Dies, on Amazon paperback, Kindle and Audible books in May. And though we had to postpone the book launch due to Chancer treatment, you've bought hunners and hunners of copies anyway. It's already in many shops and, more importantly, Chancer treatment and bereavement centre libraries in Scotland.

I've been invited to collaborate on a new project for women next week; to speak at an International Woman's Day event in March to input to a healing recipe book for Chancer patients broadcast on BBC Radio next week with Kaye Adams on the Mental Health Clinic and to do a Podcast with James English next week, and so it begins.

Hah! If I was chocolate I would eat myself. But, my world IS opening up to meet me again.

Of course the challenge will be the timing, punctuation and discernment in what I can and cannot do as the energy tanks are only just over half-full.

I can walk again upright and sleep without yelping when I turn over. My walking distance coverage improves weekly. My energy is slowly returning. I actually finished a (gentle) yoga class last week - albeit a Bambi on ice version.

I still need duvet half-days to restore after activity. I do get exhausted easily. I still have many chemo after-effects.

But small price to pay for life. For love. For YOU.

FEBRUARY 2020

LOVE·PRAY·LOVE 84

On the day before St. Valentine's Day, when we tend to tip our hats to romantic love (evolution's drug), I think it's nice to be more inclusive than that and to turn my attention to LOVE itself, not just the romantic flavour.

Shower the people you love with love - give random flowers to your friends, neighbours, colleagues, tell them you love them.

Give the cat, dog or hamster a Valentine's treat. Tell your family you love them, even if they test your nerves at times.

Let your trees, plants and feathered friends know how much you love them too. Imagine what life without them would be in comparison.

But most important of all - do something to mark the love of the little person who lives inside of you, who once upon a time longed for a Valentine's Day card and maybe never got one.

Your wee inner lassie or laddie.

Give yourself a flower, a wraparound heart hug, a smile and a wink. It all starts with you.

Here are some words on LOVE by my favourite philosopher Winnie The Pooh.

"Love is taking a few steps backward maybe even more, to give way to the happiness of the person you love."

"You can't stay in your corner of the forest waiting for others to come to you. You have to go to them sometimes."

"How do you spell love?" – Piglet

"You don't spell it.. you feel it." – Pooh

85

On WORLD CANCER DAY (TODAY) my hero and role model is Lily Douglas, aged 12, from Perth who has danced with The Chancer - Ewing's Sarcoma - for three years now. No known cure, just constant chemo cycles as long as she is fit enough for them.

My inspiration whenever I find myself on the pity pot. A legend.

TALK · PRAY · LOVE 86

Back in December, two weeks after finishing treatment for Breast Chancer (mastectomy/chemo/radio) I did a TEDxTalk for women on the curse of perfect. It's hopefully a heart - arming, supportive and reassuring message on living and loving.

I thought I'd share it here.

https://www.youtube.com/watch?
fbclid=IwAR1cDOpH-4B6uv6PqJb3Zi3LGUbeqmvSubog3pVF
1bDWIJ0xHOW1oL38Oi0&v=43TpYMKABls&feature=youtu.
be
Meanwhile I just finished filming a podcast with the number 1 podcaster in the country, James English.

You May remember James' iconic "Homeless for Christmas Documentary" where he slept on the streets of Glasgow for seven nights a few years ago.

James interviews a real variety of people, many of them from drug and criminal backgrounds who have turned their lives around, victims of crime and people who have battled addiction issues successfully. He has interviewed ex-prisoners and ex-prison officers.

He's also interviewed author Irvine Welsh, doctors, politicians, celebrities and comedians which is why his show is called "Anything Goes".

And I wonder which category I fit into? All of the above?

He has a very powerful mission to inform and to help rehabilitate. To turn things around for others who need a helping hand back from the abyss.

Today, we spoke at length (90 mins) about -

Anxiety, anger, depression, cancer, the law of attraction, how to rewire the brain, life, the power of change, death and dying, the soul.

I don't know about you James but I'm fair knackered and looking forward to seeing the final cut in a few weeks' time, will keep you posted y'all.

87

Back on Kaye Adams between 9-10 today speaking about Mental Health issues on BBC Radio Scotland.

I usually have plenty to say about a broken mind, life graced me with personal experience as a younger woman and I'm passionate about breaking the shame and stigma of skeletons in our basements.

88

Just spent a fascinating couple of hours with the huge hearted warrioress of mind health, Gail Porter. We were guest speakers on Kaye Adams this morning (9-10 am) on mental health issues.

Having had the rockstar husband/celebrity lifestyle and her naked body image superimposed on Big Ben at the height of her career, she experienced a hard fall from grace with eating disorders, self-harm and full-blown mental health problems. She has attempted suicide, been sectioned in a psychiatric hospital and the impact on her marriage and family was dreadful. She knows first-hand what the fall is about (you may have seen her recent BBC documentary - worth a watch) she also sufferers from alopecia.

She has courageously confronted her mind health relentlessly over the years and actively spoken out from a place of real vulnerability.

She smashes taboos and challenges the shame and fear that accompanies mental health issues, she is an inspiration and trailblazer for so many.

I love her.

My pal Gail.

REACH·SUPPORT·LOVE 89

Are you sitting comfortably? Then I'll begin.

Once upon a time, five years ago, there was a young man from Scotland who emigrated to the land of Oz with his love and had some nice times.

Then the really, REALLY hard times roll into town. Ill health for him, many hospitals, financial problems, especially after the "lover" disappears and serious depression settles in for the long haul. No family was available to help out so coming home wasn't an option.

Soon our friend finds himself sleeping in cars in ridiculous temperatures, sofa surfing with friends and living in compromised circumstances just to stay alive.

He is homeless with a serious health condition, no employment and no money.

He is desperate and expresses on FB just how low and desperate he is beginning to feel on a couple of occasions, not a good state of affairs at all.

So, team Oz is created in an evening of reaching out to folks in our tribe over here. Can we help from here with support, he needs friends, prayers and possibly a little bit of money support short term, etc.

That was enough, Scotland responded. A tribe was established, team Oz.

A small crowdfund was created, research and advice was sought into options on all fronts, FaceTime calls were made and after many false starts and fall-overs, rocky and tricky times (with some folks understandably throwing in the towel when it got too much, too heavy, too much in their own lives going down) Team Oz managed to support 'Jim' on to his soul path back to life over the long haul.

Miracles do actually happen.

Today Jim has been in a loving relationship with a beautiful woman for several years now, has established his own really successful dog walking business, is fitter and healthier than ever on every level, his partner breeds his favourite breed of dogs, champion dogs (ye couldnae write it) and he enjoys sharing his hobbies, cars and motorbikes with his lady.

His hobbies were always dogs and bikes/cars.

Never, ever give up

Don't ask HOW?

Reach out whether FOR or to GIVE support (we need to alternate between both throughout our lives).

Know the power of prayer, sending love and distance energy healing. Contemplation and action are needed in our messy world.

Know that it's okay to support for a while and to back off when it's too much and you need a break.

Here are a couple of "live" posts from five years ago -

No.1 is from a scary night when J was ready to throw the towel in.

This was the reply I sent -

"J, Sometimes we feel we can't go on. That's when we need to hand it over, to be carried by the love and support of others... even strangers, who are really just friends we haven't met yet. The dark often steals the light, but the light will always steal the dark back again if we just hold on. Just one small step on our own behalf can be the step that takes us along a new path- even if we can't see the road ahead. Many people are holding us in their hearts and prayers that we don't know and are urging us to take that step. Just one tiny thing, each day, over time, really can make a difference. The past is NOT the future. Sending a big hug to you today."

And from the day after the appeal for help was launched in Scotland, No.2 -

"Team Oz - you are playing a blinder. Jim has at least 10 new Facebook friends/coaches that he didn't have 24 hours ago, has been out for a walk with the landlord's dog, is considering writing a blog "A hairy arsed Scotsman in Australia - The Wizard of Oz" and is considering sharing some photography with us soon. At least another 20+ people are sending Reiki/prayers his way. You guys really do make a difference. Thank you.....grateful. xx" Never give up, love never dies.

GREET·PRAY·LOVE 90

Our minds are magnificent.

They know how to anaesthetise us via shock, dissociation and adrenaline to get us through the really tough and tricky times we face in our lives.

We are able to function and get through the terrifying events, whether those be facing the terminal illness of a loved one, the pre and post events of a funeral, the experience of trauma or some of the hellish events we have to endure and overcome in our lifetimes.

Context-dependent memory is an amazing thing to behold. It slowly allows the filters to come off and releases some of that buried emotion (or affect) that we were able to experience "some relief" from buried back at the time of the chaos and distressing situations we found ourselves in. It takes the opportunity to release some of the gas in our internal pressure cooker of stored unprocessed emotion.

This occurs where we find ourselves in a similar or the same situational environment (context) was when the original stressful events happened but we are further down the line. So our feelings seem disproportionate or even inappropriate.

I know this stuff from work, but it never fails to amaze me how that doesn't matter a toss when it comes down to the process.

So I had my very first aura migraine in my life last night, which I was happy to ascribe to the low pressure weather. The vice-like headache was pretty stupendous.

And, oh yes, by chance, I was revisiting the Chemo unit today for six-monthly treatments.

The very same unit I sailed in and out of last year from June until October for IV therapy every three weeks.

This time it was for IV Bone strengthening drugs but the same routine, place, people and process but only one visit, until August.

All went remarkably well until after three different clinic checks over four hours at Wishy Healthspital, and 90 minutes hooked up on IV, we headed to Carfin to light a candle of gratitude at the grotto, all was still well but I felt a shift inside as I began to let go of my shoulders which had grafted on to my jawbone. My neck had disappeared tortoise style over the previous 12 hours.

We went for a late lunch early tea.

All good if a little tension begins to present herself in the non-neck area.

By 5pm as we headed home, mission accomplished, I truly had stars in my eyes.

I was blinded by the light in my left eye.

I was all aura and sparkly stars with a stormer coming down the track.

The FULL MONTY of three sizes too small, steel helmeted migraine.

I taught about these things for years using hypnotherapy, but that made it worse because I now knew it was too late, I was in full flight.

Two Kalms, a pint of chamomile tea, some hot and cold hands (glove anaesthesia, twisted sister reiki (this is where you're swearing as you're delivering self-reiki, because you're too bloody sore) and two paracetamol didn't touch much at all.

There was nothing else to be done. I curled up on the couch and settled in, the blessed release of a good greet. Now, that was the very fellow.

Some of the "stuff" that had been so successfully repressed over the months had been both stirred and shaken up and up it came.

The relief was immediate.

A hot bath and a wee neck rub helped too.

Feelings buried alive never die, they wait for a chance to surface when the coast is clear, and we are strong enough to handle them.

Cellular memory is a phenomenal thing to behold.

Our body and mind are always trying to protect us with these incredible survival skills. It's always on our side. Just wish it had chatted the plan through with me first, so I knew what the feck was occurin'.

Yes, I have just discovered "Gavin and Stacey" on box set.

"Let it oot, let it oot, canny haud it back anymore." lyrics from the Scottish version of the film Frozen '.

It's called "Brass Monkeys".

ON BEING KIND and CAROLINE FLACK'S LEGACY: 91

All of the "be kind" posts are wonderful and the hairdressers have joined hands to ban gossip magazines from their receptions.

And it's amazing. It's bloody wonderful, really it is.

HOWEVER, nothing will ever really change until we take a long, hard stare at what is really going on inside of US and what WE get out of it when we:

Gossip.

Spread rumours and hearsay as if they were fact.

Recruit others to our point of view.

Exclude people.

Become involved in groups with people excluded for the sole purpose of talking ABOUT them.

Bitch regularly (oh come on! You just KNOW when that's what yer doin').

Think the number of folk who seemingly agree witcha make you right.

Come from a place of self-elevated judgement and criticism, not care and concern.

Until I AM READY to look, really look at what this behaviour is about, I am part of the problem. I am on the same page as one of those mud-slinging, gossip magazine news hounds.

This "accepted as norm" foul play is now a large boil on the face of our society, a boil that needs to be lanced.

Haters hate and we can ALL be haters at times. Baying for blood didn't die out with the colosseum or public executions. We seem, as a tribe, to still get a thrill from the public destruction and downfall of others and we seem to have a penchant for sending people into exile, all classic bullying behaviour straight outta the playground.

Let's not smooth it over and absolve ourselves with simply posting new profile pictures eh? Maybe if I take a long hard look inside and reflect on how, where and when I do it myself and reflect on the why, I might be massively enlightened and THAT may cumulatively, across our tribe, create a lasting change.

No time to ponder? I'll do it for you.

It's an artificial power grab/steal.

It's temporary and highly addictive behaviour that inflates the ego fast and furiously and it quickly takes root as a habit, a really dodgy, destructive, toxic habit.

We are effectively trying to steal someone else's toy in the nursery to feel more powerful ourselves.

It's THAT regressive, we are operating from a child-like stance. It's our own low self- esteem and self-loathing that we are trying to work out, out there.

And it disnae work... so we do it more.

It's a very dangerous game we play and we know now just how deadly it can be.

I'm off to work on my inner bitch.

Thanks Caroline for the wake-up call. I wish for you and all the other victims of shaming, exclusion and the alienation of being exiled by your tribe, that you may find peace now. Your work here is done.

CHANGE·PRAY·LOVE 92
When we become ill, whatever the illness, It's not a mistake.
It's our body's way of getting our attention, it can be circumstances forcing us to rest and sometimes it's anything from genes to toxicity, to biochemicals to hormones that are out of kilter. There are many, many origins and cocktails of reasons.

What matters is that we pay attention and investigate the best we can, but that firstly we do everything within our power to redress any imbalances and that we heal and rest.

Convalescence has all but disappeared from our modern day vocabulary. We usually get better and dive straight back in, trying to make up for lost time. I read recently a piece by an old Austrian Naturopath who said we should rest and recover for the same length of time we had been ill.

Can you imagine?

So I am now "convalescing", not ill, not in treatment but recalibrating and decompressing from The Chancer journey of the last 10 months.

Time now to rebuild and renew the immune system, with the help of my pal Janice who is a bona fide food scientist, though the snow today has delayed our plan.

We are gonna explore together all things probiotic and prebiotic, microbial and life giving.

Time now to look at the energetic landscape going forward and how to redesign my work life balance. I need a new map with new coordinates.

We really need at times like these to spend some time in contemplation and evaluation before we jump back into the same landscape, as that landscape will perhaps have been a contributory factor in our immune system crashing, before many of our illnesses and conditions had taken root.

I'm taking stock of mine. I'm gonna spend a few days next week on retreat at my favourite convent (I know, can you believe it? they are letting me back in) contemplating on "Life B.C." - "Before The Chancer."

And then I will begin on the blueprints for "Life A.C."

If we don't take the time to scan the emotional hotspots of our lives, the exhaustive demands and schedules, the toxic people and relationships we endure, our toxic habits, our toxic thoughts, conscious and half-conscious, and the ridiculous timetables we respond to like clockwork mice (who said a five-day week? and who said 9-5?).

We may prepare the ground for more of the same results.

We need to plough and furrow before we replant a new crop on our land.

MARCH 2020

BLESS·PRAY·LOVE 93

I'm up early and off to speak at REAL WOMEN'S International Women's Day Event in Airdrie with about 50 women attending for the talk, a couple of workshops with a therapeutic movement workshop (NIA) and international dance teacher followed by a networking lunch. I'm looking forward to it.
No organising for me, just turn up and speak (get me to stop).

I thought I'd share a wee bit with you this morning to kickstart your day with a wee reflection.

These days, I usually start my talks with a prayer or you could say some "words of blessing" from the late Irish mystic and poet John O' Donoghue. Perhaps I'll begin with -

"Gradually, you will return to yourself,

Having learned a new respect for your heart

And the joy that dwells far within slow time."

And I'll end the talk with the lyric from the very last song ever recorded by all four Beatles together: "And in the end the love you take, is equal to the love you make. Love you, Love you, Love you".

WAIT·PRAY·LOVE 94

I've been in self isolation since Tuesday after a call from Public Health to say I had "been in contact with a confirmed coronavirus case."

And so I was told I needed to self-isolate for 14 days from my visit to the dentist, in Cumbernauld on 2nd March. My dentist had been on holiday in North Italy.

That deadline took me up to THIS Sunday, stuck in my bedroom again but with the very excellent company of Dr Ian curled up and purring healing mantras beside me for the duration.

After a lockdown for me on immune compromised grounds due to Breast Chancer treatment from May-Dec last year, it was pretty tough to resign myself to the fact that my bedroom was gonna be home again apart from an allocated seat in the living room to watch TV at night - yards away from Lord G.

Clothes were to be washed at 60 degrees, dishes done in dishwasher only, good air flow through windows, disposable cloths of Dettol all around and hand-washing galore.

But I came through with flying colours and was just called a few moments ago by public health to say I can stand down. I am free to roam.

New Government guidance today is that seven days of self-isolation is plenty if you have no emergent symptoms (I've had 12 days pass and I am made of titanium). They are much more clued up now about how symptoms disclose themselves if they are going to. I had none.

What joy, what relief.

But I will continue with the health precautions. I used them last year and had been vigilant with them.

They make good sense.

The freedom of a walk outside, to freely move around my own home, to drive again, to be independent, all feel like pure gift.

Sometimes, you don't know what you've got until it's gone.

Maybe we will ALL end up more grateful by the end of this.

And I will keep all my fellow self-isolators (I already know a few, one related to and another couple unrelated to the Cumbernauld incident) in their mini-biospheres of life in my heart and in my prayers, as I do the people who are not so lucky as me.

But spare a thought for the Public Health nurses and officials who called me EVERY DAY (sometimes twice) went through extensive interviews and ensured I had everything I needed. They were full of compassion for every one of theme. What a country truly. Will you keep them in your heart and prayers too.

95

The most beautiful words I've heard yet to inspire and fill your lungs with love.

LOCKDOWN

"Yes there is fear.

Yes there is isolation.

Yes there is panic buying.

Yes there is sickness.

Yes there is even death.

But....

They say that in Wuhan after so many years of noise

You can hear the birds again.

They say that after just a few weeks of quiet

The sky is no longer thick with fumes

But blue and grey and clear.

They say that in the streets of Assisi

People are singing to each other

across the empty squares,

keeping their windows open

so that those who are alone

may hear the sounds of family around them.

They say that a hotel in the West of Ireland

Is offering free meals and delivery to the housebound.

Today a young woman I know

is busy spreading fliers with her number

through the neighbourhood

So that the elders may have someone to call on

Today Churches, Synagogues, Mosques and Temples

are preparing to welcome

and shelter the homeless, the sick, the weary

All over the world people are slowing down and reflecting

All over the world people are looking at their neighbours in a new way

All over the world people are waking up to a new reality

To how big we really are.

To how little control we really have.

To what really matters.

To Love.

So we pray and we remember that

Yes there is fear.

But there does not have to be hate.

Yes there is isolation.

But there does not have to be loneliness.

Yes there is panic buying.

But there does not have to be meanness.

Yes there is sickness.

But there does not have to be disease of the soul

Yes there is even death.

But there can always be a rebirth of love.

Wake to the choices you make as to how to live now.

Today, breathe.

Listen, behind the factory noises of your panic

The birds are singing again

The sky is clearing,

Spring is coming,

And we are always encompassed by Love.

Open the windows of your soul

And though you may not be able

to touch across the empty square,

Sing.

Brother Richard Hendrick, OFM

(Capuchin Franciscan Monk)

96

"Tonight before falling asleep

think about when we will return to the street.

When we hug again,

when all the shopping together will seem like a party.

Let's think about when the coffees will return to the bar, the small talk, the photos close to each other.

We think about when it will be all a memory but normality will seem an unexpected and beautiful gift.

We will love everything that has so far seemed futile to us.

Every second will be precious.

Swims at the sea, the sun until late, sunsets, toasts, laughter.

We will go back to laughing together.

Strength and courage".

A prayer by Pope Francis.

97

I know there are tough times ahead. Facing up to Chancer treatment taught me one or two things about life and how to deal with the cards you're dealt, when your carefully considered plans don't work out.

Most of our grandfathers and great grandfathers or great uncles went off to fight in distant wars for years on end, in bloody, muddy, hellish wars. So many didn't return or came back as shells of themselves, six million people murdered in the Holocaust, only 75 years ago.

The majority of us will probably be asked to stay in, sit on the couch and watch Netflix and boxed sets for a few weeks or so and it sounds like we will quite possibly be paid to do that.

Perspective is everything.

Ahm just sayin'.

DANCE·PRAY·LOVE 98

Managed to film Lord G, out early this morning, blessing the earth.

Seriously though maybe we all need our own version of this

even quietly in our hearts just now.

All forms of prayer, whatever the source or tradition, are simply the whisperings of the soul, spoken from the heart.

Taking a stance in deep connection, whether in movement of energy (body prayer), spoken or silently through words (mantra prayer), blessings, touch (kinaesthetic prayer) using beads or prayer wheels or rituals (outward signs of inner grace, a spiritual and indigenous traditions use prayer of one form or another).

All have the same purpose, connection and relationship with the immortal, the eternal, the sacred.

The bigger picture outside of ME/MY/MINE.

Connection to love itself and showing gratitude for the gift.

Life itself.

99
PRAYER FOR TODAY
Great source of love/god/mother -

Please fill me up with the SERENITY to be able to accept the things I can't change.

Please give me the COURAGE to change the things that I can change and please bless me with the WISDOM to know the difference between the two.

Thank you, amen.

APRIL 2020

100

And so now, just imagining in your mind's eye, sending a waterfall of these beautiful, bright, healthy, white blood cells, full of grace, cascading down from the sky like a moonbeam or sunbeam, depending on the time of day.

You may even hear the gentle sound of that steady flow, the whispered downpouring of those healing vibrantly lit, white cells of grace, pouring down through the crown area on the top of your head, through each and every part of your body. Into every nerve, every cell, every fibre of your being. Going right to the core of you, deep within into each and every organ, permeating even the marrow of your bones.

These are the vibrantly healthy healing white cells of your immune system that keep you so well and so healthy and protected.

They cleanse the system of any intruders or tired and faulty cells and carry them off for repair outside of your system, releasing out through the soles of your feet. Down into the ground as if pulled by the earth's magnetism.

Flowing down, out and away from your body into mother earth out from the soles of your feet to where those tired, faulty, toxic cells can be repaired, restored, recharged, recycled and later released into the atmosphere as new vibrant energy.

Leaving you healthy, fresh, revitalised and well and restored and regenerated. Vibrantly alive, aglow and full of vitality.

All is well, all is safe and all is secure.

And say aloud, or sing out.

"Every little cell in my body is healthy,

Every little cell in my body is well.

I'm healthy, so healthy,

I sparkle and I shine.

Every little cell in me is full of Grace Divine "

Every morning, noon and night.

Every kettle boiling.

During the adverts.

At a red traffic light.

In a queue (sing silently though).

In the shower/loo/bath.

Sing those cells around your system with powerful images and music to stimulate your brain's right hemisphere and autonomic nervous system, your vagus nerve, regulator of the healthy relaxation response that SO impacts the immune system function.

Trust me - I'm NOT a doctor, but I AM a clinical hypnotherapist with 33 years' experience and 30 years teaching my subject to MSc Degree level here in the UK, Portugal and Asia.

Whatcha gotta lose?

Amongst other things, this helped me get through Breast Chancer and Ki-More-Therapy.

101

Happy Birthday Dad, "Hello, from the other side."

You're only ever a breath or a heartbeat away. I know that, but what I wouldn't give to hear you sing, to hug you tight and to see that twinkle in your eyes.

We saw the two robins on the fence today at lunch. Saw them and thought of you.

Love you to bits and see you in the morning.

RETREAT·PRAY·LOVE 102

I made a few retreats last year to rest and prepare between my master-ectomy, Ki-More-Therapy and Ray-Joy therapy, quality recovery time and preparation at a soul level for what was to come.

A part of me knew I would need this time to realign at a soul level to restore and to ready myself for the next leg of this journey we call life.

Sometimes in our lives we've managed to "park" our tiredness, our doubts and fears, and our anxieties on ice. We may pack them up deep into the heart of an enormous iceberg in our very own mindscape.

But when we slow down and stop, this arctic fridge store can begin to thaw out.

For some of us it may even produce a flash flood, releasing emotions we didn't have the time, space or desire to deal with at the time. These may go back years in origin, depending on how adept we have been at trying to outrun our feelings with distraction and popular anaesthetics like food, alcohol, drama, busyness, drugs, spending, accumulating stuff.

So many of us may have felt poleaxed and disorientated as the isolation period settled into our bones, a forced rest was imposed on us by factors outwith our control and we may be feeling discombobulated.

Humility is usually learned from our arse hitting the deck.

And so here we are.

And here is an explanation borrowed and abridged and re-jigged by me from Richard Rohr on how we COULD put just some of this enforced home time to use "naturally indwelling" for a few weeks or so.

When I go to my own depths through the silence, solitude and contemplation of retreat, I will eventually uncover an indwelling presence. It is a deep and loving "yes" to the love and to the life force that is within all of us. Love is the very ground of my being.

Some mystics have described this presence as "more me than I am myself." My true self. My connection to big love, higher power, mother earth, Maya, Gaia, God, Allah, all that is the mystery, the Mysterons.

The paradox is that this true self is immortal and indestructible and yet it must also be awakened and chosen, it must be consciously received.

It needs to be recognized, honoured, and DRAWN UPON to become a living presence like drawing from a wellspring. It needs work, it needs feeding, it needs pruned. It needs direction.

We are all divine souls, but we surrender and awaken in varying degrees and stages.

Grace is not created by our actions or behaviour. Sacred love is naturally indwelling.

When I live out of my ego, my reputation, my image, my role, my job title, my looks and my wardrobe, my possessions etc, these things will fail me. They always do in the end.

But my true self will always guide me, if I create enough stillness and space to listen.

My true self is pure compassion and from this much more spacious place, I find I naturally connect, empathise, forgive and love just about everything.

We are made in love, for love.

Do you recognise your need for some stillness, space, silence and contemplation. This could be the time to find it, to make the time for relaxation, journaling, inspired reading, reflection, contemplative walking, mindful eating, meditation, mindful movement, tai chi/yoga (all available and taught on YouTube for free).

Especially now, at this time as the world is slowing and stilling herself like never before.

If it helps, you can download the mindfulness body scan by our Graham Watts or the STRESS FREE self-hypnosis (25 min session) by me, Angela Trainer, by anonymous donation of whatever you can manage (or even NOT as the case may be - have it on us for free, and do at pay-it-forward' for someone else) from www.harvestclinic.co.uk from the CD Download page .

ON HOPE: 103

HOPE is a fruit that grows on the tree of life lessons. Its roots are fed and watered by our ability to suffer wisely, calmly and generously.

The EGO demands SUCCESS to survive.

The SOUL needs only MEANING to thrive.

Somehow HOPE provides its own kind of meaning, in a mysterious way.

And we already know that LOVE moves in mysterious ways.

Abridged and over-simplified by moi from the writings of Richard Rohr

SUFFER·PRAY·LOVE 104

For most of her life St Teresa of Avila suffered serious pain for part of her life she vomited daily and couldn't eat until noon. She also suffered from high fevers, fainting spells, heart trouble, neuritis, tinnitus, a maimed left arm, a three-year paralysis, severe convulsions, a four-day coma, and the influenza that almost killed her in 1580.

She said that we can learn patience and how to surrender through ill health and suffering. We can learn how to transcend the body and rise above both sickness and health altogether.

Through this, as in everything else, Teresa learned how to let go of her own will and to trust in love in the mystery in God, source, the Mysterons in "that which cannot be named" or described in mere words. That which can only be felt, experienced. The I AM.

She wrote to her sisters,

"Courage, courage, my daughters. Remember, God gives no one more troubles than they are able to bear, and is WITH those who are in tribulation."

And in a letter to one of her spiritual directors, she reflects:

"One must not think that a person who is suffering is not praying. She or he is offering up their sufferings and praying more truly than one who goes away by themself and meditates their head off, and, if they have squeezed out a few tears, think THAT is prayer."

Richard Rohr comments that -

"Suffering can make us very bitter and close us down.

Or, it can make us wise, compassionate, and utterly open.

Our hearts open because they have been softened, or perhaps even because suffering makes us feel like we have nothing more to lose.

It often takes us to the edge where we fall into the hands of love itself."

May our hearts soften and open today, and every day.

WORLD BETWEEN WORLDS: 105

We are in an embryonic state right now, not quite half-cooked but on the way. One reality is over, finished, kaput, the next way not yet birthed or even formed.

This can feel utterly terrifying depending on who you listen to and how you view things. Or it can in fact be very exciting and we can feel really privileged. It may well be a bit of both. We stand just next to the threshold of a whole new way of living and being.

Can you feel the charge of that in the ether? What a responsibility. What a time to be alive.

Let's face it, we were in utter denial and on the brink of watching our beautiful planet have a complete and total nervous breakdown over the next few decades on OUR watch. We really thought we could have it all, without regard for the cost.

And so now, the maps on the drawing boards have been torn

up, all bets are off and all is to play for.

We are betwixt and between. My teacher Richard Rohr refers to it as LIMINAL space.

When our lives hit a transition point, a beloved dies, we lose our job, get a diagnosis, our relationship hits the skids, there is the birth of a child, it is a special time of grace.

But it sure as hell disnae feel like any kinda grace at the time.

We feel upended in a tailspin and confused and totally not in control.

Just like now.

The vulnerability of liminal space creates a gap for something new to enter stage left. We are wide open, receptive, a clean slate and chalk in front of us.

I've said before, we are at our most humble when our arse hits the deck. We are more reflective, we see our faults and failings in the glare of space and stillness. Our egos shrink (well, okay then, apart from Donald "Duck" and Boris Balloon, some of our egos shrink.

We have time and space to question the old "norms".

Richard says, "It's no surprise that we generally avoid this LIMINAL space. Much of the work of authentic spirituality and human development is to get people into liminal space and to keep them there long enough, so that they can learn something essential and new."

My darling soul friends, the mystics (sound like a pop group) St. Francis of Assisi, Dame Julian of Norwich, and Gandhi tried to live their entire lives in the gap of betwixt and between on the edge of the culture of their time.

I'm sure you can think of many more examples: "the words of the prophets are written on the subway walls and tenement halls and whispered within the sounds of silence."

This space we are incubating in invites us to see with a broader perspective and clearer vision.

In LIMINAL space we are forced to drop our usual "successful" patterns because we fail when we depend on them.

We need to be silent instead of speaking (harder for some of us than others), experience emptiness, anonymity instead of persona and image and have less instead of more.

In LIMINAL space, we descend and intentionally do not come back out or up immediately. It takes time before we re-enter the world with freedom and new, creative approaches to life.

We are suspended at the moment and for the foreseeable on this long one world retreat between at least two worlds, the one we knew and the one yet to come.

Our wiring has been forever changed and so by osmosis has that of every future generation, we cannot put the genie back in the bottle.

Now what shall we do with all that magical spirit that's been released in a world that has been crying out for it for oh so long?

MAY 2020

106

Old wounds come up for air when we are immobilised.

I'm so grateful for all the self-imposed quiet times and retreats I've experienced, they semi prepared me for a split from my external identity, roles, career as I hurtled into this whole new life that began back in April 2019 with The Chancer journey and have now segued into Lockdown before I could say "Corona lager".

Richard Rohr puts it so simply:

"What mystics finally do, it seems to me, is heal within themselves the fragmentation that is evident in the world". So, Instead of hating, excluding, or dismissing IT out there in others, they heal it in themselves it would seem.

When I see the good, bad, the ugly, the dark in MYSELF and the soft, fragile, vulnerable and beautiful in me and I refuse to hate or ignore any part of it. I develop big deep sympathy, empathy, and compassion. I become a healer in the service of love.

I can then and only then begin the skill transfer and upgrade to seeing and accepting the same in YOU, in others and in the big wide world. The shadow self in all her glory (or his).

There are plenty of high-profile working examples at this point in our time and I've had the joy of meeting one or three of these clowns on my life path.

It's my and our hunger, thirst and greed for bigger, better, faster, cheaper, easier for power, wealth, success, popularity, looks, fame, the winner, in all its forms and disguises (EGO) that has driven us to this point on our planet.

Now what are we gonna do?

It canny and disnae happen in reverse. Anything else is counterfeit, phony baloney, saccharin coated.

How on Earth can I develop the required ownership, collective responsibility, empathy and compassion needed to unpack this car crash scenario otherwise, but within myself?

Without fanning any more flames of them and us with a cry of "It's ALL out there: it's THEM".

It's not. It's in ME. It's in YOU.

We need to grow up to show up and work with something far more powerful than our puny and brittle egos.

Until I put the "H" letter first and make it planet heart on the inside and the outside, the miracles we need will elude us.

But love has boundaries too and sometimes love says "NO". Tough love - love will always conquer fear and its derivative hate.

Despair, outrage, blame, indignation, scapegoating and drama igniting are all FEAR based and can become counter-productive when they inevitably drain us. They quickly become toxic and counter-productive but the excitement and thrill can be quite addictive, haven't you noticed?

Focus, reflection, contemplation, ownership, forgiveness, responsibility, pro-activity, accountability, energy conservation, connection, clarity.

Compassion, empathy, grace (not force) are all LOVE-based.

Miracles do happen and they grow best planted in the soil (and the soul) of love.

DAILY HEARTMELTS: 107

Eat and taste, pray out loud to love itself, hug anyone who'll let you as long as they are in the same house, sleep or snooze for 20 mins, dance, write, sing.

Talk out loud to yourself and the great mystery, converse with your guardian angel whether you believe or not, study the clouds, stroke a cat or dog for a while and have a chat, remember to listen. Stand under a hot shower for a free massage, light candles to remind you of how the light and fire comes in from nowhere, but the power is always there.

Remember love moves in mysterious ways, stay open and receptive to the signs.

Because you're worth it!

JUNE 2020

108

Real compassion kicks butt and takes names and it is not pleasant on certain days. If you are not ready for this FIRE, then find a new-age, "sweetness-and-light", soft-speaking, perpetually smiling teacher, and learn to relabel your ego with spiritual sounding terms.

"But stay away from those that practice REAL compassion, because they will fry your ass, my friend."

– Ken Wilber.

Genius, Prophet and Ass-Fryer (my words, not his)

109

The Veil is ever so thin and we have far more help than we may remember or realise available to us at all times. Prayer is simply poetry from the heart. Ask for help.

"If you knew who walked beside you, you'd never know fear again." - By Dr. Wayne Dyer.

110

To my friend Rab who gave me such comfort during my "terror times." Your wife was a year ahead of me in Breast Chancer treatment but you shared tips, thoughts, love and hugs.

You worked as a painter and decorator and have worked for our family for years and by God you painted the path ahead of me and G with hope and honest sharing.

I met your wife.

You introduced us a year ago at a function, she told me, as you did with no sparing of the truth of what to expect from the Chemotherapy, the Radiotherapy, the "mean-well folk", the conscience clearers, the duckers and the REAL FOLKS who would turn up and walk beside me on the path.

And how to discern where to put my trust.

You were both so right.

And I was so grateful.

So your wife grew strong in her second year of bloom - her hair now long and shiny, as I grew green shoots of healing and recovery with my head resembling a prickly pear.

Then YOU were diagnosed with a brain tumour last October. I sent you this book.

Your wife, Agnes, read it to you. You told me in a recent chat that you enjoyed it. We talked about the wisdom in it just a few weeks ago. You told me how excited you were about your first grandchild coming any day soon.

Tonight I was told that you've have passed over the veil - just two weeks after baby Cody was born.

The circle of life.

I send my deepest love and blessings to you and your family - especially Agnes.

"Here, There and Everywhere."

Robert Donnelly 22.6.20. R.I.P.

ON THE MIRACLE THAT IS YOU: 111

Walter Truett Anderson suggests we taste the blending of science and spirituality that the Indigenous cultures manage well, using the big bang theory of evolution as a starting point.

He proposes we assume that it's true we started out with an explosion out of nothing, gases turned to matter stars and planets grew, then life on earth began and then consciousness arose and progressed to a self-reflective human consciousness.

If you don't believe yourself to be somehow separate from this series of events, you might try, when you are brushing your teeth in the morning, contemplating the rational proposition that what you are doing and seeing is an integral part of those processes. Fair enough.

The Universe is not only going about its mysterious business with quarks, black holes and supernovae, IT IS ALSO BRUSHING ITS TEETH.

Try it and see where it leads you. It drops me into a pool of freakin' AWE, a discovery of BEING like some of the fresh experiences described in many old spiritual texts describing enlightenment.

From a Zen text: "What miracle is this? I draw water and I carry wood."

What miracle is this indeed!

Something emerges out of nothing and, 14 billion years later, takes the form of words being typed on a phone screen.

Molecules spinning about the galaxy settle into the form of huge green trees I behold out on my walk, others take the form of the flying rainbow of a butterfly.

Play with it the next time you are reading a book, making a coffee or brushing your teeth.

What miracle is this?

The settling debris and dust of long dead stars takes the form of YOU reading this post.

YOU are a miracle.

JULY 2020

EAT·PRAY·LOVE 112

Sometimes these days I wake up a bit weary. Today was one such day.

My "aunt" Irene and my cousin Stephen both died a year ago yesterday and I think I was too numb last year with my "Chancer stuff" to take it fully in. But the anniversaries took the wind out of my sails.

My heart went out to my cousins who lost their father, his wife who sees his face when she closes her eyes. Irene's niece dropped off a box of her possessions left to me the other day, some Japanese plates and her own crafted needlepoint of a Geisha, knowing of our mutual love of Japan, home of our beloved Reiki. I was deeply touched by the thoughtfulness.

I was felled by the wave of love and loss, the reminder of impermanence of change.

Of the fragility of it all.

Of the blessed and precious gift of life and of my next breath.

And I had to sink down and rest my way through it.

I had to stop.

And of course, when this happens, any and all other repressed emotions take their opportunity to enter stage left, hijack the show and soon there is a full supporting cast of the missings, the losses.

Grief likes company.

Both Lord G and Sir Ian gave each other a knowing look, left my green vegetable slimy but healthy juice on the bedside cabinet and withdrew downstairs to wait it oot.

They know the drill.

I slept in and rested late.

Well, no real reason to rush.

But in time I knew where I needed to be.

It's good to recognise a place or places where your soul can sing its song. Where words are surplus and just being present in that place is a heart prayer.

I made for my Campsie Hills for the first time in four months.

It was quite the reunion.

Do you know where you need to go?

Can you and will you?

As Talk Talk sang… "Life's what you make it."

113

Just for today, BE GRATEFUL for someone, some little thing, or for life itself.

Just for today, LET GO OF WORRY, hand it over to the source of all that is.

Just for today, LET GO OF ANGER release it safely and with care for yourself and others. (breathe it out, walk or jog it out, write it out, shower it away, talk it out, soak it out, shout into a pillow it out and if all that fails, just SIT with the anger, put your arms around it and hold it for a while. It'll probably turn into hurt pretty quickly.. and maybe tears.

Just for today, go about your business honestly, LIVE TRUTHFULLY though speak your truth gently.

Just for today, BE KIND, be gentle, be graceful with everyone past and present including those who taught you the most however hard and painful that life lesson was.

Just for today, feel love flow through you and radiate it from your heart to the world - she really needs it.

I really need it, we all really need it and so do you. Remember, when you give it, you get it.

(Interpretation of the five Reiki principles of Dr Usui by moi, even though I've done seven)

ON THE MISSING: 114

I've really been missing my dad these last few weeks. He was my go-to for advice, he always had my back and I sure could do with some of his worldly wisdom right now.

I have "felt" his soft blue jumper, touched his fine white hair and breathed in the scent of him in my mind's eye's imaginary hugs in recent days.

'Twas my first trip to M&S at the Fort today for four months. I call mum to ask her if she would like some new shoes to try at home. "Yes please" she says, "and I'm about to watch my favourite film..STAND BY ME is just starting on TV."

There was a long pause and I took a long breath.

It was my dad's favourite film of all time and reminded him of his childhood.

She knows this.

Love never dies.

ON WRITTEN LOVE: 115

I was looking for a special book I kept locked in the filing cabinet.

I struggled to open the drawer, chock full of all the cards I was sent last year during my treatment, hunners of them.

I spread them out. I held bundles of them to my heart. I swear I could feel the love surround me. A rosy glow settled in the room as I sat cross-legged on the floor and read every single one again.

The healing power of love in the written word is severely underestimated, a text, an email is not, repeat NOT, the same thing.

I would not have been able to revisit all those beautiful outpourings of love and affection (some of the writers are now on the other side of the veil) if they had been virtual.

Last year, all during my Chancer treatment (nine months of it) I displayed every last one of them all over any surface that would take them to lift my spirit. To remind me of who I was.

But today, the glowing cheer, the vibrant colour and the delightful designs of the cards, some with enclosures of prayers, favourite poems, talismans, made for a couple of hours of immersion in memories, friendship, wisdom sharing, appreciation and deep love. I think the depth and breadth of the shared words blew me away the most. What a shame to NOT tell the people we appreciate and love how we feel about them, what we value most, how they have impacted our lives, what they've taught us.. BEFORE they die.

Why wait to share it with the family afterwards?

So, what to do with these amazing bundles of healing words now? Stuff them back in the drawer?

Nope. I will do what I always do with cards of love. Place them in a basket by the side of the fire and over the autumn months with each fire that I light, I'll kneel and reread each card, hold it to my heart, absorb and rekindle the love contained within the written words and then say a prayer, a blessing for the person who sent it as I use it to light my fire. As I do I will imagine the love from my heart going up and out the chimney, returning to sender via the great universal love angel air mail.

I will still be doing this next spring I reckon, with the size of the bundle.

When did you last really express your appreciation, love, share a memory with a friend, colleague or family member? It only takes a minute or five but you can never fully know the impact that investment of time will have. The written words of love and remembering sink deep into the human heart and flourish there.

They can be read, re-read and digested at the pace of the beloved.

They are pure gift.

116

As the world speeds up more and as our lives unfurl little by little into the outside world, other people and commitments of work and social connection, we may have a challenge adjusting and adapting to this new altitude and speed.

We may over-commit, over-extend and fill those diaries from a sense of what we used to be able to take in our stride.

We may encounter the "tyranny of the urgent." This is a wonderful term used by Charles Hummel in his book of the same name. He encourages us to ensure that life demands don't squash and overpower our "key desires." The needs of the soul.

Urgency can become a way of life again and we could easily lose the abilities we may have discovered during lockdown to do things more peacefully and from a more connected place within.

I realised I was pleasantly relieved when a colleague postponed some online recording work for later today. She isn't feeling too great and although I was sad for her, I soon realised I was pretty relieved. I had overcommitted for the capacity of my current energy tank.

It's easy for us to make appointments with our heads that our bodies and more importantly our souls have difficulty keeping.

What if we choose to simply do one or two things in our lives?

What if we do those whole-heartedly?

"Even too much GOOD work can become a violence to ourselves and to those around us." says Richard Rohr.

Come out of the cocoon as gently as you can and stay vigilant and aware of what you learned during "The Great Retreat."

Take YOUR time now and pace gently, factoring in the needs of your soul. I'm trying too. Happy Monday.

AUGUST 2020

ON BEING ODD AND SPEAKING OUT: 117

I have heroes and heroines that may be considered odd by many. Truth be told, many people think I'm odd. Truth be told, I'm okay with that today. I prefer it. I reckon I'm probably doing something right when I'm NOT following the herd in these recent times.

I followed the herd, mildly miserably, for the first part of my life. It didn't serve me or anyone else around me, for that matter.

So, back to my heroine – well, one of them. Hildegard of Bingen was a 43-year-old mediaeval visionary nun who experienced what she called a "Living Light", a light which appeared as a swirling spiral and eventually "spoke" to her.

She was also a musician who has written the most graceful, timeless and ethereal keyboard music which I use a lot in my workshops and meditations. Hard to believe it's centuries old. It sounds familiar yet eternal.

Hildegard mostly kept her experiences secret during the first half of her life, but in 1141 she couldn't contain it any longer. By now it was far too real and clear that divine guidance was at work in her life.

"Write what you see and hear.. Make plain the things that are hidden" was the instruction given to Hildegard.

"Speak Out!", said the voice.

She assures us the voice carried such authority she was convinced its origin was divine but she felt unworthy of this strong connection and direction.

And the more she resisted, the more seriously ill she became. "Until at last," she writes in the first chronicle of her visions, "compelled by many infirmities, I set my hand to writing and rose from my sickness with renewed strength."

Now, truth is, there are already enough prophets around if you have eyes and ears to see and listen without us all declaring ourselves as the next big thing in town.

But we can learn a thing or two from Hilde.

We can refuse to continue for another moment in a life our hearts have been crying out against for years.

It could be time to cultivate a daily contemplative or reflective practice. We can learn to pray, to speak or think the poetry of the heart.

It could be time to guard one day a week of our lives or even a few hours to keep Shabbat or Sabbath.

Interestingly this is one thing Christians, Jews and Hindus all agree on. The need for a day of rest and wholeness where we renew our connection to love/source (a Holy day). A day of rest and repair.

We could notice our over-consumption and sign up to a

simpler life.

We could explore a path of "non-violence" in everything we do, in our conversations, in our relationships, in our world. In how we relate to nature, in what we spend and invest our money and our time.

"Speak out," the voice said. When you do, when you recognize that inner voice as the voice of love and say what it has taught you, the sickness in your heart will melt away. The fatigue you have lived with for so long that you did not even notice it, will lift. Your voice will ring out with such clarity and beauty that you will not be able to stop singing,so Richard Rohr' paraphrases her message best.

To speak my truth, Hildegard' teaches me, is love in action.

REPEAT·PRAY·LOVE 119

So today was treatment number three of six IV infusions at the chemo unit at Wishy Healthspital. I get them every six months to strengthen my bones. I love to think that it's based just outside Motherwell - The Well of The Mother.

Although not nearly as rough as chemotherapy treatment, it's a case of same room, same smells, same cannula procedure, same IV process, same sounds and ropey side effects for a while. It all feels like a step back in time.

This time last year I was only half way through my chemo treatment, baldy as a coot and wondering how much more I could take.

Nurse and NHS cancer complementary practitioner Patricia McCabe MBE, as I explained earlier, started her training with me 20 years ago in Hypnotherapy and in Reiki.

I was amazed when I was referred to her for some of my NHS complementary treatments during my Chancer journey at Monklands Healthspital (The Land o' the Monks) - an amazing reunion after over 15 years, we realised.

So imagine my surprise, dear reader, when she turned up in the chemo unit today. She has been transferred and seconded to work there in her previous incarnation as a nurse during Covid changes. She was the first smile I saw and I had the honour of Tricia doing all my vitals.

And now here I am post-treatment, resting in bed with Sir Ian beside me, booking a wee trip to the Heartland, the Motherland, and Monklands of Iona – my first visit in nearly two years rather than my usual four times a year, so it will be quite the reunion.

And I'm exploring "CAMPERVAN: THE REAL THING" - a hippie campervan for a few nights at another time (with a B&B back-up plan if required).

These were just some of the dreams that kept me going through it all.. and now it's Dreams-Alive-Time!

Lying here feeling pretty bushed doesn't feel nearly so bad with an eye on my dressing table pic of the aquamarine waters of St Ronan's Bay.

Who knew that Ronan Keating had achieved sainthood while still alive?

BREATHE·PRAY·LOVE 120

After an IV of chemicals on Thursday I had been feeling pretty toxic and wobbly. Sleep helps but I needed some distraction. The revisit to the Healthspital chemo unit was a robust trigger of all things emotional and unfinished.

I call them the "what, if, who, why, when?" cycles of thoughts.

"The Ruminations" - a great name for a band.

I could feel myself sinking. There is a four stone monkey who comes along and sits on my shoulders at these times, pinning me to the chair/bed, resting her head and hands on my head, whispering in alternate ears "you're too tired Angela, just sit here. I'll keep you company with my incessant chatter, my litany of pointless commentary."

So I shook monkey off and promised her a much better time and took her by the hand off to The Cafe at Canada Woods, just outside Falkirk.

Yes, I said Falkirk!

Monkey, me and Lord G had the best of days. I still felt a bit wobbly and ropey but the clear air, the oxygen levels, the effects of forest bathing (Shinrin Roku - look it up) and the delicious food and pep of a perfectly decorated coffee, as well as all the history, were a perfect foil. The 1746 Jacobite Battle of Falkirk - 16,000 men - who knew?

The walks are stunning, there is bike hire available (a wheel too far for me today) and the views are really stupendous.

Not everyone will GET YOU, and you don't need to try to squeeze yourself into their favour. Stop playing small, let 'em go, but bless first, then shed them with love, just

like the autumn leaves fall.

There is a whole new world out there of new people with whom who you really don't need to try so hard if and it's all there just waiting just FOR YOU.

SEPTEMBER/
OCTOBER 2020

THE LEAF PILE: 121

We've probably all created our own leaf pile of the people, relationships and projects we want to release just as we begin sweeping up the autumn leaves outside.

But hold on just a minute, it's not that simple.

If we are gonna hold them, out there, to account - would it not behove me also to do a scan, an audit of my own inability to "love yet."

Are there aspects of me that need to be swept on to the pile?

Perhaps before I write them off completely, I should also consider answering some of these pretty tricky questions myself.

How fully and well do I love?

How much of my love is conditional?

Whose presence am I indifferent to?

When and with whom do I refuse to listen?

Who and how do I exclude, subtly offend, forget or easily ignore who give (or have given) time to me, even though it might have been at some time in the past?

When and how am I less than thrilled about another's joy and success. How does that serve me or them?

How deep do I go in my friendships and relationships?

Who am I not ready to love yet?

And does that list include MYSELF?

ON BECOMING A WITCH: 122

As part of my Chancer journey last year - which continues to this day of course, I've had to make many changes to my life and lifestyle.

And what I fed my gut microbiome was a major part of that. I had great teachers and role models to help me.

As you know one of those was the amazing Janice Clyne's "I never looked back."

So I jumped at the chance to go into the woods at Cadder Wharf on the John Muir Trail by the canal with Janice and foraging guru Vicki Manning. We went to learn about the wild foods packed with super-healing properties to be found in nature, to add to my healing repertoire.

We tried a veritable banquet of teas and plants, made sauerkraut with mugwort, nettles dandelions and hogweed. We learned about lady's mantle, red clover, sorrel, wild garlic, hawthorn leaves, mallow, redcurrant, brambles, leaves and the weirdly named nipplewort.

Wild camping pees were tricky but memorable and challenged by the occasional passing dog walkers - all those dried herb teas do help the kidneys ramp up their game.

The sage and mugwort sausage rolls topped with wild carrot seeds were ace, roasted rosehips in garlic and olive oil along with rosehip harissa, nut cheeses with nettle seeds, beetroot pate, herb scones and more.

I've not had as much fun since.. I'm just having such fun it's hard to say.

Life is for learning and I'm learning loads.

Now all I need is a new broomstick.

ON BECOMING A WITCH PART 2: 123

So today was for foraging for nettle seeds. This is no mean feat and real witches must have asbestos hands. I wore big man gloves but the feckers get you up yer sleeves.

Then it was back to the cauldron to clean and dehydrate them (hours in a cool oven) et voila - my jar is full to overflowing.

Nettle seed is considered a Western adaptogen herb that supports the adrenal glands and endocrine system. This is why, in herbal medicine, it is used as a tonic for fatigue and adrenal exhaustion for people who are burnt-out, run down and low in energy, zest for life and libido. Look out G, I'm a comin' for ya!

You can think of it as "Hippie Speed". I have the cleanest house in Condorrat.

And then another of the Coven dropped by for an alfresco garden cackle. Three and a half hours later we had both run out of words and our ears were bleeding.

Time for some more nettle seed sprinkles!

ON GIVING THANKS AND GRATITUDE: 124

Gratitude is not a thought, it's not the words "I'm grateful for".

It is a spiritual act, an act of the soul.

It is an elevated state of being that is soooo good for us on every level of mind, body, spirit and liveability.

I just made that one up! Liveability means you are much more pleasant to be around and easier to live with when you come with an attitude of gratitude.

The word gratitude comes from the Latin root gratus, meaning "pleasing, welcome, agreeable". Gratus is also the root of the word "GRACE". When we are grateful, we are in a state of grace and we emanate that all around us, like a perfume.

But just reciting the mantra - "I'm grateful" or declaring "thanks" is not enough.

Gratitude is an experience, a movement of our full attention and appreciation, a mindless moment of time travel when we stop thinking, lose our minds and STOP.

At that moment we breathe and enjoy the magic of true seeing, sensing, touching, inhaling, listening, tasting ... not just with our physical senses but with our soul senses the eyes and ears of the heart.

To drop regularly into the state of gratitude, to walk appreciation into my life requires that I understand WHY it's worth doing. It's a game changer and a week of regular daily practice will demonstrate that unequivocally. We grow new neural pathways, we think differently, the world opens up more to us, we live at a higher altitude and the air and views are clearer from there. Enough for ya?

Then I simply need to alter my warp speed and take the time as I go about my day, to feel and touch, to stroke with my eyes, to touch in my listening, to hear with my heart, to taste with focussed perception, with the senses of a person newly born and doing these for the first time.

Thinking and speaking are overrated in gratitude practice. Showing up fully is all that's required.

In these tricky times gratitude can be a really helpful soulmate.

Victor Frankl, Edith Eger and Anne Frank wrote much of the value of inner joy and gratitude during the horrendous years of the Holocaust.

We could learn much about how to handle our tricky times from those who endured far more than we can ever imagine; and feel the grace of gratitude for their sharing of wisdom.

PLAY·PRAY·LOVE 125

When we have had trauma in our childhoods we often shut down and close off parts of ourselves and our histories to protect ourselves.

Revisiting the things of childhood can be too painful for some.

For many, childhood itself was such a loaded and painful time, it is stored in deep freeze conditions a bit like the movie Frozen – yes, really. Worth a watch for the deeper mind benefits of the metaphorical story.

I was chatting with a friend recently who was telling me he felt clumsy and uneasy about playing with his sons while his wife is a complete natural at it.

His childhood was a Frozen job and he had never really learned how to play.

Some feel too self-conscious, too wooden and approach play as a project or a problem to be solved. Not a spontaneous deep dive into the realms of the imagination and the world of curiosity and magic.

I suggested to him that he should let the kids teach him how to play as he had possibly never really learned, or had forgotten because he was too busy trying to survive his childhood.

"Let them teach you".

MARCH·PRAY·LOVE 126

Getting those cobwebs blown away doon the water!
Get your walking shoes or boots on and get yourselves out

there, into the light, absorbing the ions of the trees, beach, grass or lochs and the infectious spaciousness of sky.

A wee flask, a Morton's roll and Spam and you're away!

You know it makes sense to increase your Vitamin D, the old oxygen levels, and it's so good for the soul. Some of the best immune system support there is.

Not including of course the increase in the Dopamine, Serotonin and Oxytocin levels with all the added health benefits from those feel good hormones and chemicals.

This is the Turnberry stretch, near Girvan, of coast at the Lighthouse (built by Robert Louis Stevenson's dad) and next to the ruins of Turnberry Castle where Robert the Bruce was born.

Lots of smugglers' coves, pine martens, hawks hunting and brambles to up your pro- biotic levels.

What's not to love about this country?

NOVEMBER 2020

A COOL CLEAR MIND: 127

Things are hotting up out there with Brexit, Christmas lockdowns and the American election.

Two very wise older ladies (my gran and sister Jean separately) told me, decades apart.

"When it's getting too hot in the kitchen - open the window, the door or better still get outside for a while and cool down. You'll only ruin the meal."

This is very good advice.

Christmas is one day - a few hours. Who is to say it won't be the best ever, without the fandango being danced around it?

What will unfold in USA will be, rogues have come and rogues have gone before.. no doubt rogues will come again.

Brexit will change some things and we are such an adaptable species.

Remember to switch off the TV, open the window, the back

door or better still get outside.

Look up to that moon and those stars and remember to be grateful for all that you DO have.

Clear your mind on a regular basis: stop, breathe, sit on a cushion and reset to factory default setting.

A cool clear head is gonna go a long way right now, for you and everyone else you come into contact with.

ON LIGHTENING UP: 128

Suffering in this life is unavoidable - all traditions and religions agree on this. Sometimes we new-agers like to pretend it's not, that we can "affirm" our way out of this fact.

I laughed out loud when a therapist friend told me recently of a client who had declared "I've been looking into this affirmation thing you've been suggesting and I've come up with one that works for me, all men are bastards."

I don't think she had quite grasped the concept.

So difficulties and suffering may be inevitable while we live and breathe, but how we respond and react to that suffering is pure choice.

We are free to choose our response, if we work on our knee jerk reactions of old and our justified reactivity.

When we hit the PAUSE button.

When we step back and surround difficult situations with a blanket of compassion for all involved (usually a lot of damaged/wounded souls) inject some humour into same, add a healthy dose of humility, drop our unreasonable expectations, a dash of generosity of spirit, a ladle full of forgiveness; and downgrade the whole scenario from Red Alert to Amber – "I can handle this, lousy as it is."

The Dalai Lama and Desmond Tutu had a week together and discussed this suffering theme in relation to joy. Some of these factors were considered to be the pillars of joy.

I call it The Scaffolding.

When I'm weary, feeling small, when tears are in my eyes, if I can go through the above checklist and apply it (it will often require external support to do so) I am able to transform my response to the pain and difficulties in my life.

With generosity and humility I see my connection to all others. I recognise my place in the world and acknowledge that at another time I could be the one in difficulty.

With a sense of humour and ability to laugh at myself we do not take ourselves or others too seriously.

We can find the acceptance where we don't push the river, don't force life to be other than it is. There is a gratitude for all that we have been given.

And as the Dalai Lama put it "Helping others is the way to discover your own joy and to have a happy life."

Tutu gave this blessing "You are loved with a love that nothing can shake, a love that loved you long before you were created, a love that will be there long after everything has disappeared. You are precious."

And love says: "Help me to spread love and laughter and joy and compassion. As you do this you will discover Joy. It comes as the gift, the reward for this non-self-regarding caring for others."

DECEMBER 2020

INTO THE GREAT SILENCE: 129

Just in time - they changed the tiers just in time.

And so we made it here to Kinnoull and the Monastery of St Mary's.

Two nights of silence on an Advent Adventure.

And the surprise of Sr Jean (ex-Iona) being over from Dalkeith. She booked last night when she heard we'd be here. Just beautiful.

"Still the light will pierce the dark

Still the dark will steal the light

And everything will be all right

Though change won't be denied..."

Lyrics by Beth Nielsen Chapman.

ON A TRICKY TIME: 130

Christmas is a tricky time, all that love and peace malarkey we are supposed to be feeling and "goodwill to all men" – erm, what about women?

I saw a programme about the Hindu religion recently and arrogantly tutted my judgement about the caste system, some are high born, others lower caste and never the twain shall meet.

Then I realised I have my own wee caste system inside of me. Those who meet my standards and approval and those who don't (which I don't actually manage myself) who are cast out, exiled.

When I find the extra room in the smelly old stable in my heart for the broken, the damaged, the vulnerable, or as Richard Rohr says, "the nobodies, those who can't play our game of success, who cannot reward us in return', I experience a DEEPER LOVE from where I least expect it."

I begin to see life through the eyes of my soul.

The nativity story that wee Ella Rose starred in last year (okay then - she played the Innkeeper) says a lot.

The Wise people (who says they were men) on a journey of searching, the outcast (shepherds were just that - unwelcome), the animals, the shitty smelly stable, the abject poverty of it all, the innocence, the vulnerability, the birth of love, the messages from nature - the guiding star, the invisible whispers of grace from the angels.

What an amazing metaphor.

A one-stop shop of pure gift.

Richard Rohr and Caroline Myss, mentors and writers, both independently remind me that to love is to recognize the sacred in everyone - even those I hold in my inner dungeons. Rohr says, "either we see love in everything, or we don't see it at all."

We only see a counterfeit copy of love.

When I fully stretch my heart and empty my dungeons, my heart gradually expands outwards, widening its loving embrace.

Our outcasts, our "enemies", our prisoners locked in our inner dungeons are sacred. Love created them too.

The ability to respect the outcast, the poor - whether in finances, in health or spirit - the different, the "enemy" is the ultimate test of the heart and that includes respecting the cattle, sheep, birds, trees and oceans. When love grows and expands, we experience more light within. Everything becomes enchanting. Everything belongs.

As Bono and Bob Marley both sang there is only one love, one world, one truth. It's tricky, but not impossible. It means taking risks, moving position, taming the ego, guarding the tongue and opening our weary and tired, bruised and damaged hearts.

Last word to Richard Rohr' "One Love: All we can do is participate."

MY MORNING PRAYER: 131
(A lovely way to start your day and worth a re-share)

"Mother, Father, Creator God - spirit of love in all that is.

This morning I say "thank you" for that warm, dry, cosy, comfy bed I slept in.

I'm so grateful for the fact I have a roof to keep me warm and dry, heat and light to make my life so comfortable and safe, and those soft carpets and rugs keep my feet warm.

Bless you for the softness of the sweater which hugs me, and the clothes and shoes that keep me warm and dry as I walk outside.

Thanks so much for this ever-changing beauty in the world I woke up to today. I loved the jewels you left out for me, the icy teardrops of the 'dew-els' on the fence.

Many didn't wake up today. Many won't see this magical frosty day. Some souls I know, it seems, are waiting to cross over the veil soon - so I appreciate it on their behalf.

Thank you for this Christmas time frosty morning that reminds me of the cloud of unknowing, the liminal and imaginal space where I meet you best, when I drop the masks and costumes I wear and eventually I even drop the words - not easy for me - and then I see your love shine most fully and brightly.

I feel you inside, aglow in my heart space. My heartscape.

Thank you for reminding me on the frosty path which I see before me, that every step I take is a pure gift. A gift given to me for the unwrapping and every day a magical mystery of lessons and learnings to be explored.

Thanks a lot. I love you."

Angela x

A BOXING DAY GEAR SHIFT: 132

If you sit soft, still and quiet for a while each day and breathe the love in your heart deeper within yourself, all through yourself and then to those around you, directing it towards those who could do with some extra, your view of the world may begin to change from abject fear to a curious loving connection.

When I do this, I stop living inside my brittle and encapsulated wee self, with my castle walls, in the kingdom of ME-ME-ME.

When we make a shift from ME-ME-ME to awareness of our expansive unbounded soulself, we begin moving from being "fear-driven to being love-drawn", as Richard Rohr puts it. Everything shifts.

When great love, which breathes love and life into our world every moment (the loving presence that has no one name) is holding you, dissolving your fear and allowing greater connection with everything and everyone,

we can live with a natural vitality, a gracefulness and flow that seems heaven sent. It is the presence of big love spinning and flowing through us.

Take some quiet time and breathe some winter love into yourself and others today.

LIVING WITH LOSING AT XMAS: 133
Grief is a journey of exploration of ever deepening knowledge and understanding, combined with handfuls of Kleenex, forced smiles and much higher than normal vocal range.

It is not about recovery and 'getting over it'. There is no target.

I lost my father four years ago at the end of November. It's STILL fresh at this time of year, but with a gentler acceptance.

And I have so many friends, colleagues and a neighbour who have lost husbands, parents or grandparents, brothers or sisters, uncles and aunts and in one case -a 16- year-old relative in a road traffic accident, all this past year. Linda, Adrienne, Paul, Lorraine, Michelle P, Tracy, Sr. Jean, Michelle C, Agnes, Helen, Claire, Tara, Lilia, Dougie, Christine, Shirley, Ángela, Chloe, Carolyn, Jane.

And no doubt others who I may not recall right now.

The challenge of the Covid-limited funeral numbers and sparse gatherings impacted on them all.

There is no time frame to be measured. No score card for stoicism and bravery. There are no brownie points for the speed of returning to "normal" (as if you could).

Loss burns inwards and the warmth of her fire can melt our defences. She coaxes us inside the living room of the heart to heal and to discover the hidden depths.

We learn to watch the perhaps previously invisible and unseen world unfold, opening the eyes, ears and senses of the soul

Grief can become a soul friend on a circling, ascending path of light, night and half-light. She guides us gently to new views and vistas previously unseen. A new altitude and perspective on life.

Loss CAN awaken us, purify us, open our hearts and open our eyes to the subtle energies which are the divine ingredients of our world. Or it can shrink us, weaken us and we may shrivel wounded from the pain of it and hide out in the shadows.

It often does both, alternating in cycles.

But if we surrender and take her hand.

Love Never Dies.

A NEW YEAR'S EVE GIFT: 134

Here is an advanced reflective practice for Ye Olde Hogmanay Clear Oot... but not for the faint-hearted. Some people get awfy bogged down with clearing out drawers and cupboards, emptying bins and throwing out old clothes at this time of year.

This is folly! A complete and utter waste of your valuable holiday minutes and hours, equivalent to trying to put an Elastoplast on a burst artery, if the objective is energetic flow. Yes, your sock collection will be colour co-ordinated and you'll find the corkscrew more easily in the utensil drawer. But the temporary elation of order and control will only satisfy your OCD and your perfectionist-driven ego for a day, or three.

If you don't clear out some of the clutter in your heart, if you don't consciously release some of the prisoners in your inner dungeons and torture chambers - where you are still punishing them for offences of many moons ago – if you don't open the windows of your mind to fresh energy and flow, making space for new challenging attitudes, the promise of trying new things, expanding your viewpoints and horizons, all the clear-oots in the world are a waste of space on an energetic level .

Light a candle, for illumination - enlightenment-ality.

Who do you need to pardon, forgive, release, unshackle? Are there parts of YOURSELF locked up in a cell down in the bowels of your inner castle, denied the light of day?

What wounds and hurts are you still nursing, possessively? What do you get out of that? How does playing victim serve you?

How much payback do you receive from carefully nursing and nurturing resentment, bathing in the waters of self-pity. It can be really addictive, soothing and comforting - can't it?

Where and with whom do the seeds of forgiveness need to be planted? How can you prepare the ground within your inner landscape? Don't forget you may need some self-forgiveness too.

What have you learned from all of the above?

Rest and digest. Smile a while.

JANUARY 2021

A RIGHT GOOD CLEAR OOT: 135

So, I'm starting my "Bag A Day For 30 Days" tomorrow. Wanna join me?

Say "Hell yeah!".

To really kick start your year, create some space and let go of some of that STUFF. Recycle, pass on, sell, dump. Make some external space for new things. It feels good!

And the Feng Shui guys say as we clear and allow energy to move more freely in our outer spaces, so we do the same in our inner space. We feel freer in our minds and feel less burdened. We travel lighter than before.

Don't worry about the size of the bag, it could be a pedal bin size, a supermarket bag or huge garden waste bin size, the trick is to leave a variety lying around in different places to remind you and once you start, you are on a roll.

Just think how much space you will have cleared by the end of the month.

Love from The Bag Lady.

ON WALKING: 50 SHADES OF WHITE: 136

After a party a deux on Hogmanay, I kicked off the inaugural day of the "50 Miles in January Challenge" for The Maggies' Centres.

It was a skaters' paradise up our way but I dusted down the ski poles and set off with G, David and Tara who came to see me off at the harbour on my long voyage.

I got 2.2 miles in the bag. Not bad for a Torville and Dean extravaganza.

But a ways to go EVERY DAY IN JANUARY afore I can honestly claim my so far sponsorship of £800 and counting!

But it's a drop in the ocean for the help and support I received from them during my Chancer journey last year which still continues to this day and beyond while I fully complete IV treatment in Feb 2022. A truly marvellous service which changes and, I'm sure, saves lives.

We finished with an outdoor cuppa and hot roll, some harvest-style relinquish and intention practices.

The Clootie Tree loves this stuff and our silk cloths hang resplendently flapping in the winds of the heavens.

It's a prayer tree by any other name.

Have you taken time to reflect, to release the old unwanted aspects, to set your compass and to set sail on a voyage of squeezing the juice out of 2021?

Every day is New Year's Day and it's never too late to begin.

137

Okay my little Baggers, let's get started.

All you need is a deep breath, a bag of ANY size and we are off.

Don't think too much, just begin chucking out. Think of how

good you're gonna feel by the end of the month.

Have a recycle bag for charity shop, a book and DVD bag to offer to pals, an "I'm not sure" bag you can keep for a week for those feelings of indecision.

The rule of seven can be helpful. Do you really need more than seven of ANYTHING? Seven scarves? Seven jumpers? Seven T-shirts? Seven dishtowels? Seven brides for seven brothers?

Lift your spirits, this need only take 15 minutes.. and we're off!

SURFING 2021: 138

Remember this is a tough time of year for us all, it's dark, it's cold, the usual viruses and bugs abound and there is often a "downer" that hits now after all the rushing and pressures of Christmas and New Year plus the effect of coming off the uppers of alcohol, chocolate, stress and any other you care to mention.

The "anti-climax effect" of a NEW year knows no bounds.

And all of that is notwithstanding that which shall not be named here (CV) and its relentless impact on our psyches.

How can you make it a gentle and loving transition, taking account of all of this?

What if you were to commit to just ONE THING that if you did it EVERY DAY, would make a tremendous difference to your life over the month, the season, the year?

Little daily acts of self-love and self-soothing that cumulatively make a huge impact.

It could be as simple as:

Get up 15 minutes earlier to have some time to yourself for watching the light in the sky, just pondering.

Walk/skate for 10 minutes a day.

Soak in a candlelit bath with a couple of cups of Epsom salts/ Himalayan salts or bicarbonate of soda, a rerr wee detox of the system. It pulls all the c@&p outta yer pores and your field.

Drink more water - hydrate to feel great.

Reduce stimulants - coffee/tea, caffeine, chocolate, salt, sugar, alcohol.

Eat more brain food like seeds, nuts.

Eat more vegetables, living foods.

Eat a healthier breakfast.

Give yourself a five-minute hand or foot massage with lovely lotion.

Sit or lie down and REALLY listen to some music for 10 minutes.

Sit quietly and meditate or pray for 15 minutes.

Read some inspiring writers for just 15 minutes a day.

Journal for 15 minutes a day writing about feelings rather than noting activities undertaken.

Reach out to someone every day with a phone call or a smile.

Ask "How are you?" and REALLY listen.

Organise your space spending 10 minutes a day, decluttering a drawer, cupboard, handbag.

It doesn't take much but doing just ONE of these every day will have a cumulative and very powerful effect in your life.

You are exercising your emotional CAN DO muscles.

You can do it: YES, YOU CAN!

ON RESPONDING TO TRAUMATIC EVENTS: 139

Denial and ignorance make great bedfellows.

A lofty dissociation from reality and being "too spiritual" for the things of this world make excellent growing conditions in which extremism will easily flourish.

"If I ignore it, it'll go away."

Nope, it thrives like a bacterial mould.

Hysterical reactivity, grandstanding, energetic stone-throwing and name-calling help set the necessary stage for them versus us.

Baiting and baying on any level allow our own prejudices to fester and a lifetime of repressed anger to hitch a ride on external issues we can easily justify.

The world has never needed contemplation so much, for sure, but it also requires action to balance and to create the changes.

That means showing up.

If the "showing up" doesn't come from the still, small voice within it's simply more reactivity.

And THAT drama has been playing out for centuries.

Can we find a new way to discuss and debate, to understand, to love our enemies, to hold good boundaries and to protect our freedoms? Can we have compassion for the exhausted, the afraid, the weary, the terrified and terrorised, the misinformed and manipulated?

They are me. I am them. We are one.

Or do we come from a place of judgement and disdain?

Or simply denial, dissociation and disconnect. All the classic trauma responses.

If I canny do it in my own life and world, how can I expect to find it in the bigger picture?

It starts with me.

ON PACING: 140

This is no time for throwing ourselves into cycles of manic activity, nor utopian plans and striving. This is a time for retreat and quiet, slow and cosy.

Mother Nature is showing us how.

Withdraw, hunker down, coorie in.

Ponder and contemplate. Read inspiring books. Journal and reflect.

Meditate and sleep.

Let the winds blow away the dust and cobwebs, let the rains wash and clean, let the snow and ice freeze and freshen. Mother Earth is busy underground and within. So should we be.

St. Angela Trainer of Condorrat

"Close your eyes and follow your breath to the still place that leads to the invisible path that leads you home."

By St. Teresa of Avila

ON EASY DOES IT: 141

January has over time become the month of universal self-loathing.
It's always in someone's interest for you to hate yourself and purge, diet, join a gym, buy exercise equipment, join weight clubs and give EVERYTHING UP - by yesterday!

Why not try loving yourself a little bit more instead and watch what happens? Be gentle. Talk nice to yourself. Slow it down.

Self-hating, self-loathing and negative self-talk create a hateful tug of war inside, then we seek to anaesthetise our pain with all the old behaviours and substances. What we resist really does persist.

Baby steps. Try it, give love and encouragement to your inner baby, one tiny step and tumble at a time.

GRIEF·LOSS·LOVE 142

Stars reach our eyes long after they have "died" light years away.

Endings and loss affect us all every step of our path through life.

Grief is not restricted to the loss of a parent or a pet. Our old dreams may die. Friendships are lost in the changing seasons of our lives. Relationships end. We retire and we move away from people, places, roles. Our children leave home, things change and we have to deal with endings and loss on a regular basis.

Grief is neither a system failure, a control tower error, a slip and fall to be righted or a hurdle to be jumped over.

I've been studying the mystics in recent times and am currently going for long walks and chats with St John of The Cross (of the Dark Night of The Soul), a 16th century mystic and poet. It's much more uplifting than it sounds and the wisdom is timeless, honest!

The skill set of healing through grief and dealing with a broken heart is a necessary part of our soul's development. There is a divine intelligence embedded within us like an eternally sparkling jewel, which recognises the value of the punctured and sacred heart, broken open in vulnerability. Naked and open.

Working with loss and disappointment is not about fast-tracked recovery.

It does not require a Teflon coating of the heart or a life lived in protective isolation, striving to become invincible and unbreakable. In fact, extreme independence can be seen as a trauma response.

We are all broken open, punctured, wounded and left scarred in our lives, usually way more than twice and by God, we are all going through a collective Dark Night of the Soul at the moment on this planet.

But the heart is bottomless - vast and beyond wide and we can learn to dive deeper still in her endless oceans of love, learning from the gifts of grief and loss.

As the ego dissolves in the depths of confusion and shock, the shoots and eventually the fruits of grief and endings becoming more tangible and visible.

In time, the boundaries and sharp edges of grief become blurred and she becomes a soul friend, shining her torch on unwalked, fresh pathways. Her light also shines on the previously menacing, dark corners of our lives. They wilt and shrivel from the exposure. We, however, grow bolder and stronger, with our emotional muscles strengthened.

There is a light in the darkness that only loss and the felt experience of the pain of grief can teach us to trust and know.

But we don't travel a straight trajectory on this path. It winds around, it spirals and circles, it twists and performs figures of eight in various combinations.

We can begin to learn to trust this mystical dance in the shallows and then in the depths of loss.

We can begin to discover how we navigate this gateway into this mystery of life and love in trust and with deep reverence.

Difficulties, suffering and loss can become opportunities for us to receive the gifts of grace deep within us the jewels in the treasure chest deep within our heart.

ON THE SEARCHING: 143
This is a time of year when so many of us are making resolutions, lusting goals (yes - I left that very apt typo in)

and deciding that what we really need is yet another new job, partner, car, hairdo, exercise routine or body shape.

Nothing terribly wrong with seeking something more or new but it's often futile when what we are often really seeking is a sense of CONNECTION.

We crave a sense of AWE. A sense of the SACRED in our lives and that is an inside job, it will never be sustained by the externals in our lives in any truly satisfying way.

We simply become "Hungry Ghosts" as labelled by Dr Gabor Mate, looking for the next increasingly shorter and faster fix, growing a bigger appetite.

We thirst in the dry night of the material world with empty and growling bellies and move on to the next thrill of excitement, hoping to be satiated, with an ever-increasing appetite, and deeper hunger.

When we practise detaching with love from our exterior world from our ego-driven appetites from our need for competition, perfection, the need to win, from our hurting places, the need to be right - we detach from fear. The fear of lack, the fear of not being or having enough, or the fear of rejection, exile, being forgotten.

Surrender is usually a precursor of healing, a necessary step and there are many ways to surrender - meditation, contemplation, self-hypnosis, mindfulness and reflection are all ways of surrendering and going within.

But so is "quiet" walking, sitting soft and still, watching the sky, snowfall, birds at the feeder or light changing first or last thing, candlelight, bubbles in the bath, the following of our breathing for any extended period of time.

Maybe on this bright fresh sunny January day, you can detach a little from the fear and go inside a little with a bit of quiet, space and silence.

And we find in there the still small voice of intuition and wisdom. The voice of love.

And love will always conquer fear.

ON RECEIVING: 144

I STILL find it hard, after all these years of working on myself to receive.

I feel the muscles tighten in my body, my teeth clench at the jaw and I fix a grin with a too high by an octave voice and squeak.

"Oh thank you, you shouldn't have."

I wish I could find it easy to just sink into the heart of gratitude, to unfurl and uncurl and connect to the beauty of the moment of receiving, whether for an oh-so-appropriate card, gorgeous words during a phone call, a touching compliment in a comment, a thoughtful gift.

But at 61 there is still a touch of the "I'm not worthy" around, I guess.

Ah well, more work to be done.

Or maybe I simply need to develop a loving acceptance of the shyness inside and learn to negotiate the overwhelm of receiving.

I had a wonderful lockdown birthday on Thursday.

I WAS in fact REALLY overwhelmed by the beautiful messages, comments, cards, gifts, sentiments and the big blanket of love that enfolded me.

I'm still unwrapping the pleasure of the last few days and still have a few presents to open yet. I call it a birthday weekend.

It was different under the circumstances but we managed two

"tea in separate flasks, car windows down", birthday present drop-offs and two accompanied walks with Michelle and Dougie on separate days.

Kim dropped off a delicious afternoon tea for a pre-birthday day of celebration and Ella Rose dropped off a magnificent rainbow and a card promise of a plant for my new studio (which she thought was hilarious, "why would anybody ask for a PLANT for their birthday mum?").

Too many beautifully thought-out ideas and a house that could sell tickets as a botanical garden - The Condorrat Flower Show.

Love my new Kombucha factory, ultra-super walking sox and pom pom hat and my all singing and dancing walking gear.

I'm fully kitted out for walking the length of the country, top to bottom with my well-chosen wardrobe!

So thank you - all those well wishes and loving words have filled me up for the journey.

I'm deeply grateful, chuffed and revisiting those lovely messages, cards and gifts until I can feel them sink ALL the way in.

And keep them there.

FALLING DOWN: 145
I "fell" the other day.
Not physically, emotionally.
Though they are really one and the same, when you break it down.

I found myself crying in the car in the Tesco car park. "Full moon!", I tutted as I eventually locked the car and headed inside sporting my Hannibal Lecter mask. It matched my mood.

Was it when I was almost doubled over the trolley handle, hanging my head in exasperation at the Chatty Cathy serving her pal at the checkout, while I stood waiting for at least three hours (okay five minutes). My lower back was throwing the towel in, concrete floors, fluorescent lights and the bing-bong of all the electro-magnetic equipment drain me dry these days.

Or was it when finally being able to begin to pack my wares, I couldn't reach the feckers because of the shiny new perspex barriers that required the skills of a contortionist to negotiate. Chatty was practising Zen minimalist effort at moving them down the not so slidey slide.

I did attempt to keep my voice level even neutral - but on reflection I guess it verged on a snarl: "Do you think you could pass them further along DEAR? I'm struggling to reach."

All delivered with an acidic grimace, starting from the nose down.

She didn't chat with me.

I was so grateful to be able to hide underneath my mask as I left.

Comfortingly invisible.

Alienated and disconnected.

I felt safely camouflaged and anonymous.

I was a jumbled ball of sadness and rage.

A needy, restless, empty, whiny, drained, homicidal thing.

My next Post-Chancer treatment, due in February, has been cancelled.

I have had three now and this was to be number four. But because of Covid, it's been sacked. It is hoped it may happen in May.

I have to have blood tests and a consultation before treatment to check I'm fit to have it and those were all scheduled with two weeks to play for. I thought I was in the clear.

Then I received a call to pre-warn me before the letters to confirm NOT happening.

And it took me a day or two to process that fact, a double-whammy during this crazy time.

Now it's really NOT the end of the world but it sure as hell felt like it.

My stamina deserted me. The fear and the grief stepped in as dance partners.

We are all so open and raw at this time of year anyway that when you add in a pandemic and a lockdown any extra baggage or weight to carry can feel impossible.

Just too much to bear.

Falling down is very important at these times.

It's good to fall like a wee drunk man or woman. To not stiffen (you will break more easily if you are rigid).

It's better to surrender and to crumple. To roll into a ball and to howl.

And to breathe, to sit, to sob.

And to wait.

It WILL pass, I promise, but only when you cough up and release the emotional furball then get your breath back. That's best done by giving in.

The relaxing into powerlessness is vital in these strange and unpredictable times and we can find it hard to admit and acknowledge how powerless we are. However it can feel like a tremendous comfort blanket when we soften our warrior stance and let go. All sorts of comforting energies can be released and we allow reality to be our friend.

The tears do stop and the fear does subside. A terrified child is piloting our body for a time.

On return from the Tescofest I read some bubblegum glossy mags with a glass of Barosso until I was deactivated and ate a comfort dinner whilst Helen Reddy did her thang on Netflix and sang to "Angie Baby" – really.

G used his phenomenal psycho-therapeutic skills this morning - free of charge.

Pals have offered phone chats over the weekend but we often thaw out slowly and need time to self-soothe too.

So I'm away to walk with G in the sacred landscape of the Campsies.

And taking with me in my heart the prayer I found for just now.

May you find solace in it too, if you need a prayer today or identify with any part of my post:

"May I be free from inner and outer harm and danger. May I be safe and protected.

May I be free of mental suffering or distress.

May I be happy.

May I be free of physical pain and suffering.

May I be healthy and strong.

May I be able to live in this world happily, peacefully, joyfully, with ease.

Amen."

APPRECIATE·PRAY·LOVE 146

Almost all of my life, well from at least the age of 14 onwards, I have moaned about facial and body hair. No doubt brainwashed and encouraged to spending thousands of pounds by the marketeers during my lifespan as a lassie on products and gadgets, haircuts and treatments to control this vagabond substance - hair, which was most unwanted and unwelcome so much of the time.

Hair that was the wrong colour, texture, length, style. Hair that grew in places it wasn't allowed. Eyebrows that were too thick, then when over-plucked too thin, leg hair which sprouted like a summer lawn and eyelashes that were invisible without a coat of tar. I shall leave it at that.

Nowadays after losing the lot to Chancer treatment in 2019, I say a prayer of gratitude for hair in all her fine forms and glory. Long live hair, grow wherever the heck ye like now! I love you. I now have a full and bouncy head of it again.

I bless my long-lost eyebrows and my beautiful vulnerable wee eyelashes which eventually made a cautious and tentative entrance back on stage.

Even the hairs up my nose have come out of the ether, I had no idea they were so valuable and important for dust and germ protection.

And you've no idea how much any kind of hair keeps your head warm, until it's gone.

Stop bullying your hair and God bless the hair fairies.

FEBRUARY 2021

THE CELTIC SPRING: 147
It starts today, February 1. It even has a Celtic name, Imbolc - the return of the light.
But the wee snowdrops are just peeping, it's only the TURN towards spring, the light is changing, we can see and feel it but it takes such tiny, incremental baby steps.

February is a month where we need to be gentler still as it's been a long winter and we would do well not to force a SNAP to attention, instead putting down deep roots and strengthening them.

The fragility of the tiny snowdrops should remind us of our own pacing. The peeping buds on some of the branches are hesitantly testing the elements, as should we.

Even the birds are choosing the easier option of the offerings of seeds and nuts, the fatball feast that Ella Rose and I prepared last week during outdoor home-schooling. They are not joining Slimming World or Weight Watchers just yet, or digging for keto-style worms.

They are taking the path of least resistance and practising energy conservation.

As for the heavens, we are moving into a mercury retrograde until February 20, I am advised, so this is no time of pushing, forcing or forging ahead if you have any interest or trust in the studies of the planets.

It can be helpful to do things which encourage alignment with this energy. Slow it all down, take YOUR time, know that mistakes and misunderstandings possibly have a higher chance of happening now. Focus on improving your communication, open-ness and honesty are the order of the day. Be sure to double check important documents and arrangements before finalising them.

Don't push the river, go with the flow - even if it circles around a time or two.

Retrogrades are great times to surrender, remember, reflect, release and rest.

Happy, gentle, soft and restful Imbolc to you.

ON CHANGE: 148
I want a life where the green grass comes to meet me at my doorstep and a nearby tree welcomes my hug, as I lean my back against its support and sink my toes into the warm, pulsing heartbeat of the Earth.

I want a life where joy is second nature to me, not something I have to chase or buy or save up for.

Something that is made every day, by me, through me and shared.

I want my work to be about giving of myself, of my talents, of my heart. Where I reach out and out again to the world to share, impact and to love.

I crave a slower life.

A simpler life.

Yet a full life – full of moments.

I like to wake up and rest on the movement of my breath.

I like to wrap up my patchwork blanket, hug the cat and feel my body stretch and realign as I come out of sleep and dreams.

I like to open my eyes and stay there for ages, doing absolutely nothing.

I am learning slowly after this period of global retreat how to feel "enough" when I don't have a schedule knocking at my mind's door along with a raging "to-do list".

I want to live a life where simply BEING is the way - my new job description.

Is it weird that if I've never dreamt of wearing Prada or Louboutin?

Instead, I find my greatest comfort from soft sweaters and faded t-shirts that hold memories like a hug.

Is it weird that I just want to do what I love without explaining "why"? Oh the freedom of not needing to justify it to you or, for that matter, to me.

What if my greatest goal is to be filled up with a sense of peace and serenity for as many hours a day as I can stand it?

And what if I withdraw my investments in what other people think?

Is it allowed for me to create a career of moments after moments of sharing and contributing in ways that will never really be recognised or lauded?

And getting a cheap thrill from the completely under-the-radar invisible ones - they are between me and my God.

I don't want what the world seems to want for me. I want to follow the coordinates that my soul whispers into my heart now, moment by moment.

ON TUGGING AT THE ROOTS: 149
It's not yet time - Spring has not yet sprung.
I've found myself resisting the recent extended snow downloads, mildly irritated by them and in complaining mode.

The lower vibe that had lasted too long revisited yesterday and is today demanding another day or two of rest. It is still winter, I'm reminded. It's not yet time to push forward.

On chatting to friends and listening to clients I realise I'm not alone. They too are frustrated by the long winter and all its demands on mind and body.

Our ancestors adjusted their rhythms to the available hours of light and constraints of weather, to the rhythms of Mother Nature. They slept when it was dark, stored up supplies of fuel and food, entertained themselves quietly indoors and rested (often sleeping much more) until the first true signs of spring arrived.

Now we expect we should have the same productivity and energy levels all year round, perhaps due to the advent of electric light, 24-hour TV and 24/7 shopping. A time to rest doesn't seem to have its place in our seasonal calendar.

The snowy weather and the return of the lower ebb/vibe

reminded me it's still a time to germinate, incubate and hibernate. It's still a time for fires and cosy blankets, hot baths with candles, good books and box sets, steaming bowls of soup and stews, woolly tights and warm boots, scarves and hats, snugly duvets and throws.

Can I surrender to these last few weeks of wonderful winter things?

The push through and growth of the blossoms of springtime ARE on the way, just not yet.

ON LOVE: 150
Love is a decision.
Love is a verb.
Love is not a feeling
Love is a discipline.
Love is a practice.

Love in action

is a thing to behold;

the soul knows and

the heart sings.

Love is for giving

to be shared.

and to be fully received.

Love is forgiving -

it doesn't count.

You can refuse love,

but you can never lose it.

Once given

It never dies.

You are Love.

And Love Never Dies.

St. Valentine's Day 2021

ON GRACE: 151

Grace is the breath of love.

Only love can melt the invisible chains which imprison us in the misery of our inferiority, alienation and isolation. Our human despair.

Love breathes on and through us, love unlocks, unblocks and blows the breath of grace into our lives and of those around us.

We are called to breathe this love, this grace on to and into others locked in human misery and despair. It's why we're here.

Who needs your breath of love and grace today?

AFTER THE PANCAKES (ON LENT): 152

When I ran residential retreats down in the borders or on the island of Iona, we always had a fire on the Saturday night and sat around it, sharing what we wanted to let go of in our lives. Then we gave it away symbolically to the flames with a nature bundle of twigs and leaves wrapped in twine. Fire is a great symbol of purification and release.

We revisited next morning early doors and reflected on the previous night and how we wanted to move forward from this point, often incorporating a Vision Quest (a mindful walk to you or me) and took some ashes from the remains of the fire to cast upon a stream, a river or the sea - the tides of life. The living waters – the symbol of life itself.

Before we left the fire we each placed a thumbprint of the now cooled ashes on each other's foreheads (on the third eye chakra) as we recited the words I had grown up with from my Catholic origins that were always shared individually on Ash

Wednesday in this way:

"Angela, remember woman (or man) that you are dust, and into dust you shall return."

I have always loved this ritual.

The reminder that life is short, that I am blessed to be here, that I have THIS day and this day only, it's a pure gift and I should live it fully.

Keeping death on my shoulder is inspiring for me. It is truth that puts everything into perspective.

The reminder of the theme of impermanence that runs through all of the spiritual traditions of the world.

Everything changes. Nothing stays the same.

So this is the traditional ritual for the start of the Lenten season - six and a half weeks before the celebration of spiritual rebirth or resurrection. Forty days in the symbolic desert heading for home, the homecoming to the sacred heart.

Again, the traditions of the world all have their own way of "going into the desert", their initiations, retreats, withdrawals into the cave for purification to draw closer to God, the Great Spirit, Allah, Pure Mind, the Divine Creator, Maya, Gaia, The Mystery, The Mysterons... whatever word one might use to describe the totally indescribable - all that is.

After the reminder of impermanence from the ashes, Lent asks for a form of "fasting" - a form of self-denial as a purification tool.

This is far more than an ego trip of giving up chocolate and announcing my self-denial to the world for strokes. God could care less if I give up red wine/swearing (fat chance anyway) or meringues.

I can "fast" from my destructive or judgemental thinking, from expectations of others, from self-loathing. From self-harming attitudes, beliefs or behaviours. It can be a practice of adding value to the world and others in my life. Giving more of myself away in love to people or situations.

It should always be an act originating from love and practised with loving intention.

Fasting in whatever form is a deal with my soul that I will "sharpen my saw", bring my awareness into sharper focus. I am taming the tiger of my physical appetites and drawing closer to the God of my understanding. The creator, mother, source of life.

The I Am.

I mostly prefer to call her love.

And Love Never Dies.

For the record I'm a Catholic, Tibetan Buddhist, Jew, Celtic, Christian, dash of Wicca, Hindu, Zen, Part Pagan, Honorary Native American Yogi these days! Or in other words, I am ME.

ON LIVING WITH LOSING: 153
Elisabeth Kubler Ross wrote "the book" on death and dying.
Graham trained with her many years ago. She told him she regretted putting on paper the stages of grieving for the dying, the grieving, denial, anger, bargaining, acceptance etc.
She said people used it as a tick list and thought they were "doing it wrong" if they didn't fit the template/timeframe. She had noticed that about two years was quite common for some to visit the various stages. She felt she was taken too literally.

There are dozens of books on Amazon on grieving.

I've grieved before, lost friends and grandparents, beloved pets, miscarried, all were different. I've worked as a therapist for 35 years and sat for possibly thousands of hours with people going through loss and grief of many different types. Losing my father four years ago was different again.

I feel the notion of "closure" is foolhardy.

The stages and pathways of the dying and the grieving are NOT the same.

The dying die and get closure. The grieving do not. The notion of "acceptance" can be unhelpful. It can give us a destination to achieve a target, a goal.

For sure, we get on with our lives, we recalibrate, we re-adjust, we have fewer meltdown moments further apart, things get better over time but "closure"?

I'm not so sure we should be aiming for that.

Birthdays, anniversaries, movies with a death theme, a song on the radio, happy events without a loved one, a stranger with similar stature/features, similar handwriting can all be triggers that put us in touch with the loss, the "missing" of the beloved.

And we remember. RE-MEMBER. The event or trigger re-embodies us in our heart and the physical loss is reactivated.

This can take us by surprise, usually does and it doesn't understand time or the calendar. It may be three months, three years or 30 years after the death of our loved one that the even-deeper-still pain is felt.

These Heart Openings are not faults to be corrected. We are not on a disorganised timeline. Elizabeth Kubler Ross would be most apologetic for the confusion.

Time does not exist - it's a man-made concept. We need to take OUR own time.

When we allow the loss to be felt fully, no matter how far down the line we are, we open more to life in the present, not just the past.

If and when we don't, we will usually try to close down by anaesthetising ourselves with something, anything.

Alcohol, food, work and busy-ness, or any compulsive behaviour of avoidance. Or we create dramas and real-life painful experiences that we can hang the unwanted reawakened grief pain and anxiety on and declare "Ah! THAT'S why I feel so bad!"

So what CAN we do instead?

We can REMEMBER.

FEEL IT, through crying, smiling, laughing and crying some more. This is NOT Bi-Polar,

TALK IT through with an empathetic soulmate who won't shut you down, tell you to move on, shape up or get over it.

WRITE IT in a journal to express our feelings.

TAKE TIME and SPACE to reflect, remember, visit the grave, old home, special places, pull out the photos, cards, wear their jumper, scarf, slippers.

And most of all be warm and accepting of ourselves when we feel this vulnerable part in our heart asking for HEALING and ATTENTION... not CLOSURE. Not to be closed down.

We discover a beautiful landscape of vulnerability within which produces tremendous fruits and gifts, softness, empathy, awareness, connection and intuition. They all deepen as we connect within and beyond.

These are the Pearls of Grief however and whatever way, we need to live it without time or limit, no matter what the books say.

ON BEING REAL: 154
What on earth does that mean?
What does being authentic look like/feel like?

Well, as I sit here writing and preparing the content so I can deliver a Zoom conference tonight on my work as a Psychotherapist, I realise I'm still considering that question way down the line in my 61 years on the planet.

But maybe THAT is the point, the asking of the question.

What does "being real" really mean?

John Powell wrote a great wee book years ago entitled "Will The REAL Me Please Stand Up?".

It was timeless wisdom and one of the first "serious" books I ever read as a teenager, when I really needed that book.

Is it being a blustery version of myself and asserting my views like fireworks (with absolutely no humble opinion), telling it like it is - regardless of the impact? Is that being real?

Is it going a day without make-up?

Or is it something far deeper and much less simplistic?

As I revisit and reflect on that question, I'm reminded that it is all in the asking.

"What does it mean to be real?"

And what is the cost of straining and striving for the utterly impractical and impossible perfect version of me that cannot and does not exist. We are glorious in all of our messiness.

Well, I am today anyway.

MARCH/APRIL 2021

ON GOD: 155

How very dare I? Well ...I dare!

I woke up this morning with random thoughts and recent readings mingling and felt moved to share.

Richard Rohr talks about God being a VERB, an experience, an interactive relationship not a static notion or rational answer to a question. So, if asked what I'm doing today, my reply will be, "I'm away oot to God the world and I'm probably going to be God-ding most of the day."

What if there's a wee bit of God in us that wants to find herself? How awful if we ignored that longing inside and outside though, as quantum physics now tells us, that's really the same thing.

What if THE LONGING, the constant craving for that sense of

connection and security we all seek, IS the point?

What if THE SEARCHING is the meaning and it's not that we've failed because we don't know, can't be sure, are still seeking and exploring, looking for answers.

What if our EGO (though it does a marvellous job in so many areas, got us outta those swamps and works on so many levels evolving us and getting things done) has no effective built-in braking system and can become a relentless and ruthless driver. It drives us towards "perfection".

Just how is that working for me and my planet today?

Dr. Wayne Dyer used to say, "If you knew who walked beside you, you would never know fear again." What if that's true? How would I do things differently without the fear.

What if I actively practiced changing channels in my head and my heart from the "lack channel" and the "self-pity and resentment channel". To the "gratitude" and "sense of awe" channels. They are ALL there on your inner remote control. Where you put your focus, you will BE.

But this requires daily practice to establish a good quality signal and reception.

There are ways of the heart which function like keys unlocking the chains, padlocks and the prison cell we find ourselves in, so that the breeze of eternity can breathe on us and in us. Gratitude and appreciation breathe grace and blessings into our lives.

ON THE SEARCH FOR GOD: 156
You need to work up to this, start small, baby steps and easy does it.

St. Bonaventure in the 13th century said we should start by loving the simplest things and then move up from there. "Let us place our first step at the bottom, presenting the whole material world as a mirror, so we may pass over to God who shines in created things."

Richard Rohr advises -

"Don't start by trying to love God, or even people.

Love rocks and elements first.

Only then move to trees, then animals, and then much later, humans".

It works.

In fact, it might be the only way to love, because how you do anything is how you do everything.

"Why wait until Heaven when you can experience divine flow right now?" he asks.

I tweaked above what he ackchewally said just a totie wee bit, for ease.

Why indeed Richard?

How can you and I wake up to the innate beauty of the natural world and connect with the soul in all things?

When I learn to appreciate and to BE in nature, he tells me I am "situated in the one loving gaze that unites all things".

This is enlightenment. I don't actually need to get a sore bum sitting on a cushion for forty years in an ashram on a mountain in Tibet, or up The Campsies.

As I spend more time in the natural world with slow, quiet focus and attention, the connection strengthens, my relationship grows and contentment deepens, with more silence and stillness. I meet deep appreciation and total awe.

I can progress from pretty crystals and rocks to the scent of herbs, the perfume and vibrant colour of flowers and the pulse and vibration trees, to the language of clouds and stars, to the music of streams, stillness of ponds and lochs, vastness of landscapes and views, to the winged birdsong of feathery angels and the inherent majesty of animals.

And soon enough, I can be using the same practice with people, starting off with easier-to-love people. Then in time working up to the "more challenging" of the human species.

And in time, with practice, I will progress to the source of all of the above, love herself. Which I call God.

ON HOW REAL LOVE WORKS: 157
A REAL friendship is a way to experience love and helps us access divine love.

If you have never let Mother Earth love you, you'll have a challenge loving from a deeper place.

But grace can help here.

And so can Richard Rohr and, first, St. John of the Cross:

"You give a piece of yourself to someone.

You see a piece of yourself in them (usually unconsciously).

This allows them to return the favour.

You do not need or demand anything back.

You are engaged in 'Bigger Gazing and Loving'.

This creates an inner aliveness.

(Simply to love is its own reward)

You accept being accepted for no reason and by no criteria whatsoever.

This is the key that unlocks everything.

Both in me and for others.

And towards love itself (which I call God)."

Richard says:

"What I let God see and accept in me becomes what I can then see and accept in myself, in my friends, and in everything else.

This is why it is crucial to allow our higher power - whatever that is, whatever we call it, and at least one other trusted person to see us in our imperfection and even our nakedness. To be seen as I really am.

Rather than as I would ideally like to be seen.

And that's why I must give others this same experience of being seen in their imperfection."

Warts 'n all, even my messy, narky, whiny, moany, bitter, twisted, raging, selfish, bitchy bits.

This love, this grace, is the only love that validates, transforms and changes us at the deepest levels.

It's what we are all searching and longing for, it's why we're here.

Once I allow it in, I become a conduit for others. In fact, nothing less will do any more.

ON THE THRESHOLD: 158

We are in an embryonic state right now, not quite half-cooked, but on the way. One reality is over, finished, kaput. The next way not yet birthed or even formed.

This can feel utterly terrifying depending on who you listen to and how you view things. Or it can be very exciting, we can feel privileged. It may well be a bit of both. We stand just next to the threshold of a whole new way of living and being.

Can you feel the charge of that in the ether? What a responsibility. What a time to be alive!

Let's face it, we were in utter denial and on the brink of watching our beautiful planet have a complete breakdown over the next few decades on OUR watch. We really thought we could have it all without regard for the cost.

Now the maps on the drawing boards have been torn up. All bets are off and all is to play for.

We are betwixt and between. Richard Rohr's LIMINAL space.

When our lives hit a transition point - a beloved dies, we lose our job, get a diagnosis, our relationship hits the skids, there is the birth of a child, it is a special time of grace.

But it sure as hell disnae feel like any kinda grace at the time

We feel upended, in a tailspin and confused, totally NOT in control.

Just like now.

The vulnerability of liminal space creates a gap for something new to enter stage left. We are wide open, receptive, a clean slate and chalk in front of us.

We need to be silent instead of speaking (harder for some of us than others), experience emptiness, anonymity instead of persona and image and have less instead of more.

We are suspended at the moment and for the foreseeable on this long one-world retreat between at least two worlds - the one we knew and the one yet to come.

Our wiring has been forever changed and so by osmosis has that of every future generation. We cannot put the genie back in the bottle.

Now what shall we do with all that magical spirit that's been released in a world that has been crying out for it for so long?

MAY/JUNE 2021

CHAMPAGNE ON A SCHOOL NIGHT: 159

Mammogram result in for the remainder

First full year since treatment ended, ALL CLEAR.

I cannot describe the feeling.

Just canny.

NOTHING matters but your health.

Not the weather, not rotten TV programmes, not your weight or football scores.

NOTHING!

Love your body like the precious temple it is and remember to GREET-PRAY-LOVE.

LIVING IN THE MOMENT: 160

Today may be a very momentous day, after a few days or weeks of heightened anxiety.

All during what has been a very momentous week, Chancer results, 20th wedding anniversary, mum turning 85 and now possibly another life-changer and page-turner.

But it may not, so I have to learn to hold the tension.

It is all to play for and out of my control.

I'm trying to stay in the moment to get me through this momentous day and embrace it.

Many friends and their families are going through tests and procedures after investigations, some with real big stuff to deal with and I'm really familiar with that kind of waiting, anxiety, terror.

It's all about the breathing, I find, and how soft and loose I can keep my hands - no claw- like gripping.

And how soft I can keep my jaw and neck - with my shoulders not up round my ears like a grinning chimpanzee.

And how soft I can keep my belly, like kneaded dough, how long and soft I can keep my toes - not curling and gripping in my sandals like staples.

Even though it's a bittersweet time.

I suspect today will be one of those days I will never ever forget - IF it happens today.

To be continued.

END OF AN ERA: 161

With a heavy heart, I handed over the keys yesterday to the new owner of our beautiful Harvest Clinic building, Saad from Iraq. The family will be wonderful caretakers of our nest, a family of doctors with open hearts and such a great sense of humour.

We clicked from the start.

Gifts were exchanged, though my tin of Scottish shortbread and book entitled "Things To Do In Glasgow" (Saad is moving up from London) paled into insignificance against the stunning homemade plate of baklava and sweetmeats Amina had brought, along with gorgeous summer flowers.

But we were handing over the building, NOT the BUSINESS. The Harvest will reshape in a simpler, gentler, quieter form over the months.

We all exchanged blessings for the future and hugs in the reception hall and hopes that we can meet up for a promised afternoon tea in the garden to see how the journey unfolds for us all.

It has been a fraught time with many challenges as commercial property is different and more complicated than residential.

This was my baby. We were in THIS building for 26 years (though I had been up in Park Quadrant for nine years prior working solo). It was a huge chunk of my life.

But things change. The loss of my dad, a year of Breast Chancer treatment, Covid dancing, lockdown yo-yoing, fearful therapists leaving. The signs were becoming pretty clear late last year that it was time for change. Everything was pointing to a new chapter.

And so now, that new book begins and it's good to know that everyone seems settled in their new abodes.

Irene is now hosting Marian and Elaine up at Kelvingrove Park, Maureen has just opened her new place round at Firhill and Morag is gonna be in the area shortly too.

So the Harvest seeds live on through all of their new ventures.

Of course most of the others (too many to mention) have been in their new spaces for a while and we continue referring on.

Me and G though just want to draw breath for now, enjoy the sunshine and the summer and will introduce our new Harvest @ Home Studio shortly, which will be our base-camp out in the countryside overlooking the Campsies.

No commute, no traffic, no parking issues and the sound of birdsong, not the M8 as background.

It's bittersweet of course. I'm grateful for all of it and we are delighted we found such gorgeous people to hand over to, who I know will care for the building and who recognise its healing energy.

But I'm ready now, after 26 years of working within a community, sharing my space, negotiating with and supporting up to 20 members of staff at a time.

Running a training college as Principal of Scotland, working most weekends lecturing and having the responsibility of employees was pretty much 24/7 on the brain power

but we loved it (mostly).

I couldn't have done any of it without the immense support of Lord G, Marian and the team - you know who you are.

We will arise in different form soon enough but now is for reminiscing, grieving a little, and dreaming of new beginnings. The Harvest indeed.

LOVE NEVER DIES: 162

"You have the strength and dignity of that oak tree centred in the field on the road to Perth, the tree you loved.

You bring the warmth of sunshine whenever you're around.

When you smile the world smiles with you too.

Like the surface of Tannoch Loch, where as a child you took me to feed ducks on Sundays, you have a stillness and a depth that calms and reassures.

You share the comfort blanket of a night sky with the silent power of an owl in flight and wisdom in its wide stretched wings to enfold.

Your faith is a radiant light beam.

Your patience deep as the rocks around Columba's Bay.

You crossed the veil four years or more - why write in present tense?

Your love lives on right here and now.

And with it your presence."

By Angela Trainer

June 2021

Happy Father's Day Dad

Love NEVER Dies

JULY 2021

KEEP YER HAIR ON: 163

I posted a photo lately that a lot of people kindly remarked on, my hair was looking particularly healthy and full. So many people comment on my new post-treatment mane.

I had thin fine baby hair all my life.

I lay the credit for the long lustrous locks I am enjoying today at the feet of three wonderful and super-skilled women: Irene, Caroline and Janice.

I kept my nails, my hair grew in like Coco the clown and my skin has never been better. It wasn't luck.

Don't be like Ange, don't wait until you have the Chancer, support your body to be the very best it can be NOW.

Do your body and hair a favour - check out these women.

www.irenemccabe.com

www.homeopathfife.co.uk

www.blognourishedbynature.com

BEING IN THE PRESENCE OF LOVE: 164

My soul reveals herself/himself when I ask, "how can I look for Love's presence in my day?".

How do I expand my heart, not contract?

How can I keep my heart, mind and soul open, even when I feel utterly closed and shut down?

Richard Rohr says contemplation is a way to bring heaven to Earth - but it usually involves losing.

Losing my fixed views and my solid overprotected stance.

I need to enter with curiosity and openness.

I need to stop defending myself and my ego.

We try to protect ourselves from our shadow with an armour of steel over our soul and over our dodgy, unconscious motives.

I settle for being right instead of being whole and therefore holy.

I say prayers instead of being a prayer.

Contemplation is really quite down to earth. It does not require life in a monastery.

But I do need some "social distancing" and detachment from the distractions and delusions of our world and my false self.

When I try to use my limited 'thinking tool' for problems, I rarely get very far.

But when I allow and encounter mystery, worlds open to me.

Oftentimes mother nature or simply the contemplation of colour, opens the gateway into my soul, my true self and I can find a path into my soul and to love's presence in gardens and woods and in nature.

I find the soul's garden.

A STUDIO IS BORN: 165
The Harvest Clinic @ Home

It was January. It was freezing when the rebirth of the Harvest was conceived, the original Harvest Clinic in Charing Cross wasn't even sold yet - what were we thinking?

But we were not thinking at all of giving up our practices, or me running some retreats and workshops in the future, so lockdown provided the time and the space to gestate some ideas about how to transform our oversized garage into a steampunk loft space in a rural countryside location.

And tomorrow we have our inaugural and very small Reiki 2 group by special request. It's exciting and nerve-wracking all at once. I last taught Reiki before my Chancer journey back in April 2019.

ON HEALING: 166

Sometimes people steal our power, sometimes we give it away; sometimes we steal it from others. We don't always recognise that's what we are doing but if we scratch the surface and look deeper, we often find that we are.

Life can be a series of power plays if we sleepwalk through it or we can awaken from the trance dance and learn how to EMPOWER our own circuits without downsizing others, or bigging ourselves up with the usual external trappings (money, power, status, stuff, looks, achievements).

Sometimes we are very afraid of our own insignificance. As a therapist, I see so many clients with self-worth and confidence issues. After all these years, I still wrestle with my own, perhaps just not so often or for so long.

Perhaps we just learn to live with our vulnerability more comfortably, befriend our fearful and insecure selves and return the broken parts back to the love which lives at our centre. Always waiting and welcoming of our return.

I love what Ram Dass says about being around people who make us feel intimidated or insecure around them. The people who play power games. He describes the very intimidating and powerful "Grand Man" he met who mirrored back irrelevance and insignificance in his response to meeting RD.

He glazed over in his lack of interest in anything RD may have to say or offer. He felt himself shrink and wither, felt off balance, knowing he had to spend two days at a conference working with him.

He noticed the collapse within himself and the loss of his essence around this colleague. He simply stayed with it, watched it, noticed the desire to compete, impress, or run and hide, criticise or dismiss "Mr Big".

He did none of the above. He simply stayed with the feelings as they arose, noticed them and observed his internal reactions to the "Grand Man."

Not immediately but in time, they dissolved like clouds parting in sunlight. Soon all he saw was not an intimidating "Grand Man" at all. Just someone who was doing the best he could with what he had available to him. Some of his behaviours and attitudes were not appealing but no longer intimidating or threatening to RD. He simply saw a good man doing his best.

He found himself softened, open, receptive, welcoming the other - just as he was. He felt love and compassion for the "Man"- without judgement of either of them. It was a healing experience on the inside.

James Taylor sings a song by Carole King called "You've got a Friend". I like to sing it every now and then to someone special who really needs to hear it.. ME.

ON LIVING HELL: 167
Sometimes in life we are faced with what we perceive as the lowest of the lows.

What mostly gets us through is knowing that from experiences of things we don't want, always in time comes a growth opportunity.

And then, from that growing comes an equal amount of joy later on. But not yet.

In these moments of crisis in life, if you can stay fairly calm and centred, as best you can, realising that "this too shall pass", you will come out on the other side stronger and wiser.

Love conquers all and real love never dies (counterfeit "love" will always fizzle out like sherbet).

Even when those you love act like they hate you, if you refuse that hate with love, even though you reject the behaviour, the hatred dissipates over time and all that is left in the end is that true, sacred bond of love.

And that is the elusive UNCONDITIONAL love we read and hear about but struggle to sustain.

Everything else pales into insignificance in its wake (but it is tough work).

Today, dig deep and find the source of love within you. Let it flow through you no matter what circumstances you find yourself in.

You may need to take yourself to be in nature for some time, lie in a salt bath with a lit candle to focus on, or immerse yourself deeply in a book that inspires and soothes you.

Lie out on a blanket and sky-watch.

Make tea and put on meaningful music to really listen to with no distractions. Or just lie on the floor with a cushion and a blanket over you, wet tea bags over your puffy eyes, surrendered to the world.

Find the chunk of light and hold on tight. DO NOT LET GO.

If you lose your hold, get right back on it and re-find your grip.

Know that the "not so good" or even the 'living hell' will pass in time and remember to breathe whatever you do.

Keep opening your palms and your arms wide and physically release the pain as you fully exhale and even release a big sigh of lamenting. Laments are prayer of pain release, usually mostly just gasps, sobs or tears.

Tension builds up in that heart space to keep it open, soft and free.

Literally hand over the broken bits of you and the broken people of your life, the wounders, the wounds and the scars, back to the source of love for healing.

Pour love on yourself and your situation and let it dissolve.

Good breathing, nourishing foods, movement, rest, rays of light and lots of hydration work well (a big glass of water NOW).

The more you can soothe YOURSELF, the more powerful the growth.

Elevate your way out of the pain body/field - that's where we get sick.

No matter what the messages from the world outside of you.

You are love and you are loved.

Repeat hourly until the crisis passes and the second stage of healing begins - the insights/messages.

ON THE WISDOM OF NO ESCAPE: 168

Nobody escapes.

Pain and suffering are part of the deal, it's just the type and frequency that vary. Even Jesus and Buddha agreed that to live is to suffer.

Love hurts - it costs to love and beneath the pain of living and losing lies a reservoir of even deeper love, the timeless, endless variety that our wee spiritual circuits have trouble sustaining.

Loving and living break us open.

They rewire us, upgrade, increase our capacity and raise our frequency if we allow it. But there are growing pains in the process.

Pain and suffering are not mistakes or obstacles. They transform us one way or the other.

Sometimes pain makes us twisted and bitter. We withdraw into misery and isolate ourselves, becoming cynical and critical.

Or we may shift into denial, morphing into the manic hysteria of phony surface positivity and synthetic optimism.

We can give ourselves and everybody around us a headache with our lack of congruence.

We may alternatively employ the old defence mechanisms of

Projection - "It's all you not me!"

Regression - "Where's my dummy/booze/chocolate?"

Displacement – "I need a new job, new house, new car, new partner, a holiday.."

Denial - "I'm brand new thanks, La De Dah!"

Much better we explore and digest our suffering to sit with it, unpack it and befriend it.

This is best done with a trusted soul friend or a competent therapist. But some long solitary walks, journal-writing and quiet thinking time may well be of great use as long as self-pity and resentment (victimhood) have a limited amount of airtime and healthy exploration is the goal.

This prevents us playing pass-the-parcel with our pain and reduces our knee-jerk responses to life.

It helps us stop returning any volleys of hatred or hostility, malice or spite that come with the territory of living alongside human beings.

Especially during this time of high volatility emotional tsunami living just now.

We are "only human after all."

Pain and hurt can be our greatest teachers when we stop denying or trying to hide, fade or fix things that are bringing us to our knees.

When we stop, embrace and accept our pain breakdown we allow a breakthrough to a deeper level of understanding.

I need to surrender first, to hold my own hurt and allow love to enter and transform my sacred wounds.

When we simply hold the tension, embrace the pain, it CAN transform us. But we often want to chew on it with our minds, ruminating and asking "why me?".

This disnae help.

Why you?

Just because. Why NOT you?

It's SUPPOSED to be hard!

And remember there will be people in therapy because of you too.

To grow in love and not float on the surface or live on the margins means to hold the poles, the feckin' maddening polarity of life, lightly. Until our horizons expand.

When we do this, we move beyond our own personal pain and ego. It's like we drop through time, identify and connect with every tear ever shed.

I remember when my father was dying, feeling a connection with every person who had ever sat watching by the bedside of their loved one as they were dying. I felt their circle of grief and love surround me and carry me through the thresholds of loss in the months to come.

When we hold it and allow our own pain to be transformed, we embrace the wounds of the world and when we work on our own healing, we help others work on healing too.

I borrowed the title for this piece from Pema Chodron's book - one of my favourites. If you related to this post, you may find her book helpful – it is called "Wisdom Of No Escape". She writes from a Zen Buddhist perspective. Richard is a Franciscan priest - but they are a perfect fit.

169

Some of my favourite things for healing the soul when the tides are low.
Sitting by a tree spine to trunk.
Telling the coos all about it.

A favourite prayer.

A welcome visit from nature, be it butterfly, bird or bee, a candle and a dose of silence.

What are yours?

AUGUST 2021

HOW LOVE MOVES IN: 170

Two of my circle have just lost friends very suddenly, others are wading through anniversarial grief and some are deep in anticipatory grief. These are all grief in familiar form - unfathomable.

There are various layers of grief not easily identifiable - the pain of watching a world on fire, melting or flooded and still the mindless violence and wars which roll on unabated.

There is violence around us closer to home too in the ongoing Covid dilemma. The pain of the disrespect of various views - words like "bullshit", "nonsense", "idiots" and worse - are bandied and hurled around by BOTH sides.

Views are slammed down, the anxiety and fear from ALL ANGLES sneered at or ridiculed.

So much certainty - no middle ground, few concessions or understanding of confusion and very little respect from so many humans for each other at this time and it's all growing like the wildfires we see in the world. Some folks are drowning in the confusion and conflicting information they are being flooded with and the sniper attacks are on the increase along with the terrorism of judgement.

Then there are les petit morts (the little deaths) that spin us into loss we don't always recognise or acknowledge. Loss of health or mobility, loss of the known and familiar, loss of looks, loss of relationships, friendships or colleagues, loss of face, loss of career or change of working environment.

Loss of faith or trust in the world.

Loss of faith or trust in the universe/God/Love/Gaia/The Mystery/The Mysterons or however you refer to any power greater than you in the world.

I've had some grim times in recent years there is a still a hurting place easily bumped against. Do we ever really "get over it" perfectly for all time?

Absolutely not. They all move on, but we don't always keep up pace.

And as with any loss, the world slides on - oh usually about a month after the funeral - but the heavy heart canny keep up the pace.

Sure, we can practice toxic positivity or emotional repression but there is a cost for that. We often bleed out in another area of our life.

But even the most resilient, revered, connected and plugged-in teachers, saints and masters had their long, dry times of deep grief, loss and fear.

Yep, Christ, Buddha, The Prophet, Luther King, Mandela, Maya Angelou, Malala, John of The Cross, Gandhi, Eckhart Tolle, to name a very few.

"Gonnae take this cup away fae me..." was one famous line but reiterated by most who felt they had reached their limit. What chance have WE got?

But it's what happened next that made the difference.

After the surrender, the realisation. When ego moves over,

when all else failed, when they handed it over, there was more room for LOVE to move in.

How can I, you, we, make the space and allow pure love into our own life and then into the world?

171

Hearing from so many in heightened turmoil through the clinic phone line and emails from chronic insomnia, wagon-falling-off, smoking habits revisited, coke uptake (and not the fizzy stuff), relationships crumbling and joint rolling (not yoga).

Seems the sunshine gives only a fairly temporary lift before the angst returns.

I know. I have felt my own feelings and emotions rise and rise at various times and stages of our Covid paindemic - the chocolate tin has become a guilty secret hidden behind the crispbreads.

I found solace and comfort from Richard Roger's writings today so I'll share. It's mostly him - but I've adjusted and adapted for a wider audience.

Elisabeth Kübler-Ross defined the well-known stages of grief and dying, denial, anger, bargaining, resignation and acceptance.

That fella Job in yon olde book exemplified them aeons ago.

The first seven days of Job's time on the "dung heap" of pain are spent in silence, the immediate response matching the first stage - denial. Then he reaches the anger stage, where he shouts and curses at life, at God. He says, in effect, "This so-called life I have is not really life, God, it's death. So why should I be happy?".

Perhaps some of us have been there - hurt and devastated by our losses that we echo Job's cry about the day he was born.

"May that day be darkness.. may no light shine on it. May murk and deep shadow claim it".

I think today we'd just scream "F*** you!".

But he uses beautiful, poetic imagery.

He's saying: "Uncreate the day. Make it not a day of light, but darkness."

Where Genesis speaks "Let there be light", Job insists "Let there be darkness."

The day of uncreation, of anti-creation. We probably have to have experienced true depression to understand such a feeling.

W. H. Auden expressed his grief in much the same way in his poem "Funeral Blues" which ends with these lines:

"The stars are not wanted now: put out every one,

Pack up the moon and dismantle the sun,

Pour away the ocean and sweep up the woods;

For nothing now can ever come to any good."

There's a part of each of us that feels and speaks that sadness.

Not every day, thank goodness.

But if we're willing to feel and participate in the pain of the world, we must also allow grace to lead us there as the events of life show themselves.

We must go through the stages of feeling, not only the last death but all the earlier little deaths.

If we bypass these emotional stages they take a deeper form of disguise and come out in another way.

Many of us learn the hard way by getting ulcers, by all kinds of internal diseases, depression, addictions, irritability and misdirected rage because we refuse to let their emotions find some appropriate place to share.

I am convinced that people who do not feel deeply finally do not know deeply either.

It is only when we are willing to feel our emotions that we are able to come to grips with the mystery in our head, heart and gut.

Then we are working our way through our fear and loss.

THE GIFT OF TEARS: 172

The human instinct is to block suffering and pain. This is especially true in the West - as anyone who has experienced grief can attest, it isn't rational. We really don't know how to hurt. We haven't a Scooby what to do with our pain.

The wisdom traditions try to teach us grief isn't something from which to run. It's a liminal space, time of transformation, an initiation if you like.

In fact, we can't risk getting rid of pain until we've learned what it has to teach us and grief, suffering, loss or pain ALWAYS have something to teach us.

Unfortunately, most of us have been taught grief and sadness are something to deny or avoid. We would rather be angry than sad.

Grief is "unfinished hurt". It feels like a demon spinning around inside of us and it hurts too much.

We have to learn to remain open, to wait with patience for what it has to teach us. When we close in too tightly around our sadness or our grief, when we try to fix it, control it, or understand it, we only deny ourselves its lessons.

In days of yore, Holy tears were a common experience. Saints Francis and Clare of Assisi reportedly wept all the time for days on end. The "weeping mode" really is a different way of being in the world. It's different than the fixing, explaining or controlling mode.

We are free to feel the tragedy of things, the sadness of things. Tears cleanse the lens of the eyes so we can begin to see more clearly.

Maybe they even help us clear our world and world view.

Sometimes we have to cry for a very long time because our eyes are so dirty that we're not seeing truthfully or well at all.

Tears only come when we realise we can't fix or change the picture. We may be in shock, the reality absurd, unjust, wrong or impossible. How can they be dead? How did it come to this? How can this paindemic be happening?

It's usually when we are led to the edges of our resources that we are moved to tears.

The way we can tell our tears have cleansed us is after them we don't need to blame anybody, even ourselves. It's an utter transformation and cleansing of the soul and we know it came from beyond our own will.

I , Angela, have often referred to tears as heart melts and crying as tenderising the heart.

It is what it is, and somehow love is present in the gift of tears.

By Richard Rohr

With a wee bit of help from me.

THE WAY: 173

Things heat up as the numbing effects of shock of recent times wears off and the novelty of returned freedoms wane.

For many, emotions heighten, inner repressed emotions come to the boil and yes, it really can take months for things to sink in, reality to bite and reaction formation to unfold.

I see it in my own life, my friends and family and the folks I've been working with in therapy.

And we all see it on our TV screens.

The old unhealed, buried alive stuff will come up for air from the becalmed deep time of lockdown and percolate to the surface.

Apologies to the really busy frontline folks whose lives became more busy than ever and who desperately need some quiet and still time, I hear ya too.

We may feel out of control.

Well, we ARE to a degree.

But we CAN have our feelings without letting them have US.

When we feel out of control, we often tap into very old feelings from early childhood - think of that rage, that sobbing, that huff, that stomping upstairs with accompanying slammed door. Ring any bells?

If we were to follow through, act out then FEEL the feelings without stuffing down the doughnut/s, half a ciabatta (okay - whole ciabatta), smoking the fags-vape-joint, downing the Shiraz, bottle of cucumber gin (pretending it's one of your five a day) plink- plunking the co-codamol for the phantom pain, we would see feel and hear a frightened child saying, "I want my mum."

Do not shame for love's sake and do not blame. Be the loving "'mum" to your terrified inner child. YOU are the parent now, it's YOUR job.

It can be overwhelming.

Feel totally out-of-character.

It's not, it's you.

They are YOUR feelings - I promise.

They have just been in lockdown for a long time in a pressure cooker.

Soothe yourself, hug yourself, listen to what your inner child has to say about how she or he feels, write it all oot in a journal).

Take them to the park, wear something playful, bright and colourful, sit wrapped in a fluffy blanket, read them a lovely story, play in the bath bubbles, sing out loud, draw pictures or make some fun creative play stuff just for fun. Sleep 'n' weep with your arms wrapped tight around you, wear the zany earnings you talk yourself out of (and that's just the guys), spend close-up time in nature, or around animals, dance to loud music.

Order a hula hoop, skipping ropes, a childhood game, mindful colouring-in books, acrylic paints, talk NICELY to yourself, hold hands with your wee scared child inside and be there with them and for them THIS TIME AROUND.

And remember, you are loved and you are LOVE.

ON TURMOIL: 174
"When things go wrong, as they sometimes will when the road you're travelling seems all uphill.."
QUIT! Yes, you heard me right. QUIT.

Quit ruminating in the fallout, or "the sting of your setback". I love Tim Storey's take on rumination and resentment - "stop cursing, nursing and rehearsing". I don't know about you but I can get stuck in that loop so easily, like a CD track on repeat.

It can be a latent side effect of early trauma so don't beat yourself up about it, just catch it when you can.

We all experience diversions from our well-trodden path and the life map. According to my ego, on a regular basis we are redirected from where WE think we should be going.

If you live long enough, you're gonna go through more tricky times and we begin to recognise that the core meaning and design of my life really isn't based on MY outcomes, MY ego's desires and MY goals. We can however live in "authentic hope."

Sure, we can influence our life's design - goals and intentions are helpful as ski-poles but the design of the ski run? I rather think not.

When my life is in turmoil, I need to STOP as soon as I spot it and pull over into the next soul service station.

When we are heart sick - it's time to tune into the frequency of love.

We need inner and outer peace to find the presence of love. The answers are already inside of us, we just need to remember who we are.

We may find a way to remember and find direction by praying it upwards, by meditating on it inwards, by going outwards in nature, in creativity, movement or by reaching out to others. But we do well to watch what we "consume" at these times of vulnerability to what and who we let into our energy field.

GET OFF THE COUCH OR OUTTA BED.

TAKE BABY STEPS: ONE AT A TIME

REPEAT "What I am about to do today (say what it is), although a tiny step, will create and influence my tomorrow".

REPEAT LAST ONE AGAIN

IT'S NOT ABOUT THE HUGE STUFF, IT NEVER EVER WAS. THEY LIED!

REPEAT "SMALL IS THE NEW BIG."

WRITE DOWN THREE THINGS THAT ARE GOING RIGHT OR YOU ARE GRATEFUL FOR (e.g. I am breathing).

Dr Martin Seligman has scientifically proven this to improve

mood within a couple of weeks but do it DAILY. It helps you access resources and resilience pockets in your mind. You begin to get your mojo back.

WALK WITH THE WISE: find your tribe. Connect with people who will help you feed your soul, there are a million groups, organisations, traditions out there - just find ONE.

Here's a clue: art, dance, reiki, learn a new skill, music, film club, choir, walking, rambling, church groups, meditation, tai-chi, yoga, politics, eco-conservation, 12-step groups, befriending, volunteering.

Some people can suck the life out of us, especially when our tanks are low but often when they are full too. So watch out, they don't know how to properly fill their own tanks so they steal from ours.

Avoid while you are low ebb.

AND before you feel too superior here, we do this ourselves at times.

Raise your vibe with like-minded empowered people.

REPEAT "MY LIFE IS NOT ALL ABOUT ME, IT'S ABOUT HOW I CAN EXPAND MY HEART AND ALL THE PEOPLE I CAN LOVE AND TOUCH HEARTS WITH."

HUG YOURSELF TIGHT NOW FOR READING THIS TO THE END, YOU ARE A FINISHER.

SO GO DO ONE TOTIE WEE PART OF IT NOW.

ON HOPE: 175

It's easy to lose hope. It's easy to become overwhelmed, to rant and rail against our circumstances. I regularly and often felt a sense of despair overtake me, especially when tired, when things went wrong and on days where it seemed like too high a climb with on the Chancer journey.

On days like those, I find the words of Clarissa Pinkola Estes very comforting and empowering.

She rattles my chakras, straightens my spine and strengthens my core. I feel reminded of who I am and am reminded that I am part of a team. When I walk through the storm, I never walk alone.

I paraphrased, shortened and edited a fair bit. She writes beautifully and poetically but it can be too flowery for some. Apologies to the purist fans, the cropping and alterations are all mine.

"We were made for these times.

We are in shock about the state of our world. We are bewildered and enraged over the degradation of people, especially the vulnerable and our planet that's happening on a daily basis.

The hubris and arrogance some engage in while endorsing callous acts against those who are vulnerable, heinous acts against children, elders, the poor, the helpless, is breathtaking.

Please don't spend your spirit dry by bemoaning and bewailing these difficult times.

Especially do not lose hope.

WE WERE MADE FOR THESE TIMES.

For years, we have been learning, practising, been in training for and just waiting to meet, HERE.

There have never been more awakened souls, never more able

vessels in the waters than there are right now across the world and they are fully ready and able to signal one another, as never before in the history of humankind.

There are millions of boats of righteous souls on the ocean with you. Even though you may shiver from every wave on this stormy sea, I assure you, your boat is made from such strong wood, from a great magnificent forest and it will withstand the storms, hold its own, and sail on regardless.

In dark times, there is a tendency to faint over how much is wrong or broken in our world. Do not focus on that. There is a tendency to become weakened by dwelling on what is outside your reach, by what cannot yet be.

Don't focus there. That is wasting the power of the wind without hoisting your sails."

SEPTEMBER/ OCTOBER 2021

ON COMPASSION: 176

Compassion means to suffer with.

It isn't a pink, fluffy, hippie love for others.

It is the ability to walk beside, to understand to "stand under" another no matter where they are at.

It is the ultimate exercise of the spiritual heart and is one of the fruits of meditation, reflection and contemplation.

My guiding light, Richard Rohr writes in his book "Eager to Love" that through meditation and prayer... "we will naturally become much more compassionate and patient toward just about everything."

When we sit still and quiet with ourselves in love and simply "hold space" for ourselves in stillness and quiet in the presence of love, we become better able to do this with and for others.

"Compassion changes everything. Compassion heals. Compassion mends the broken and restores what has been lost. Compassion draws together those who have been estranged or never even dreamed they were connected. Compassion pulls us out of ourselves and into the heart of another, placing us on holy ground."

"Compassion springs out of vulnerability and triumphs in connection," writes Judy Cannaton.

And me, I say, this compassion rises above the cynicism and bitterness, the suspicion and blame culture of our failing world.

The judgemental and sarcastic, the toxic and inflamed place our planet is fast evolving into.

It lights up hearts. It inspires minds.

It restores weary souls.

It is the fuel we've been looking for to replace the fossil type.

It is the sustainable energy to heal and save the planet.

It begins with compassion and that begins with how I learn to sit with and hold some space and time for myself, unplugged and unshackled from the busy and distracting world.

No matter how fidgety, irritable, cranky, hurting and hollow or twisted and dark my mood and disposition.

I suffer WITH.

Then I can move out into the world with clarity, insight and the wisdom to discern what needs to be done and where my input is required.

I can see the wood for the trees.

ON STAYING SANE IN CRAZY TIMES: 177
"Deep within us all there is an amazing inner sanctuary of the soul, a holy place, a speaking voice to which we may continually return" - Thomas R. Kelly.
In the wild and vindictive craziness that is evident around us in a pretty narcissistic world, remember that the Earth is wise

and love has great intelligence.

What can you meaningfully do in the way you think and the way you act and how do you walk that into these times of arrogance, posturing, disdain and judgement? In fact, these times of terror?

How do we engage the energy of the subtle realm of love?

We live on the border of the physical, visible world and then the invisible world – the actual source of all abundance and life itself.

We need to develop the spiritual courage to live from that place in the border and draw strength, guidance and inspiration from there.

To see, hear and sense with the heart I need to spend quiet time tuning into the deeper place, whether through silence, meditation, contemplation, reflection or prayer. They are mostly different methods for the same purpose to connect with the still small voice within (remember to listen though).

There are many places and books that store and downpour energy, we can spend time in or with them too.

Develop your inner sanctuary, your holy place.

Love flows from here and that love and courage is in short supply in our world right now, adjust the base conditions. What is usually missing are the elements of love, joy and laughter.

Create more of them in your world and share liberally around you.

They are infectious.

A HAPPY ANNIVERSARY TO ME: 178
Two years ago today I finished Ki-More-Therapy after a

mastectomy in June.

I had 15 days of radiotherapy ahead of me soon after, followed by six IV treatments six months apart (the last but one is in a month's time) and daily hormone blockers for eternity.

To all of you potentially facing it, supporting others with it or actually going through it, keep your attitude as high as you can, say yes to all offers of help, greet your eyes out regularly and often to keep your pipes clear and do it one spoonful at a time. Find even the tiniest reason to be grateful every single day and smile though your heart is breaking, at least once every day for an hour. It keeps the muscles working. Sing out loud daily, hourly on the shaky or darkest days.

Use every single resource that's available Maggie's Centres, MacMillan Cancer Support Groups, Beatson Centre, hospice outpatient support, chat forums.

Ask for your area what's around, do not put the leaflets in the bin, these are available long after physical treatment ends for the emotional and spiritual wounds.

Change your consumption habits, both oral and psychological, get advice on supplements to boost your immune system, drink gazillions of water, hang out with high- altitude folks more, reduce exposure to and protect yourself from exposure to "negs" and vampires. Carry less seen and unseen, laugh more, put yourself first!

Appreciate and connect with every single angel you will meet on the road - some you knew already others will appear as if from nowhere, you will meet so many and a lot of those will wear NHS uniforms.

Keep your focus on ringing that bell like your life depends on it.

You got this.

179

The Empowered Woman dances to her own drum or castanets She knows the power and the pull of early morning rises for a quiet time of solitude and silence, listening to the whispers of the universe.

She loves to sit on the floor wrapped in a blanket with her back to the wall and watch the light change from night to day, from day to night, tuning in to the rhythm

of the birthing of light, half-light and night.

She can be all four seasons in one day, that's part of her mystery. That's the way she's made.

She can be a too demanding, too loud, too moody, too needy, too difficult. Too stormy, too deep. TOO MUCH.

Too bad, she is wild, untamed. OLE!

BREATHE·PRAY·LOVE 180
You are gonna die one day.
I am gonna die one day, fact.
But only the really strong of gut are willing to go near the subject of death and dying with someone who has had a "diagnosis."

Is it tempting fate to even sniff around the edges? Some in the health and positive thinking fascist society would run from the word.. DEATH!

I said it again and look, I'm still here.

The truth is I could get hit by a bus next week.

But during treatment I found myself clearing out, organising better, explaining things others don't know/need to know should I be unavailable in the future for any reason - putting my house in order.

Negative thinking? I like to think not, more a WAKE-UP CALL to that best friend, REALITY.

It's easy to think we will live forever. I happen to believe we do, just not in these clothes.

I listened when my teacher recommended we keep death on one shoulder as a soulmate and a reminder to live fully on this earth.

Chancer treatment is a destructive process, your body dies a little with each treatment, but in time you learn to trust the rebirth of your system as you gain strength again in time. It's serious, big-time ebb and flow, dark moon, full moon, sunshine and storms.

Just like the circles and cycles of life.

It helps me to really tune into nature for supportive guidelines and metaphors.

Autumn is a metaphor of great volume and she reminds me that I need to let go.

I have begun clearing out over the past week or so. I sifted and sorted through lots of paperwork including some of dad's stuff the other day. It was tough - seeing his signature on things, wee notes with smiley faces he had drawn for me, scribbled messages.

I've had to let go of a lot of "stuff" this year as we sold the clinic building and moved to the slimmed-down version in the studio out here, from 20 therapists to two (albeit with some external consultants in the city).

But if the trees can let go of their leaves of fire, so too can I.

I had to let go.

When we acknowledge, breathe fresh air, shine some light upon and let go physically of stuff, things, people. When we let go emotionally of the holdings, the denied thoughts, the sat-upon feelings, the terrors, the raging, the guilty secrets, our leaves golden and glow with fire. Before the gentle release and fall into grace where they are transformed into new life energy.

When you look up from your life and check in with your spiritual sat-nav you may need a re-route. The soul will gently guide you - one way or another - to where you need to be.

The process of transformation and letting more light in mostly ain't pretty and is rarely done sitting on the meditation cushion, tinkling your tingsha bells or lying prone on the yoga mat, according to most of the magnificent teachers I've met or read. These do help root and prepare the ground and shake the bough, though.

It's mostly a process of guts and glory, tears and snotters, dragons and dens. In 35 years of working with people as a psychotherapist I never yet met one client who made a truly worthwhile connection, discovery or recovery by tap dancing or by waving their arms through fun and giggle sessions or without a handful of Mr Kleenex's finest by their sides.

It's a peeling back and stripping away job, a shaking down, a complete rewiring and replumbing project and it's not easy –

nothing worthwhile ever is.

Despite what the wishful thinkers would want you to believe in their "I Can Make You Wonderful" books, "From Gremlin To Goddess In An Afternoon" workshops and early bird online courses £17.99 with free bonus personal FaceTime live from the bath (now there's a thought).

So if you are struggling today - regardless of whether it's a physical challenge, an emotional crisis or your spirit feels like a burst balloon - know that you are not alone. You are part of a huge community of people who are too, and some very deep shifting will be happening IF you allow it to teach you what it can about this short life.

Maybe as you watch Autumn do her thing she will whisper some guidance into your ear for the next step on your path.

Adapted from a previous post from 2019 by Angela Trainer

BEACHES: 181
Beaches are great places for feeling spaciousness - which is very good for us, for our hearts (which are boundless) and for our minds, which need to be reminded to be as wide and deep as the sea.
Beaches do not need to be hot or sunny to activate their magical healing properties, all you need is a tea-cosy on your head and a duvet coat from this time of year onwards.

Bare feet are good especially in the sea as you can give yourself a bit of cold water exposure in order to tone your vagus nerve (your relaxation response). Just a paddle is really good wild medicine, it's the lazy version of wild water swimming.

Sand on the feet is a superb method of exfoliation and a free pedicure while you walk, plus the fantastic salt and sea minerals are absorbed too - without pricey bath salts.

The sea gave me up some ocean diamonds this week - sea glass.

Precious souvenirs of a day on the beach.

Get out there! There is a beach waiting for you, somewhere close to home. Go!

182

"Or walk through lightly with little luggage ready to imagine another world and ready to fight for it."
Arundhati Roy, telling it like it is.

ME: Are you ready to help raise the vibe?

Placards won't turn this around on their own.

A change of heart - yours and mine - will.

Stop with the constant focus and reactivity to the negative and all that's wrong with our world.

Stop feeding it.

There's a lot that's right, a lot that can be done, look for the light and feed that for a change.

Guard the tongue.

Imagine this world anew.

Below is a reply I offered to someone recently who was drowning in fear and anxiety.
It helped her, perhaps it may be helpful to others.

"I have found in the past and still find nowadays that when I surrender to the feeling of fear and breathe my way deep into it, feeling it fully (rather than letting thoughts run away with me) and keep breathing through it exploring where I feel it, how I feel it, just being really present in the feeling, I can recognise that it's an old, old feeling of a small child (or even baby).

I may even get a sense of how old or have a sense of the circumstances around me at that time.

But when I locate the name and identify the original fear or "pain body" I can begin the holding and healing process.

I don't feed the fear, I hold it.

And I grow bigger and stronger.

I heal just a little bit more.

Now, often the discomfort intensifies at first (which is why some people don't persevere or even want to go here) but it's a bit like driving into a skid, you go a little more out of control to get some traction and to gain more control. We move into a wider, stronger and deeper stance.

When I put my arms physically around myself and hold "her", just allowing her to feel the feeling but whilst being held and supported by "me" - the adult me - in time, that feeling of overwhelming fear dissolves, it dissipates.

The fear melts.

I begin to lose my fear of the fear.

And I grow in the skillset of fear management.

Love will always conquer fear.

You got this."

NOVEMBER 2021

CANDLELIGHT·PRAY·LOVE 183

On All Souls Day (today) there is an old Celtic tradition based on the belief the veil between the two worlds is at its thinnest at this time of year.

It is thought those who have left us can come back for a brief visit on this night. Your energy and love for them is the path they follow, though to be honest I think they are with us all year long.

Love Never Dies

A candle is lit symbolically as the light that guides them to your home and two small vessels, one of salt and one of water, represent the essence of life itself.

The salt and water also represent the meal you would have prepared for them were they on this side.

As they pass through your home and your hearts they leave their love and blessings and take away your troubles.

What a beautiful ritual! I'm doing this tonight, wanna join me?

My candle will be lit for my dad Patrick, my gran Peggie and grandpa Charlie, my soul baby Emma, Gran T and Papi.

For all of our relatives over the veil, G's parents Mary and Arthur, Billy, Liz and Liz W, Ron and Vi, Clare and Liam and those not mentioned but who are in our hearts.

And especially remembering those who passed over in recent years.

Aunt Irene, Stephen, David and Elizabeth, Marlene, Gordon Sr, Mary Elisabeth, Lewis, Michael J and Noreen.

Sending earthly blessings to you and looking forward to some heavenly graces showering down on us all.

ON WISE AND WILD WOMEN: 184
The Empowered Woman knows the value of detox and often commits to a diet.

She will follow "the diet from jealousy" for weeks or even months on end, detoxifying the impulse and desire to envy and resent others their erstwhile good fortune.

She observes the arousal of envy, treats it as bio feedback and feeds the hunger inside with GRATITUDE for what she herself already has. She then explores the unmet needs and appetites which lie dormant under the surface of envy and jealousy and is creative in sourcing new satisfying and nourishing ways to feed her needs.

She may choose to follow "the diet from competition" or combine with "the diet from comparison" and restrict her intake of these inflammatory culprits.

She knows that detoxifying from these addictive mindsets is an investment in her energy reserves and in her emotional and physical health.

She practices good energy conservation in this way. She knows that in a short time a sense of self-worth, clarity of mind and purpose will replace that empty, restless feeling of low-level resentment and life-draining bitterness.

She knows how to move from bitter to better.

By Angela Trainer

"The Empowered Woman" Event - October 2017

185

To all the overtired, spiritually exhausted, energetically overwhelmed and pretty fecked and decked people out there:
Don't forget the energetic detoxing value of salt baths, Himalayan/Dead Sea/Epsom.
Remember the restorative power of a few early nights in a row.

Switch off the telly and social meeja except for uplifting movies or heart-warming programmes, music, dance, comedy for a while.

Take a detox break from news or limit to 10 minutes a day, earlier in the day.

Rinse and charge all your crystals and use them.

Get a small piece of Selenite and clear your cords.

Seeds and nuts are full of it, they're pure life force energy, get them into your mouth.

Hydrate, hydrate, hydrate. Power flush your system through water, herbal teas, clear soups.

Go drink a pint of Mother Nature's liquid crystal waters right now, fresh from the sky.

Supplement with vitamins, minerals and probiotics.

I am not a nutritionist but I do these daily.

Read only uplifting and inspiring stuff.

BREATHE - open windows.

Hug a tree, lie on the ground on a bin bag, take off your shoes and earth yourself on grass, soil or sand.

Go to the coast and fill your heart with your heart with the ocean and her ions.

Go to the hills and fill your heart with their power and strength.

Make soup.

Nap.

Remember to meditate, pray or just nod off if you are past the point.

Stop, you are tired.

Don't end up with a soul like a prune. You need to hit the pause button and refuel.

Another wave will carry you in time and remember we are all here together and going through it together.

Reach out.

Support each other.

And allow yourself to be loved by life itself.

186

So today was number five out of six treatments back on the Ki-More-Therapy day unit at Monklands. Only one more next May then I'm down to a yearly check, Inshallah.

And how encouraging was it that The Isley Brothers' "Harvest For The World" was playing on Clyde Two in the ward as I sat down.

I was a bit surprised then that it took four canulas before they were happy with the drip. It seems your veins eventually put up a bit of resistance to all these chemicals, no matter how much they may save your life.

And mine were protesting vigorously today, I'll have an arm like a half-chewed beetroot burger tomorrow.

I could sense that the clock was against us all, we had clocked up an hour at this point and I could also intuit the image of a ring with towels being thrown in shortly.

That was until the angel that is Nurse Patricia McCabe appeared.

She has appeared out of the blue at every visit over the past three years even though I've moved between two hospitals, Monklands and Wishaw - so has she.

She gave me my complementary therapies out here in The Land O' The Monks but was seconded back to nursing practice at the Ki-More-Therapy unit during Covid. We've "bumped" into each other EVERY visit.

Seeing the kerfuffle around my arm she announced, "RIGHT, get your hand over that arm and let's blast it some Reiki".

We were only half-joking as we did a 30-second mock up.

I'm no time the drip dripped and the resistant vein surrendered.

It worked.

Well it would, wouldn't it?

LILY, MY INSPIRATION: 187

A special lunch and afternoon with the incredible Lily and her mum, Jane Douglas at the Radisson Red Sky Bar in Glasgow.

Lily is my inspiration, the whole way of my Chancer journey and beyond. The girl who danced her way through life and who smiles that smile. The true dancing queen.

Wishing you both a lovely few days at the Rad Red with the Weegies and a change of scene.

Remember big panda and tiny dragon will always have something to say.

And delighted to get a catch up with Marcus who took care of us and later meet up with DJ Michael Kilkie who was doing a set before and after Fatboy Slim's Hydro gig.

We were well tucked up by then.

But interesting lyric on my favourite song of Fatboy's and so apt for today meeting up with the girls.

Praise You

"We've come a long, long way together

Through the hard times and the good

I have to celebrate you, baby

I have to praise you like I should."

Till next time we meet, always in our hearts, enjoy!

TAKE A REST FROM WANTING: 188

The fastest and simplest way to refresh the soul and rekindle the spirit is subtraction.

That's it, stop, reduce, take away.

Lesson over.

Just take them away.

The distractions, busyness, obsessive routines, the opinions of others, to-do lists, too much stuff, sugar, alcohol, spending, TV, social media, over-targeting, socialising, people, work, perfectionism.

And keep stripping back until you find your spiritual heartbeat again.

You may encounter a few wild things on the path through the inner forest on this journey, that at first glance seem awfy scary.

Like surfacing feelings of anger, low-grade depression, repressed fear and anxiety or irritability.

These are usually temporary and will pass but if ongoing, some support might be sought to understand and translate those shadow feelings into heart speak.

But mostly these "wild things" inside that we try to circumvent have been living there in the forests of our inner self for an awfy long time in order to protect and defend us, even though they may be a little out of touch with the reality of life today.

They are the reason why we continue to avoid the slower and lighter pace, the drama-free zone.

So don't be afraid.

Listen, chat and journal with your wild things of the inner forest.

You will learn so much.

Stretching and hydrating, resting and sleeping and feeding the soul with gentle foods and lots of oxygenated fresh air will encourage the process.

But remember it's a subtraction, a dropping, a "moving to the side of". It's not another regime to stress us.

Keep on subtracting until you find that pulse, that heartbeat and honour it with your presence and full attention.

Your soul is waiting and depending on you.

Happy Sunday.

189

If you up your water intake to two litres (not including tea or coffee or juices in that, just pure water) you will feel and look AMAZING by Christmas!
Just that one tweak can work wonders and now is the time to be focused on hydration.

Will you try the Waterworks challenge? Leave out a jug or water bottle to remind you - and keep score .

You'll feel less hungry, hydrate your brain, think and feel clearer, your complexion will glow, your skin will be fresher and less dry/lined. Water will purify your liver and kidneys flush out more toxins and oxygenate your cells.

DECEMBER 2021

ON SITTING: 188

After a day of meditation in Edinburgh with G and Alex at the helm and an unexpected night of rest and recovery at Stobo, I was moved to share this old faithful post again. Reset and reconnection is such great medicine for these times of hi-velocity anxiety and fear.

We are porous people and the crushing anxiety of those around us, can have a major impact on our own stability and resilience. We do well to remember to protect our energy body as well as our physical bodies - they are utterly interconnected.

You really need your centre and your still small voice within to gain altitude and manage your state at times such as these we are living through.

If you sit soft, still and quiet for a while each day and breathe the love in your heart deeper within yourself, all through yourself and then to those around you, directing it towards those who could do with some extra, your view of the world may begin to change from abject fear to a curious loving connection.

When I do this, I stop living inside my brittle and encapsulated wee self with my castle walls in the kingdom of ME-ME-ME.

When we make a shift from ME-ME-ME to awareness of our expansive boundaryless soul-self, we begin moving from being "fear-driven to being love-drawn", as Richard Rohr puts it.

Everything shifts.

ME BECOMES WE.

When great love which breathes love and life into our world every moment (the loving presence that has no one name) is holding you, dissolving your fear, and allowing greater connection with everything and everyone, we can live with a natural vitality, a gracefulness and a flow that seems Heaven sent. It is the presence of big love spinning and flowing through us.

Almost regardless of the external chaos going on around us.

Take some quiet time and breathe some winter love into yourself and others today.

It is a fabulous booster for your immune system too.

ON LIVING ON PURPOSE: 189

We can set an intention in our heart to help us realign and live in closer harmony in this bold, magical and beautiful world.

Here's one I wrote loosely based on the Reiki principles handed down by Mikao Usui, the founder of Reiki:

"For the next 24 hours only, I am gonna do my level best to train my attention on what's going right and what I'm doing well, noting my tiny successes and accomplishments, and encouraging and praising myself and others along the way.

I'm going to support myself today by reminding myself of what I have to be grateful for, appreciate all the little things and the kindnesses of others. I'll focus on the good in people even when it's hard and remind myself they are doing the best they can.

I will drop the high expectations I can over-demand from me and others and retire from my time as Judge Judy in my little corner of the planet.

I will go about my business with integrity doing 'enough' in whatever I do and adding value wherever I can without overextending or draining my own energy supply through neglect of self (because this serves nobody).

I serve others and care for my tribe and this still stunning planet, which is my home. There is only really one of us here, so in serving you I serve me anyway. I remember that in giving, I receive and try not to forget to give to ME too just for good measure.

I remember to hold things lightly and amazingly special and totally unique as I am, so are we all. I endeavour to be a team player, share my toys and remember to applaud, take my seat in the audience and work backstage for a while.

I need to remind myself that I can only do any of this for a while being only human after all, I forgive myself quickly with a dose of good humour, when I stumble or wander off the path (even though at times I may actually nosedive off a spectacular cliff along the way)."

By Angela Trainer, 2018

190

Today, for me, is about collecting acorns, just like the squirrels and their sustenance for the winter journey ahead.

What did I learn this year, what did life teach me, what were the lessons?

Where did I let myself down?

To whom and how can I make amends for my part in the places

where I've let myself down.

What were the fruits and gifts of this year's 2021 harvest?

What will sustain me on the journey over the pause/threshold into the New Year with the secret promises it holds.

This time is a time of punctuation which allows us to take stock to reflect and be transformed by it.

It's a soulful time and a thin time between the worlds.

I recommend a gratitude letter or grateful silent heart prayer offered up to God/Maya/Gaia/Allah before midnight.

Earth School is a pretty amazing place, if at times rather scary and lonely. You are here to learn how to polish your soul up like a diamond but it can sometimes be quite dirty work. So take a soft cloth and after rinsing off the debris, buff up your diamond to see just how much progress you've made this past year.

How much has your soul grown, deepened, widened?

A long warm bath in Epsom/Himalayan/Dead Sea Salts in candlelight before the year turns, allowing the salts to draw out toxic waste and psychic wounds symbolically. Follow by smoothing on some lovely lotion or oils representing the gratitudes for the year, the people, places, animals, knowledge, books, blessings and gifts abundantly received. Those things we hold close and carry over the threshold into 2022.

I wish you all a blessed, healthy, vibrant, abundant and right guid New Year.

JANUARY 2022

ON WORKING THE NEW YEAR BLUES: 191

This is a tough time of year for most folks. It's dark, it's cold, the coffers are empty for many, the turbo-charged hype of December can leave an abyss in its wake, our immune systems are under assault, we're tired.

Here are a few simple things you can begin today that really WILL make a difference within a short time.

1) Hydrate properly, go now and boil a kettle and drink a large mug of boiled water, cooled. Even better with a slice of lemon (or fresh ginger, good for digestion). Repeat regularly through the day, we simply do not drink enough water in the winter months and it leads to all sorts of problems. We need to flush the bugs out of our gut.

Irene, our Naturopathic Nutritionist, was telling me recently how stress leads to dehydration and dehydration leads to stress, a vicious circle. We may think we are drinking lots of hot drinks but tea and coffee dehydrate us even more.

Commit to six or more big mugs of warm water with lemon, honey and ginger and give your inner engine (and bowels) the gift of a home spa break.

2) Go throw out/recycle some clutter, just one bag. Right NOW! It takes five minutes but feels good. Letting go is good for us, it creates inner and outer space. We hold on too much and we calcify.

Do this every day for the rest of January!

3) Leave out some of the lovely bath/body stuff and a candle beside the shower/bath and have a spa break in candlelight today or tonight. Music is good, a wee 15 minutes of indulgence can be a huge act of self-soothing. Do the whole thing, the scrub, the face mask, the conditioner left on for more than a nanosecond, the body lotion. A healing ritual of self-love.

4) Get out for a short oxygen and natural light bath, a 15-minute walk will do for starters.

5) Sit and read one of those books you never get time to. Just 20 minutes a day of reading is a pure gift for your busy, thinking mind, even if it's the last thing in bed at night.

6) Perform an invisible act of kindness today. Do something lovely for someone else, without looking for gratitude or repayment. It may simply be to smile at a stranger or chat to someone in the supermarket queue or let someone else have the parking space. Phone a lonely friend or family member, send a gratitude card acknowledging someone, invite someone for dinner, offer Reiki or a massage to another - ideally someone you know! Giving it away feeds the soul.

LILY: LOVE NEVER DIES: 192
Wee darling Lily Douglas danced home tonight just after 7pm, the bravest strongest smartest girl in the world.

Her heart got too tired, she was cuddling mum Jane on the couch at home.

Heaven will be singing but the missing begins here in earnest.

Please pray for mum Jane and brother Leon.

A really special soul and an inspiration to those of us who were touched by her grace.

Love Never Dies.

FEBRUARY 2022

GREET·LAUGH·LOVE 193

I worried a bit when people consistently commented on my positivity, my strength, my fight and my humour during my healing dance with The Chancer over the last few years. Superwoman, eh?

As I begin to pull together material and thoughts and begin writing my second book in earnest, I came across this post from 2019.

"In truth It's going to be a struggle to revisit some of the dark times.

Diamonds are rocks under extreme pressure found in mines and I'm sure I will uncover some diamonds down there in the dark that will sparkle in the light. That's the plan anyway and my hope for eventual readers of the book. However, living in the dark and foraging around in it is no mean feat. It's terrifying, it can feel relentless and endless and nobody wears a cape while living through their dark night.

It's good to fall down, to wail, to release, to give in to despair.

We are not machines. We are not computers. You are not 'being negative'.

You will not die from having a good greet but you might from the effects of repressing emotions if you don't. Tears soften the heart, in fact, you will release toxins from your system in the process.

Letting go is part of the whole healing cycle.

Hauding it in is not the way, nor I would advise, being 'a wee soldier'.

These turning points in our lives, whether because of a Chancer diagnosis, a physical or emotional health breakdown or any major shift in our relationships, family situations, work life are not mistakes to be erased, disasters we must urgently despatch.

They are the natural challenges and experiences that every soul who has walked the planet since the history of time has faced in some way, shape or form. We all have cracks in our bowl.

We all have scars on our bodies.

The dark night is an opportunity for a spiritual transformation.

When things fall apart, I must not add shame and blame to the challenge of negotiating my way through the landscape of life.

It's ok to fall, it's important to fail - in fact it's crucial. It teaches me humility, it teaches me compassion for myself and others.

Falling and failing are essential and elemental parts of my life skills.

It's essential as an awakening to all that matters. It's an

opportunity to receive, to lean on, to learn new stuff about yourself, people, life. To deepen your relationship with yourself, and others, with the bigger picture, with love.

And when it hurts - you should cry.

Curl into a ball and do it well.

Tears water the heart and help it grow.

Big boys DO cry and so do big girls.

There were always gonna be twists and turns, dark woods and thick forests, wild animals, vultures and thieves.

Along with the birdsong, angels, rainbows, seascapes, starry skies, sunsets and the wise ones to guide and protect us on our way.

It's still a world of duality we live in here on planet earth last time I looked, night 'n' day, up 'n' down, fear 'n' love, the wicked 'n' wise, sugar 'n' spice, hot 'n' cold.

The dark and the light."

THE INTERIOR SILENCE AND THE LITTLE WAY: 194

I arrived last night at the Carmelite Convent, my urban spiritual home - Iona being my rural version - and melted into the rhythm of prayer, meditation, contemplation, spiritual direction, reflection and writing. Of course sleeping, eating and showering feature too.

Morning prayer is at 6am together and requires adjustment to my bedtime. However, the rewards of birdsong and walking in the dark across the grounds, sleepy-eyed and vulnerable but open-hearted, mindless and receptive were worth the price and tomorrow is a long lie if I choose till eight. Woo-hoo!

I'm here until Monday.

Although it can be seen cynically as some kind of spiritual Olympics, the circular rounds of prayer and contemplation anchor the heart. They deflate the grandiosity of the thinking mind. They nudge me closer to my spacious self which has far more room for everyone and everything. I don't need to be captain of the universe here, which is far less exhausting, believe me.

I can let go, be held, be carried.

But that also requires some effort and discipline on my part. I need to show up and engage.

Here I very much experience that sense of connection and grounding in love itself. You may have your own name for that higher power which is in everything including you, life itself.

God, The Creator, The Mother, The Mystery, The Mysterons, Allah, Yahweh, the Christ, that which cannot be described in words.

But can be experienced, felt as a powerful presence in "Aha!" moments, deep love, deep pain, rapture and ecstasy - and in the shards of light of an ordinary day.

I so appreciate this oasis of reflection. I've started to speed up in my daily life since even before restrictions eased.

There are new calls and demands on my life. I'm needed more in my personal life, I'm my own practice manager, P.A. and receptionist now - in fact I am for the others who work with us too. I'm it!

And as things move forward, I need to be clear about those time and energy boundaries and check the security of my borders vigilantly.

Health is wealth and the number one asset we possess and it's only when you stop that you can hear the birdsong properly.

So here I am emptying out, listening in, filling up and resetting the compass points for 2022 so I can move with body, mind and soul in alignment.

And a plan to also share some of these benefits in a few retreat days offered from the Harvest Studio this year too. Paying it forward is a big thing here in the convent.

Sharing and service are just some of the fruits of retreat.

When we get more, we have more to give.

"The silence of the mind is when we live best" - R.S. Thomas

CHLOE - LOVE NEVER DIES: 195
It can't be true, Chloe?
We texted lots on Friday and are having lunch with Caroline, Janice and Kate tomorrow to plan for the trip we've all booked to Iona in March.

Did I just get a phone call from your friend via husband Steve telling me you died suddenly this morning?

Yes I saw Ben (your brother's) FB post a few minutes before the call but I was still telling myself it could be someone else with the same name.

I'm in total lockdown mind escape, mindless.

You'll need to give me time to digest this.

You're 51 with three beautiful kids.

You were heading to the caravan at Loch Lomond you loved and promised to take me to this spring.

It wasn't meant to be like this.

You held me all through my Chancer journey and way beyond.

I'm holding you tonight and Steve and the kids.

I love you and will always love you my beautiful pal and Anam Cara.

Rest with the angels tonight.

Ps

I did the rose petals and candle photo just before I took the call from Caroline. I had no idea why I felt the need to do that. But do you remember how we scattered red rose petals in my garden at the earth prayer day held at mine last year together?

I'll scatter them for you tomorrow at dawn before the nuns here pray for you at the convent where I'm on retreat.

THE EMPTY CHAIR: 196

We were meant to meet at Kate's for lunch today, Chloe, to plan our Iona trip travel in March - you were meant to be bringing a gluten free/vegan something or other.

I did not miss that offering for one second.

I thought you were just late as usual and would tumble in all gorgeous, boho chic and bubbling with life.

But you were never coming, were you?

Caroline and I both "heard" you at 6am this morning.

Kirkintilloch and Dunfermline are a mean feat to communicate with simultaneously.

"It's all true - it's pure bliss and heavenly, you'll love it, I'm fine!"

Our imaginations? Start of schizophrenia? Or it just IS?

Do your worst, lock me up buttercup.

I couldn't give a toss, it just WAS!

I got the song in the car I didn't put on by myself.

"All that matters in the end is how we love" by Beth Nielsen Chapman.

It finished me.

And Caroline showed me the Mindfulness Association tribute with the quote by Jack Cornfield a couple of hours later:

"In the end these things matter most:

How well did you love?

How fully did you live?

How deeply did you let go?".

Well strike two!

You mastered o'er the veil communication module No.175 in less than 24 hours.

I could go on with the other stuff.

Why bother?

We loved you.

We love you.

And we will always love you.

Oh yeah.. and Love Never Dies.

ON LOVE AND VALENTINE'S DAY: 197
For Chloe, Lily and Jane.

Love is a decision.

Love is a verb.

Love is not a feeling.

Love is a discipline.

Love is a practice.

Love in action

is a thing to behold.

The soul knows and

the heart sings.

Love is for giving

to be shared.

and to be fully received.

Love is forgiving

it doesn't count.

You can refuse love,

but you can never lose it.

Once given

It never dies.

You are love.

And love never dies.

By Angela Trainer

Words written St. Valentine's Day 2021

A SHOULDER TAP: 197B

I was on a retreat at St Mary's, Kinnoul last weekend. G and Alex were in the driving seat, running the retreat though I did lead a Kin Hin (walking meditation).

It was immediate immersion into peace when the morning started with two baby deer on the lawn as I opened the curtains. Weather was our friend for Qi Gong outside on that same lawn and beautiful bountiful blue skies above the canopy of huge conifers and sequoias that sheltered our walking meditation through the grounds of the monastery.

But here's a wee story to chew on.

A call came through on arrival, my dearest pal had a stroke (and silent heart attack, it transpired) while on holiday abroad.

She was in hospital, tests awaited and a no-fly home ban for at least two weeks.

Feeling pretty powerless and helpless, I did all I could, pray.

I prayed every prayer I knew by rote, made a few up and sat in silence sending healing.

On Sunday I went to mass.

I sang the requisite hymns from my hymn book and I prayed for her again. I asked for intercession from every saint I knew and a few I didn't even know I knew.

I had an internal chat with her family who have passed over the Veil, dad Jimmy in particular, James Murphy.

"She needs you guys," I addressed her dad, mum, brother. "Please surround her with your love and grace and of course healing, she'll be scared, be there with her."

Mass ended, final hymn sung.

A scrap of paper fell out of my hymn book on to the floor.

I nearly toppled trying to pick up this pesky litter between the kneeler and seat in front. I almost got jammed like a penknife between them.

A kinda Catholic downward-facing dog.

What made me read that scrap of paper on which a priest had obviously scribbled a reminder of his chosen hymns and the people he was gonna pray for, when he'd inserted it into the book and forgotten to remove?

I dunno.

But when I turned it over, I gasped out loud at the name

written on the other side. JAMES MURPHY.

In black and white.

Pauline Murphy was written underneath. That's my friend's aunt's name, who is very much alive.

My friend is resting, out of hospital, shaken and stirred but grateful.

And hopefully home in a couple of weeks, heaven has her back.

Me, I'm just grateful.

In awe and reminded.

Of course, there was a wee tiny white curly feather at my feet as I stepped out of the church.

COMFORT

THE VEIL: 198

Four deaths in as many weeks - wee Lily Douglas, Christine Johnston, Chloe and Helen (Kitty) in addition to my pal's heart attack and stroke while abroad, Sir Ian (my cat and soulmate) with a cancerous eye op too.

So I was guided back to my spiritual mentors' writings and messages on life, impermanence and "what's it all about Alfie?".

I found this and it comforted me. Maybe it will some of you too.

THE VEIL IS A THIN PLACE. Part 1

"Very often at death, the inhabitants of the eternal world come out toward the visible world. Your friends who now live in the eternal world come to meet you, to bring you home. Usually, for people who are dying, to see their own friends gives them great strength, support, and encouragement.

Here we are caught in linear time. Time must be totally different for the dead because they live now within a circle of eternity.

The Celtic mind never liked the line but always loved the shape of the circle.

I imagine that in the eternal world time has become the circle of eternity. Maybe when a person goes into that world, he or she can look back at what we call 'past time 'here. That person may also see all of future time.

For the dead, present time is total presence.

This suggests that our friends among the dead know us better than they can ever have known us in life."

By John O'Donoghue

THE VEIL IS A THIN PLACE PART 2: 199
"I believe that our friends among the dead really mind us and look out for us. Often there might be a big boulder of misery over your path about to fall on you, but your friends among the dead hold it back until you have passed by.

One of the exciting developments that may happen in evolution and in human consciousness in the next several hundred years is a whole new relationship with the invisible, eternal world. We might begin to link up in a very creative way with our friends in the invisible world.

They are now in a place where there is no more shadow, darkness, loneliness, isolation, or pain. They are home. They are with God/Love from whom they came. They have returned to the nest of their identity within the great circle. God/Love is the greatest circle of all, the largest embrace in the universe, which holds visible and invisible, temporal and eternal, as one."

By John O'Donoghue

Though I added in the word "love" twice for user-friendly reasons.

THE VEIL IS A THIN PLACE PART 3: 200

"God/love" is the greatest circle of all, the largest embrace in the universe, which holds visible and invisible, temporal and eternal, as one.

In the eternal world, all is one.

In spiritual space there is no distance. In eternal time there is no segmentation into today, yesterday, or tomorrow. In eternal time all is now time is presence.

I believe that this is what eternal life means. It is a life where all that we seek goodness, unity, beauty, truth, and love are no longer distant from us but are now completely present with us."

By John O'Donoghue

From the book Anam Cara

Though I added in the word "love" for more inclusion.

ANGELA TRAINER

THE LAST WORD

To start or end your day or both.

"Give me Hope, God.

Drench me in that Grace.

I want to feel the Grace of hope fill my heart and pour into my blood and bones.

This life is your creation. I am your creation.

I know that you work through every

good thought and every act of love and every courageous word and deed.

This gives me hope.

It gives me hope each time I see a good and kind person and

every time I hear a loving word spoken.

If one kind word can do so much for a stranger,

the power contained in a prayer must be immeasurable.

So I ask that the grace of hope

flow through me to those in need on this earth.

Let me breathe in this grace and

channel it to whoever is in need.

I hold the image of a healed humanity and a healed earth.

I ask for the grace of hope

because with you, God, all things are possible.

This world is your creation.

Hover over this world, Lord,

and all who are in it.

Amen."

Prayer by Caroline Myss

THE END?

The Beauty Of Broken is also lovingly dedicated to Angela's constant companion and confidante, the much-loved Sir Ian, who crossed the rainbow bridge in July 2022 as the book was nearing completion. It seems he felt his work here was done.

ANGELA TRAINER

TIME-OUT: RETREAT AND RESET WITH ANGELA

As a nice way to round off this step of your journey, I've created a retreat and reset you can do at home, using some of the lessons you will find throughout.

Why not put into practise some of the ideas we have been sharing - it's a retreat you can do by yourself, as a couple, as a family, with friends - over either 10 or 21 days.

If that's too big a step right now, just try one or two of the ideas that don't seem too daunting, then revisit when you want to take another step.

And please.. enjoy.

DAY 1: THE RESET

Are you stuck in fog?
Tired all the time?
Treacle in your veins?
Hopeless and helpless?

IN THIS RESET RETREAT, CHOOSE AT LEAST ONE OF YOUR TRICKS EVERY DAY AND KEEP THEM GOING FOR AT LEAST 10 DAYS - BUT 21 DAYS IS BETTER.

In a week or two you will be tangoing around the house with plans for turning the world around too.

Push yourself to get up before the rest of the world - start with an hour earlier, then the next day or two earlier still, until you reach 6am (or even 5.30).

Go to the nearest hill or open space with a big coat, your favourite blanket and a scarf and watch the light change - even just sit your garden.

Spend at least 10-15 minutes with a quieter world, listen to nature and the world waking up.

Push yourself to fall asleep earlier - start with an hour earlier, then another hour earlier after two or three nights, then earlier still until you get to 10pm (or 9pm for the gold star).

Wake up in the morning feeling re-energized and comfortable.

You are not giving up the right to party ever again. You are practicing some of the principles of retreat and reset.

Sit in the garden or open all the windows wide and relax with a hot drink, feel the fresh air and light on your skin.

DAY 2: BLESS THE BODY

Start your day with a BIG glass of cooled, boiled water and perhaps a few slices of lemon to awaken your liver and kidneys and prepare your digestive system for the day.

Give it a good 30 minutes before nourishing yourself with healthy fuel (food).

Ensure it is beautiful stuff, elegantly presented - whether it's fluffy scrambled eggs, delicious mushrooms, tangy tomatoes, chopped nature's gift (fruit or berries with chopped nuts and seeds), boiled eggs and soldiers, velvety yoghurt, a colourful veggie smoothie of living vibrant greens, peanut butter and honey on rice cakes, crunchy muesli... and use the best china.

Set a place with cutlery or take it outside for some light and nature. Taste every mouthful, enjoy and savour it all. Make it a gift to your body.

DO NOT stand yawning, scraping a dead bit of cardboardy bread with greasy butter and gaping at the telly. And don't eat all of the above - choose one only.

AND/OR

Devise your own 10-15 minute stretch or movement routine.

You know your own tight bits. Do it to gorgeous music.

Lie down and start slow and gentle -or even sit.

Stretch, gently and feel into your body. Talk nicely to it.

You can even do it in bed. Flex and tighten, shake and wobble.

Get to know your body again and if you have time over the week, finish with a wee walk around the block.

Bless every bit of your precious body.

It is the temple of your soul.

Commit out loud: "I'm on this. I'll feel like a new person by the end of it and be so full of energy I can lift the spirits of an entire region, I'll radiate so much joy".

DAY 3: HYDRATE AND WRITE

Buy a water bottle. Push yourself to drink the whole thing today. Then try drinking it twice.

A hydrated body and brain is a well-oiled machine. We feel better and think clearer.

Hydrated skin glows; eyes sparkle and you'll have a spring in your step.

AND/OR

Buy a lovely diary or journal and a beautiful rollerball pen for easy writing.

Write down everything you do plus appointments, assignments, meets, coffees, what you need to do that day. No detail is too small. How are you feeling? How is your retreat/ reset going? Write it all down. It's a space for you to check in with yourself. Your space.

DAY 4: BREATHE

Practice breathing better.

It's the fuel for everything in your body and mind, it can change how you feel in minutes.

Breathe out for longer than you breathe in, in order to relax. It stimulates the vagus nerve - the body's invisible comfort blanket.

Close your mouth and breathe through your nose to reduce anxiety.

Breathe down into your diaphragm so the ribs widen like an accordion - bathe the body in oxygen.

Breathe way down into the belly so it expands and softens. Big deep full breaths, then fully out - and rest at the end of the out breath for a second or two.

Check out the legendary Wim Hof on YouTube for breathing info and exercises or my own TedTalk - also on YouTube (skip forward to 14 minutes in) - about the vagus nerve and breath. It's called "The Curse of Perfect" (20 mins long in total).

Find it here: https://youtu.be/43TpYMKABls

AND/OR

Have a luxurious shower or bath with your favourite music playing. Even light a candle.

Make bathing a sacred ritual as you bless your body. Be grateful for every part of it - no matter how lumpy or bumpy, rusty or scarred. It's served you so well.

Wash your hair. If you have a loofah or body brush exfoliate your body or just use some coffee grains or rock salt and a little olive oil. Brush and floss your teeth with love and appreciation.

Lather your whole body in moisturizer, get familiar with the part between your toes, your inner thighs, the back of your neck. Wash the old 'holding on stuff' away. Water is a conductor of energy and it washes the old energy away down the plug-hole.

You will be left refreshed and reset. This is mindful, nay HEARTFUL bathing. A sacred ritual.

DAY 5: CONNECT

Be the person you'd like to meet. Let cars out in front of you with a smile. Pay for the next person's coffee. Stick your tongue out at babies. Speak nicely to someone's dog. Compliment folk on their hair/clothes/general health - especially your nearest and dearest: sometimes we forget them.

Challenge yourself to not ridicule, talk (or think) anyone down for a whole day - then do this every day for your whole retreat. It can be a faulty habit pattern, downsizing people to feel bigger yourself.

Look people in the eye. Ask people about their day, their story. Treat everyone you meet as if they were an old friend. Some may soon become old friends.

AND/OR

Message a friend or family member you seem to be losing touch with. Because soon you might.

Remind them of a special wee memory or laugh about a time together. Reminisce. Suggest a catch-up soon, even if you think you can't follow through. Push yourself to follow through.

This has been a time where, for too many reasons, lots of us are losing contact with others – it's hard in this post-Covid world. Start with one contact and build from there: old aunties, ex-colleagues, friends from pre-Covid, old neighbours, current neighbours, cousins, old school friends, people overseas…

We get more love inside when we give it. Spread a little love: let them know they matter.

DAY 6: EXPAND

Push yourself to go for a walk no matter the weather.

Take your headphones, go to the beach/woods/park/canal/ river/loch and walk kindly. Kiss the earth with your feet. "Peace in every step", as Thich Nat Hanh said.

Smile at strangers walking the other way and be surprised at how many DO smile back.

Bless silently everyone you meet - even those who don't or can't meet your eyes. They need it most.

Bring your dog and enjoy the dog's attitude and antics, or even borrow a dog from family or neighbours. Don't steal one!

Sense the energy of trees, water, flowers. Smell the scents of the natural world - they are all so very different. Feel the textures of trees, leaves and grasses. How many colours are in nature's palette today?

Tune into the landscape wherever you are; the outer landscape and your own inner one. This is not about exercise or speed - it's about mindful walking.

AND/OR

What are you really interested in?

What would you like to know more about? Find a non-fiction book about it and read. You will find hunners of books for peanuts in a charity shop or second-hand from Amazon - but make it something that really interests you. There's bound to be one lying about the house you never got round to last Christmas.

Read every day for at least 30 but ideally 60 minutes. Nothing else. Just reading.

You're learning and expanding your mind. Neuroplasticity is a thing.

Our minds grow and develop if we feed them good stuff and new things.

No time? Reduce social media, phone time and TV.

Make reading and learning a part of your mental hygiene programme.

What we consume with our minds affects our inner and outer world - we have knowledge to share, to discuss. We become more interested and more interesting.

DAY 7: REVIEW

Some of you may have followed the whole week but I'd guess few. Life gets in the way.

This process is not about striving for perfection. It's about scattering seeds and seeing what takes root and grows.

Today is a good day for review and taking stock, either with your lovely journal or in reflective thought and inner conversation.

How have you done?

What is working?

What disnae?

What will you continue to commit to from the past seven days? Or whatever you have managed to do.

Don't pour guilt on yourself and DO refrain from shaming yourself - praise and delight in the fact you are reading this today.

Now recommit to following through.

No rush. Nae pressure. ENJOY it.

AND/OR

OPEN YOUR EYES WITH YOUR CAMERA

Develop a more mindful, creative way of seeing the world. Take some photos, inside or out, of unusual colours, shapes, angles, textures - just on your phone.

These are not for the family album - these are for creative

stimulation and expression. Seeing beyond the usual, the "normal".

There is a sacred geometry in the natural world we often miss in our haste.

It might be a photo that expresses your connection to your kettle. Trees. Car tyre tracks. Puddles. Your toes.

Use your Third Eye to see the world for a while today - get up close and personal and BE a photographer for an hour - but a very different one. And maybe share one or three of these captures with the world on social media.

AND/OR

BUY A PLANT or take a cutting, cultivate it and pot it. Or go find some wild flowers or interesting leaves/branches/berries and arrange a vase for your bedroom.

Bring some life into your bedroom to energise and lift the energy in there. Gift yourself some natural beauty to brighten your nest.

Good work troops.

DAY 8: COLOUR- IN AND LISTEN

Autumn is knocking at the door and Mother Nature will change her wardrobe shortly: she is trying a few things on already! Watch her bring a new COLOUR palette to our world.

Colour is pure gift. It lifts, refreshes, expresses and brightens our own energy and that of our spaces and places.

Wear and use colour deliberately now. Try wearing some colours you wouldn't normally - it's interesting and liberating. Notice if it affects your mood (it should).

Bright scarves, bold earrings, a fresh lipstick, a pair of jazzy troos or a colourful jumper can help make the day more cheery.

And perhaps the guys will try the lipstick and earrings too... why not?

Use coloured pens. Buy a colourful candle to light your room. Eat foods of various colours - how many colours can you get on your plate from veggies, salads and fruits? Every colour has different micro-fella properties according to Janice my probiotic guru.

Doesn't matter if you're at home all day on the colour-dressing front - do it for YOU! Your heart will thank you.

AND/OR

Really listen today.

Open your third ear.

Listen beyond the words for the person behind the words. For the meaning.

Allow silence before answering someone.

Don't interrupt.

Practice listening to nature, she talks to us all the time.

The art of good and real communication is to listen.

Listen up today.

Listen to yourself too - perhaps using your journal.

How are YOU today? What do you need from yourself?

You will see now we are adding a new trick or two every day, a whole new vibe and tool bag by the end. And a healthier vibrant you to boot.

DAY 9: BOUNDARIES

Guard the tongue today.

Watch and observe what you say.

Practice a bit of oral hygiene in terms of gossip/take-down remarks/sniper-fire and low- energy vibe comments.

Keep your words higher vibe and at a healthy altitude.

What we say has an impact on our own energy field and that of others.

It can lift me up or pull me down - and you.

If you slip it's absolutely fine. These resets take time.

What's fantastic is that you NOTICED!

Just get back on the horse.

AND/OR

SET A BOUNDARY for yourself for time on social media and exposing yourself to news.

We can become overwhelmed with the 24/7 worldwide access to news that no other generations have had to digest or be exposed to.

It is good that we are informed and can respond to our world community but we need time to recalibrate and hold our centre too.

It's all about balance and discernment.

Social media can become an addiction like any other. We can spend too much time in an altered state and a virtual world and avoid connection with our actual reality and relationships in the here and now. It's a fabulous tool and great connection for information and contact with our tribe. It can promote fantastic debate and discussion.

But it can be a bad master too.

Set yourself some limits and notice how you manage to not fall down the rabbit hole of oblivion for hours at a time.

Where, when and for how long?

And where and when is it strictly off-limits and time to switch it off?

DAY 10: NO

SAY NO.

The focus here is on discernment, checking in with your heart and gut (not just your head) with whatever you are doing, deciding, planning.

In an uber-fast world of too many choices and far too much stimulation, "NO" can be a sane and healthy response.

When I practice saying "NO, thank you", to myself it becomes easier to say to others.

We find life smoother, healthier, easier, freer, more honest, gentler and happier.

Just say "NO THANKS!".

AND/OR

SAY YES.

Check inside with your heart and gut and notice what you want to say YES to.

And when it's a definite yes - give your whole heart to that YES.

Commit 100%.

Don't hold back.

Give it or them your full undivided attention.

Don't get a sore ass sitting on the fence with fear of missing out on something else. Be there.

Immerse yourself fully in the people places and experiences you have said "YES" to - whether it's doing the dishes, an online meeting or walking the dog.

Say "YES!".

To recap, we are picking one or both tricks and committing to practice for 10 days (or 21 days) from today.

Building on the strategies from the previous days.

If overloaded, slow it down: pick something every few days and commit to practice it every other day/once a week/once a month. It's your life. It's your reset.

DAY 11: SELF-CARE

Upping the ante a little today.

Self-care is not all pamper nights and glossy magazines. Self-care is about taking a long hard stare at our lives and being pretty brutal about some of the changes - the tough, hard changes that we'd rather not deal with - that need to be made.

It's easy to drink more water. Fit in a wee walk. Photograph sunsets. Eat some carrot cake.

Not so easy to admit where you are leaking your joy or haemorrhaging your energy.

You can start by creating time to reflect, then write in your journal the who, what, where, when of where your own TRUE DEEP SELF-CARE needs to really begin.

Start with the simplest and easiest to address - but often these are the things we least want to do.

It's drawing up a strategy.

It's forensic investigating.

It's not satiating your appetites.

It's letting go.

It's choosing the new and that can be scary.

It's disappointing some people and making sacrifices for others.

It's living a way that other people won't or can't -so it may be lonelier for a while.

It's totally worth it.

AND/OR

Revisit Day 1 again – how is your sleep?

DAY 12: JUST SMILE

SMILE ON PURPOSE even if you are by yourself. Smile into yourself; smile into the mirror and wink as you do. Smile at the cat/ dog/ornaments.

Laugh out loud - let go, soften your belly and let the sound out.

Some people cry as if they are constipated emotionally and some laugh as if they are too.

Let your laughter go with the flow.

It's so good to smile and laugh - it releases all the good hormones - Dopamine, Serotonin and Oxytocin.

It's great for the immune system and I'm sure it reduces emissions of negativity into the stratosphere.

Buck the trend: what if we could beat the 'Rona and climate change with laughter and smiling?

Should we give it a try?

AND/OR

Revisit Day 2.

DAY 13: SING ALONG

MUSIC uses a different part of the brain and shifts mood.

Today's commit is to bring more conscious choices of music into your life, your ears, your mind, your being.

Can you make a soundtrack of favourite uplift tunes on your phone to start your day with?

One for later in the day to inspire and reset?

And one for later in the evening to soothe and unwind to?

Just a few choices, but to stop and really listen to. Ideally to sing along with.

If you are brave, YouTube or Google the backing tracks of your fave songs and belt them oot in the car, the shower or making dinner.

Have a dance to them.

Singing, dancing, clapping and humming are all hugely therapeutic: they are all therapy techniques in their own right.

AND/OR

Revisit Day 3.

DAY 14: DANCE

TODAY WE DANCE

Any time, any way, anyhow.

Put some music on in the garden, shower, kitchen. And best of all, even in the rain.

Close your eyes and get right into your body.

Partner with the dog, weans, your beloved, your pal or an imaginary John Travolta or Patrick Swayze. If you don't know who they were - Justin Timberlake or Pharrell?

When we let go and dance, shake, shuffle, twirl, we flood our bodies with feelgood hormones that wake up our immune systems to head the 'Rona into retreat at the first pass (Oxytocin, Dopamine, Serotonin).

Get your white cells staying alive with a jive into tip-top condition, jiggle with joy and set your defences up for the day.

AND/OR

Revisit Day 5.

DAY 15: RESISTANCE

Write down everything you do. How are you feeling? How is your retreat/reset going? Write it all down. It's a space for you to check in with yourself.
Resistance to change is simply part of the process.
Relapse is part of recovery.

If you've found this process of changing some of your habits and behaviours hard, you are in good company. Mind you, you've had a lot of choices of how to shift your energy, health and mood.

It's the keeping going.

You wouldn't think it'd be so tough to drink water, keep a feelings journal, take a walk, manage sleep better, eat more real food, be nice, guard the tongue and bless the body.

But it IS!

So today's task is to check out the part of you that might be resisting, that relapses, that shouts you don't have time, it's too hard, there is no point or we are all doomed anyway.

Take some time inside today to check out your inner saboteur.

It usually has a background intention of trying to protect us from disappointment or humiliation but can also be quite self-harming.

Our job is to recognise, understand and gently engage the saboteur; reassure and then firmly take over the pilot seat in spite of the demands.

But it's good to check out how your saboteur operates and a few of the whys.

Habit is often one. Playing the victim can be another. Sometimes we do get currency out of our own wound-ology.

Let's reflect and explore today and every day, get to know and keep in check The Saboteur energy.

AND/OR

Revisit Day 6.

DAY 16: GRATITUDE

Every single day think or say aloud, or better still write in your journal, three things that spring to mind to be grateful for. It might be stuff, people, experiences, feelings, parts of your body, events. Anything.

And starting before you even get out of bed definitely turbocharges your day.

I also like to count my blessings in bed at night instead of counting sheep.

Just reflect on your day and you will always find at least three diamonds to acknowledge from the lessons of the day (even if it's a lesson in how not to be).

It might just be the blessing of a warm, dry bed, food or a non-toothache day.

Martin Seligman researched the practice of daily gratitude and here are just some of the beneficial outcomes:

•increased happiness and positive mood

•more satisfaction with life

•less materialistic

•less likely to experience burnout

•better physical health

•better sleep

•less fatigue

- lower levels of cellular inflammation

- greater resiliency

- encourages the development of patience, humility, and wisdom

Ooft - well worth the time and effort.

AND/OR

REFLECT

Had anything been helpful for resetting and uplifting your well-being and energy levels?

Have you tried any of the resets?

Are you making any of them habits by daily practice and awareness?

How is it impacting your life?

Are there things you want to re-establish and revisit?

What's got in the way?

This is an exercise of reflection for today after The Saboteur reflection from yesterday.

Will you give the next FIVE days a committed push?

DAY 17: PAUSE

Remember to have a rest today.

No new stuff to process or implement. Just maintain your altitude wherever you are.

Holidays are important; it seems even the Divine creator rested on the seventh day.

Practice the art of pause and/or catch up with yourself regularly and often.

It brings so many benefits.

DAY 18: WALK AND READ

Picking up a couple of important revisits now as we move towards the final days. See Day 6.

WALK

AND/OR

READ

DAY 19: THE MOON

Watch the night skies for some quiet time every night. It soothes the soul.

In my time we are beginning a three-night journey with my favourite of them all, THE HARVEST MOON.

This is a great time to charge up your crystals or bless some water.

But even better PLACE YOURSELF OUT THERE for a moon-bathe.

Good farmers and gardeners know the importance of the moon's cycle and plant and harvest in tune with them.

We should too. Our problems seem so small in that vast miracle of existence.

Even start a moon cycle watch in your journal and pay attention to how your own energy ebbs and flows alongside; just like the oceans of the world which are totally under the control of the magnetic field and power of the Moon.

And we are made mostly of water so this influences us hugely too.

In days of yore women would menstruate in cycle with the full moon and all the girls' cycles would be in sync. Red Tents were erected for women to gather and rest, to bathe and massage and to decorate each other with henna. To support.

Bring 'em back, I say.

And I'd like to propose a Purple Tent for the pre, current and post-menopausal women of our tribe: a place to retreat and rest.

AND/OR

TALK

DAY 20: CHEW KNOW IT

Commit to really chewing your food.

The famous Mayr clinic in Austria charges its celebrity guests a fortune and this is the main teaching.

Digestion starts in the mouth.

When we chew properly, the correct acids and the saliva do their jobs. Food should be broken down to almost liquid before it hits your stomach.

Why?

Because your stomach doesn't have teeth so food not properly broken down requires buckets of acid to digest.

That equals a lorra digestion issues over time.

And try not to drink WITH food.

Before or after is fine but it dilutes those juices and acids so disrupts digestion accordingly.

Let your marvellous body do its job and support it.

Chew, chew, chew (Mayr suggested 30 chews or more per mouthful).

AND/OR

BREATHE through your nose and close your mouth.

You will filter out particles of dust and pollutants.

Your body was meant to breathe through your nose.

You'll feel more relaxed as it triggers the relaxation response.

Oxygen is absorbed more easily into the body, and you will have more energy.

The perfect breath is in for five and a half seconds, and out for five and a half seconds... who knew?

Breath by James Nester, out now, is great if you would like to know more.

Tomorrow is our last day!

So let's have a big final push at introducing some new ways of living to support and energise you. And to boost your immune system in time for the Winterfest of amazing cool, crisp, magical days of candles, fires, soft lighting and scarves, hot baths and hot soups, cuddly blankets and wooly tights.

DAY 21: LOVE AND HUGS

Give yourself a long and loving hug today: just for being you. Look in the mirror and wish yourself a good day - because you're worth it.

Tell yourself out loud "I love you" - and keep doing it until you mean it.

Be one with your own best friend. Take things slower and gentler until you find your pace; find your voice; find YOUR way.

You are unique. No-one else has or ever had your unique thumbprint.

Nobody can ever know your needs and wants better than YOU.

Start a love affair with yourself from today.

AND/OR

Make a wee list of the tools and techniques you've found worthwhile and helpful over our 21-day retreat. Make time to review them by scrolling back and design your own plan for the next while.

But most importantly commit to a daily practice, no matter what!

Big hugs. I'm proud of you and you should be too.

THE DAY AFTER

Well done if you participated in any of the last three weeks; and it's never too late if you didn't. Start again. Pick your favourites.

The trick is making new habits and that takes 21 days of daily practice.

Explore what you have managed and what was tougher - what gets in the way? What thoughts and messages sabotage your commitment? How do you stop yourself before you even start?

Keep things small, bite-sized and simple but mostly make them airy, light and fun.

Reduce the volume of the voice of your inner dictator, the inner drudge, the inner bitch.

Speak nicely to yourself; encourage, congratulate.

Have fun with it. Today is a new start.

A new beginning.

Love your way into it.

MY TEAM

The following people were a very important part of MY journey, with apologies to others I may have not included. There were so many who helped.

But I did see these therapists at various times on my journey and found their input helpful; not just during Chancer treatment but for after and for living life to the full.

All are based in Glasgow unless otherwise stated. Of course I am not suggesting anything should replace medical treatment or advice, but I believe these people helped me AS WELL.

Reflexology
Helen Boyle
Helensboyle@virginmedia.com

Reflexology (and Headshave!)
Elaine Gilliland
elafaraway@gmail.com

Kombucha/Sourdough/Fermenting workshops (nutritional food scientist)

Janice Clyne
www.nourishedbynature.co.uk

Jikiden Reiki
Theresa Cryans
Listed on Jikiden Reiki UK Association JRUKA
www.jikidenreikiuk.com

Homeopathy
Caroline Miller
www.homeopathfife.com

Consultant physician/Holistic wellbeing and transformative change
Dr David Reilly FRCP MRCGP HonDSc
www.thewelworld.org

Reflexology lymphatic drainage (RLD)
Marion McAdam
marionmcadam53@googlemail.com

Naturopathic Nutritionist and Food Intolerance testing using Bio-Resonance
Irene McCabe
www.irenemccabe.com

Massage /Reflexology
Patricia McCabe MBE
patricia.mccabe@lanarkshire.Scot.nhs.uk

THANK YOU
FROM ANGELA

Books are born, not made and this one had a four-year labour. It was an unplanned pregnancy. Along the way there were many midwives and folks holding my hand.

I'd like to thank our magnificent NHS for everything, from the receptionists to the cleaners, the consultants and nurses to the tea trolley ladies, the porters to the radiographers. It's a miraculous machine and is manned by earth angels.

Mrs Lannigan my consultant and Margaret my breast care nurse, Patricia McCabe and Elaine Gilliand - I will never forget your kindness and skill. I have included a list of the amazing therapists who advised me at various times on my road. I am so grateful to know you and indeed for your tremendous help.

Thank you to my family and friends over the Veil. Once again I regularly felt those whispered inspirations from you, my invisible supporters.. especially dad and gran. And my beautiful pals who passed during the creation of this book.

Graham, my husband of two decades and more: none of it is possible without your love, presence, your 24/7 support, ideas and suggestions, your wisdom and early morning veggie juices. I'm the luckiest girl to have found an eternal love with you.

To all my family: mum, you were my inspiration, having gone through a lumpectomy and radiotherapy journey 10 years before me. Your strength and positivity, commitment and courage left me in awe. You were a fantastic support on the road.

To my brothers Raymond and Chris, my diagnosis was a hard blow for you both after dad, but your help and support meant the world. Thank you. Dad was and is proud of you both.

Ashley, my niece - you are just a star. Always checking in - nothing too much bother in the midst of a busy life with a career and Aiden your young son. You are amazing and I'm so proud of you.

To David, Kim and all the Watts family, Ella-Rose, Nathan and Daniel, you brought love and family into my life mid-way through my 40s.I knew you had my back.

Gratitude to my grandparents and further back to my ancestors. I bless you all in my heart. You had tough lives to navigate and walked through many storms, wars, health challenges and losses. I hope we have done you proud.

You produced musicians, athletes, entrepreneurs, dedicated mothers and fathers, academics, published writers, champion dancers, teachers both academic and spiritual, artists and beautiful young children who are now ready to take on the world's challenges.

My friends kept me afloat too often: thank you all. You are all here in these pages along the road.

But Kate G, Lorraine, Laura, Michelle, Janice, Caroline, Kate C, Dougie, James, Marian, I value your friendship so very much. Pearls are created over a long, long time from the irritation of grit or sand inside the shell of an oyster. I think good long friendships are a lot like that. We turn the grit of life into something precious and beautiful over time.

And we have been friends a long, long time - and irritated the hell out of each other along the way, I'm sure.

To Lily, Chloe, Christine J, Jim, Helen, Irene and Antje, who all journeyed home during the period I was writing.

And of course Liz Harland, who made this journey with Breast Chancer and travelled home several years ago - but was my greatest teacher and resource along with Peter Broadhurst, our good friend who published his letters before his passing from Mesothelioma.

My beautiful Chloe, I still can't believe you've gone. Mind you, you do find a way to 'chat' on a regular basis from over there. Those sunflower shoulder taps, the dirty laughter I sense without warning, beautiful feathers and rainbows when I'm thinking or talking about you.

I miss you. Bless this book for me?

Special thanks to Morag Tester and Claire Mayfield - you'll never know how much it meant. You know the path well.

Mark McMurtrie, you made a first-class job of the cover. I love it and it was exactly as I dreamed it would be.

The cover is probably the most important aspect of a book being read and I'm really grateful to you.

Thank you Dave Reynolds for again applying your proof-reading talent, a result of your editorial skills from a long-standing career in journalism for some of the country's finest broadsheets. So many helpful and insightful suggestions.

And gratitude to Jenna Clyne who proof-read and offered her own thoughts and observations.

Thank you both, you made the birthing process so much easier.

I'm really grateful to the contributors who read the drafts for comment - I was overwhelmed by your generous and encouraging comments. It's a nerve-wracking process as those of you who write / publish words know. You were all very kind: Anne Rowan, Dr David Reilly, Donna Ashworth and Jane Douglas.

Thank you my lovely social media pals - it only happened because you acknowledged, liked and commented on my postings along the way.

I felt you every step and I know you played a huge part in this process. You were part of my recovery.
Writing can be a very healing process - I know that. But having an interactive audience was really gratifying. A writer needs a reader.

A book can't happen without a good editor and I was blessed again to work with Mickey McMonagle, who badgered me from the start of diagnosis to 'write it all down for later'.

Thank you Mickey - it was a big job and a long trip but we made it happen and I'm very grateful. I know how much you love my emojis but they didn't make the book, sadly!

We both loved Lily Douglas (who died age 14 from Ewing's Sarcoma, a rare childhood cancer). Lily was my inspiration through it all. She touched the heart of everyone she came into contact with.

I was blessed to be at her funeral when Lewis Capaldi sang "Someone you Loved" live, and that was exactly how I felt – "now you're not here, to get me through it all".

I put my energy into pulling the book together and felt her egging me on. I'll never forget our pre-Xmas lunch with mum Jane at the Radisson Red Sky Bar (one of her favourites) only a few weeks before she passed. It was one of her last outings She brought me a beautiful advent calendar. I still have the Santa.

Lily was a gift to the world. Mickey 'introduced' us online when she was only nine or 10. That smile, that resilience and her "dance in the rain" attitude carried me through many a raw day.

I was getting kinda used to being someone who loved you Lily.

I still do.

Angela Trainer, September 2022

Angela with her beloved Lord Graham

A very happy family!

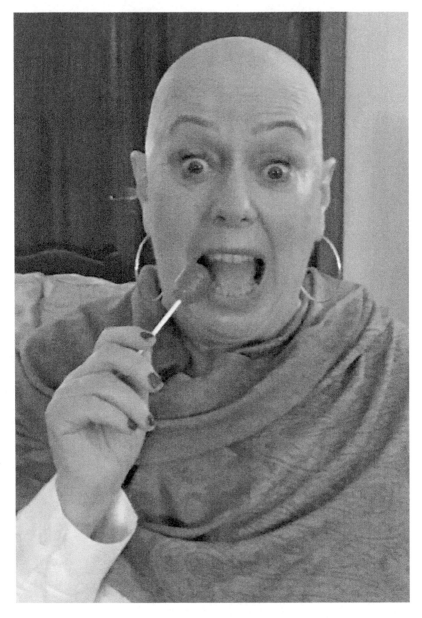

Ang and G with lovely Lily Douglas and her
amazing mum Jane at Radisson RED Sky Bar

ANGELA TRAINER

If you'd like to learn more about Angela, go to **www.harvestclinic.co.uk** or call (+44) 0141-333-0878.

Angela, along with husband Graham, offers one-to-one psychotherapy and counselling. In addition, she facilitates personal development workshops and retreats from the Harvest Countryside Studio in the hills overlooking The Campsies, just outside Glasgow, Scotland.

Her previous book Love Never Dies - also for charity – followed her through her beloved father's terminal diagnosis, passing and her grief. The book was widely praised by readers who found it helped them through their own losses.

Printed in Great Britain
by Amazon

22039365R00212